Navigating
Rhetoric:
A Guidebook for
College Writing

Carl Schlachte

Daysha Pinto

Beth Miller

hayden-mcneil
Macmillan Learning

10 9 8 7 6 5 4 3 2 1

ISBN 978-1-5339-1376-0

Macmillan Learning Curriculum Solutions
14903 Pilot Drive
Plymouth, MI 48170
www.macmillanlearning.com

Applegarth 1376-0 F19

Sustainability
Hayden-McNeil/Macmillan Learning Curriculum Solutions is proud to be a part of the larger sustainability initiative of Macmillan, our parent company. Macmillan has a goal to reduce its carbon emissions by 65% by 2020 from our 2010 baseline. Additionally, paper purchased must adhere to the Macmillan USA Paper Sourcing and Use Policy.

Hayden-McNeil partners with printers that use paper that is consistent with the environmental goals and values of Macmillan USA. This includes using paper certified by the Forest Stewardship Council (FSC), Sustainable Forestry Initiative (SFI), and/or the Programme for the Endorsement of Forest Certification (PEFC). We also offer paper with varying percentages of post-consumer waste as well as a 100% recycled stock. Additionally, Hayden-McNeil Custom Digital provides authors with the opportunity to convert print products to a digital format to use no paper at all. Visit http://sustainability.macmillan.com to learn more.

Table of Contents

Editors v

Special Thanks vi

Introduction. vii

I. Introduction to College Writing
  1. An Introduction to Rhetoric, Brenta Blevins 3
  2. Rhetoric in Academic Settings, Brenta Blevins 10
  3. The Rhetorical Canons and the Writing Process,
      Beth Miller and Carl Schlachte. 19
  4. Understanding Course Materials as Part of the Classroom
      Conversation, Alicia Beeson 24
  5. Personalizing Your Writing Practice, Beth Miller 31
  6. Cultivating Your Ethos: Class Participation, Written
      Communication, and Student-Instructor Conferences,
      Kayla Forrest 37
  7. Academic Integrity: Promoting Intellectual Growth,
      Elysia Balavage. 43
  8. Collaboration in the Classroom: Uncovering the Benefits
      of Group Assignments, Kayla Forrest and Marc Keith 48

II. Analyzing and Acknowledging Others
  9. Strategies for Active Reading, Meghan H. McGuire. 55
  10. Reading for the Rhetorical Appeals, Lauren Shook 61
  11. Thinking Critically Using Rhetorical Analysis: It's Not Just
      What You Say, But How You Say It, Kristie Ellison 69
  12. Writing a Visual Analysis, Luciana Lilley and Jay Shelat 77
  13. Topic Selection: Finding Your Foundation, Luke Huffman. 82
  14. Research Is a Process, Jenny Dale and Maggie Murphy 87
  15. Managing Sources: Finding Your Voice in an Academic
      Conversation, Kellyn Poole Luna 94
  16. Rhetorical Elements of Academic Citation, Ben Compton 99

III. Crafting and Drafting

   17. Pre-Writing Strategies: Methods to Achieve a
      Successful Argument, Kristine Lee. 109

   18. Thesis Statements: Keeping the Beat in Written, Visual,
      and Spoken Arguments, Emily Dolive. .115

   19. Staking Your Claim: Strategies for Persuasive
      Argumentation, Kristie Ellison. 122

   20. Writing with the Rhetorical Appeals: Opportunities to
      Persuade in Context, Amy Berrier 129

   21. Organization, from Beginning to End, Bryan McMillan 138

   22. Incorporating Evidence from Source Material to Make an
      Effective Argument, Erik Cofer 145

   23. Personalizing Academic Discourse: Balancing Style and
      Academic Expectations, Gia Coturri Sorenson 156

   24. Understanding Tone and Voice, Lilly Berberyan. 163

   25. Rhetorical Delivery, Brenta Blevins 169

   26. Exploring Alternative Genres: Writing Outside the
      (Research) Box, Jessie Van Rheenen. 176

IV. Revising and Reflecting

   27. Re-Seeing the Revision Process, Carl Schlachte 187

   28. De-Stressing the Peer Review Process, Marc Keith 195

   29. Writing about Your Composing Process, Jessica D. Ward. 203

   30. Reflecting Back: Compiling the Portfolio and Writing the
      Critical Reflection Essay, Emily Hall. 209

   Appendices

   A. An Example of an Annotated Text. 219

   B. Sample Prompt for a Rhetorical Analysis Essay. 221

   C. Sample Outlines 223

   D. The Annotated Bibliography. 227

   E. Sample Pre-Writing Webbing Exercise .229

   F. Transition Words Table 230

   G. Sample MEAL Plan Paragraph. 231

   H. Sample Self-Reflection Questions and Answers 232

   I. Sample Critical Reflection Essay with Peer Review 235

   Index 240

Editors

1996–2019

Write Angles: A Journal of Composition
    1996: Bob Haas, Janet Bean, Warren Rochelle

    1997: Diann L. Baecker, Timothy Flood, Jewell Rhodes Mayberry

    1998: Keith Gammons, Beth Howells, Lee Torda

    1999: Judit Szerdahelyi, Katie Ryan, Cynthia Nearman

Writing Matters
    2001: Rebecca Jones, Jackie Grutsch McKinney, Jason Tower

    2003: David Carithers, Heidi Hanrahan, Bethany Perkins

    2004: Rita Jones-Hyde, Chris Porter, Liz Vogel

    2005: Rita Jones-Hyde, Karen C. Summers, Liz Vogel

    2006: Karen C. Summers, Temeka L. Carter, Sara Littlejohn

    2007: Temeka L. Carter, Brandy L. Grabow, Melissa J. Richard

    2008: Melissa J. Richard, Brandy L. Grabow, Laurie Lyda

Technê Rhêtorikê: Techniques of Discourse for Writers and Speakers
    2009: Laurie Lyda, Alan Benson, Will Dodson, Katie Fennell

    2010: Will Dodson, Alan Benson, Jacob Babb

    2011: Jacob Babb, Sally Smits, Courtney Adams Wooten

Rhetorical Approaches to College Writing
    2012: Courtney Adams Wooten, Sally Smits, Lavina Ensor

    2013: Lavina Ensor, Chelsea Skelley, Kathleen T. Leuschen

    2014: Chelsea Skelley, Kathleen T. Leuschen, Meghan H. McGuire

    2015: Meghan H. McGuire, S. Brenta Blevins, Alison M. Johnson

    2016: S. Brenta Blevins, Lilly Berberyan, Alison M. Johnson

    2017: Lilly Berberyan, Kristie L. Ellison, Alicia Beeson

    2018: Kristie L. Ellison, Carl Schlachte, Beth Miller

Navigating Rhetoric: A Guidebook for College Writing
    2019: Carl Schlachte, Daysha Pinto, Beth Miller

Special Thanks

The Editors of *Rhetorical Approaches to College Writing* would like to acknowledge the continued support of the UNCG English Department, especially Risa Applegarth, Scott Romine, Anthony Cuda, Nancy Myers, Lydia Howard, Alyson Everhart, and Paul Cloninger. Additionally, we thank our dedicated contributors, instructors, and students, all of whom inspire us.

Introduction

Rhetoric is, according to Aristotle, the art of persuasion. As your guide for College Writing, this textbook focuses primarily on the ways that persuasive language can be used to communicate with others through writing and speaking, particularly the writing you will do in an academic context. However, in order to unleash the full rhetorical power of your writing, it is important to understand that writing is more than words and more than coursework. Writing includes all acts of creation intended to convey a message. This means that writing includes creating images and sounds, as well a wide variety of informal works, from social media posts to text messages to video chats. So, while you may be a bit nervous (or not!) about taking College Writing, you have a lot more experience with writing than you think. And while much of your academic work will involve writing words, look for opportunities to try the types of writing that speak to you the most. You can also take the concepts you learn here and apply them to be more persuasive in your personal and professional lives.

Although each writing situation is unique, College Writing will provide you with foundational tools, which can apply in any situation, by exploring your own writing and the writing of others. To help you manage the new skills you'll be learning, this textbook is divided into four parts that loosely follow the writing process. Part I, Introduction to College Writing, covers foundational concepts in rhetoric and writing as well as some more general, student-centered information that is designed to start you out on a successful path. Part II, Analyzing and Acknowledging Others, provides you with skills for working with sources, including finding them, reading them, and thinking critically about how you might have a conversation with them. Note that conversation doesn't mean that you are literally talking out loud to your sources (although you might at times!). Rather, it means that you are figuring out what they are saying, not so that you can merely report it, but so you can respond to them with your own ideas.

From there, Part III, Crafting and Drafting, helps you figure out how to communicate your response in that conversation. Here, you'll find a variety of methods and advice for ensuring that you make your voice heard and convey the message you want, including creating and supporting that message. Finally, in Part IV, Revising and Reflecting, you'll be let in on a little secret—writing is never finished. As you re-visit your ideas and the way you have communicated them, you'll continue to learn, grow, and improve. So even though you may have to commit those ideas to a final form in order to submit them to your instructor, you've really just stopped writing, not finished.

No matter where you're coming from or how much previous experience you have with formal writing in an academic context, you can be successful in College Writing. You have something to say, and we want to help you say it in the most effective way possible. Welcome.

I

Introduction to College Writing

1. An Introduction to Rhetoric

Brenta Blevins

The College Writing class focuses on rhetoric as a tool used for communication. At the beginning of this class, you may feel **rhetoric** is a term you have not encountered much before in your studies. Stop for a moment and consider what associations you have with the word rhetoric.

You may be familiar with the concept of asking a rhetorical question. Or you may have heard the term used in a negative way, for example, to accuse politicians of being "all rhetoric and no action." You may associate rhetoric with lawyers persuading a jury to vote a particular way. Finally, you may have heard the phrase "it's just rhetoric," meaning that the communication has no link with any real world effect. This existing knowledge about rhetoric can provide a good starting place for learning about the rhetorical foundations of your College Writing courses.

The previously-mentioned rhetorical question is a **rhetorical move**, or strategic use of language, in which a speaker asks a question but does not expect the audience to answer that question in a conversational fashion. The speaker intends the audience only to consider the question, thus indicating the speaker has made a choice to use language in a particular way for a particular purpose.

Elected officials and those running for office often face accusations that they focus on rhetoric. As with people who ask a rhetorical question, politicians are using language for particular purposes: to persuade their audiences. In such cases, politicians are using rhetorical moves to influence their audience toward an action: to vote for the politician, to support legislation, or to recognize a noteworthy community member. Leaders face accusations of focusing on rhetoric when their language promises more or different results than they can in fact deliver.

Some see rhetoric and action as separate. Phrases like "it's just rhetoric," "it's only rhetoric," or "it's mere rhetoric" seem to imply that what we write, say, or otherwise communicate does not have consequences. In contrast with those attitudes, twentieth century rhetorician Lloyd Bitzer defines rhetoric as "a mode of altering reality, not by the direct application of energy to objects, but by the creation of discourse which changes reality through the mediation of thought and action" (4). In other words, while words, sounds, or images do not directly physically move bodies to take actions—such as pulling levers in voting booths—communication can affect beliefs, change or confirm individuals' opinions, and influence how they choose to act.

Let's take a closer look at how rhetoric can affect reality.

» A Brief Look at Rhetoric's History

It's not surprising that one of the first associations we have with rhetoric is politics. The tradition of Western rhetoric has its roots in governance and the court system. Rhetoric scholars Sonja K. Foss, Karen A. Foss, and Robert Trapp place rhetoric's origin in the fifth century BCE during a turbulent political change from tyranny to democracy.

After a revolution overthrew the dictators of the Greek colony Syracuse on the island of Sicily, the courts faced conflicting claims about whether land belonged to the original owners or those who had been granted the land by the dictators. The Greek legal system required individuals to speak for themselves; they could not hire attorneys to speak for them. Corax of Syracuse saw the need for individuals to learn how to speak in the courts and wrote the *Art of Rhetoric* to help them present their cases persuasively (Foss et al. 4–5).

The history of Corax shows how Western rhetoric first arose in the legal system during a context of political change. Corax developed his treatise of rhetoric so individuals could represent themselves to achieve their own goals. Specifically, individuals in the court systems needed to argue legal claims so they could own the land that had fallen under disagreement. In other words, they wanted to achieve a real world effect through their language: to regain their property back or to maintain their ownership of the property, so they could live or work on that land.

Although Corax developed his advice on rhetoric over 2,500 years ago, we still seek to achieve our own goals through rhetoric. Any time we try to achieve a change in the world—perhaps not in court, but in trying to persuade friends to go to a particular restaurant or to choose a particular movie to watch—we are using rhetoric. This means that we all use rhetoric all the time. Studying rhetoric can help us become aware of the choices we have in communicating and enable us to make conscious choices about rhetoric, which can help us become more effective writers, speakers, and designers of texts.

» Defining Rhetoric

As Corax of Syracuse's history shows, Western rhetoric has a tradition that extends back for 2,500 years. As you might expect, how rhetoric has been used and defined has changed throughout that long period.

Shortly after Corax's *Art of Rhetoric*, Aristotle (384 BCE–322 BCE) offers the most famous definition of rhetoric: **"Rhetoric is the faculty of discovering in any particular case all of the available means of persuasion."** Let's **analyze**—that is, **break down**—Aristotle's understanding of rhetoric.

Aristotle offers a two-part definition of rhetoric, focusing on 1) invention and 2) persuasion.

1. *Rhetoric as Invention.* First, his words about "discovering...all of the available means" conceives of rhetoric as a tool for guiding the creation of strategies. In rhetoric, the discovery of creation strategies is termed "invention." We'll learn more about invention later in this textbook, but invention is a tool for coming up with what to say. In this case, Aristotle sees rhetoric as offering the capacity to find not just some, but multiple, in fact, *all* of the different ways to communicate in one instance. Rhetoric effectively enables communicators to identify the different choices they have to create their communications. (For more on rhetorical invention, see Ch. 17, "Pre-Writing Strategies.")

2. *Rhetoric as Persuasion.* The purpose of discovering different communication strategies is **to persuade an audience to a perspective the rhetor presents.** You might think mainly of political and legal speeches and debates as involving persuasion, but every communication has persuasive potential. For example, when you respond to an in-class discussion question, you attempt to persuade the class that your point and your evidence are credible. When you have a problem as a customer, you seek to persuade customer service to remedy the situation. In coursework, you may offer a proposal of how to divide up group work. (For more on argumentation, see Ch. 19, "Staking Your Claim.")

Aristotle sees rhetoric as a combination of invention and persuasion. Rhetoric is most likely to be effective when an individual thinks through multiple means of communication and selects one suited to the audience and purpose.

(PD—1923)

Figure 1. Raphael, *The School of Athens*. Ca. 1510–1512. Fresco in Stanza della Segnatura, Vatican Palace, Vatican State. While the identities of individual figures are contested, Raphael is thought to have based the painting on the likeness of at least 21 philosophers. The central figures represent Plato and Aristotle.

» Other Ways of Defining Rhetoric

Rhetoric has been in existence for over 2,500 years, dating at least to Corax of Syracuse. With over a two millennia-long history, discussion about language and communication has resulted in many thinkers offering different definitions and ways of understanding rhetoric. Let's explore a few of these different definitions:

Classical (1 BCE)

Cicero: "To begin with, a knowledge of very many matters must be grasped, without which oratory is but an empty and ridiculous swirl of verbiage: and the distinctive style has to be formed, not only by the choice of words, but also by the arrangement of the same; and all the mental emotions, with which nature has endowed the human race, are to be intimately understood, because it is in calming or kindling the feelings of the audience that the full power and science of oratory are to be brought into play....Further, the complete history of the past and a store of precedents must be retained in the memory.... And...the speaker's delivery? That needs to be controlled by bodily carriage, gesture, play of features and changing intonation of voice; and how important that is wholly by itself" (qtd. in Bizzell and Herzberg 291).

Medieval (C. 5th Century To 14th Century)

Anonymous, *The Principles of Letter Writing*: "A written composition is setting-forth of some matter in writing, proceeding in a suitable order. Or, a written composition is a suitable and fitting treatment of some matter, adapted to the matter itself. Or, a written composition is a suitable and fitting written statement about something, either memorized or declared by speech or in writing" (qtd. in Bizzell and Herzberg 496).

Renaissance (C. 15th Century To 17th Century)

Ramus: "[R]hetoric is the art of speaking well, not about this or that, but about all subjects" (qtd. in McCorkle 83).

Bacon: "The duty and office of Rhetoric *is to apply Reason to Imagination* for the better moving of the will" (qtd. in Bizzell and Herzberg 743).

Enlightenment (C. 18th Century)

Campbell: "All the ends of speaking are reducible to four; every speech being intended to enlighten the understanding, to please the imagination, to move the passions, or to influence the will" (qtd. in Bizzell and Herzberg 902).

19th Century

Bain: "Rhetoric discusses the means whereby language, spoken or written, may be rendered effective" (qtd. in Bizzell and Herzberg 1146).

20th Century

Cheryl Glenn: "Rhetoric always inscribes the relation of language and power at a particular moment (including who may speak, who may listen or who will agree to listen, and what can be said)" (1–2).

21st Century

Krista Ratcliffe: "But as Kenneth Burke has taught us, rhetoric may be defined very broadly (e.g., I tell the students in my undergraduate rhetorical theory class that the study of rhetoric is the study of how we use language and how language uses us)."

Christine Farris: "What rhetoric has always addressed: not the mastery and regulation of language so much as the ways in which language shapes, reflects, and changes practices among members of particular communities."

Dexter B. Gordon: "While I intend to focus on the broadly accepted notion that black nationalism entails a call for black autonomy in culture, economics, and politics, more important is my emphasis on black nationalism as a rhetoric—an ideological discourse in process, constantly responsive to the exigencies of the contingent situations in which it operates—as against the more popular notion of black nationalism as a philosophical ideal" (5).

Why might these different rhetoricians have different views of rhetoric? Consider the context—such as the place and time—in which they lived. Some of these individuals lived in eras when governments did not welcome input from citizens or individuals living in lands where they could not be considered citizens. As we saw earlier, Corax developed his version of rhetoric because individuals needed to speak before others to influence the outcomes of judicial decision, else they might be left without land.

Think too of all the changes in communication technology the millennia have seen. For example, until recently, mail delivery relied on couriers traveling long distances, arriving perhaps a long time after the letter was finished. Rhetors could also encounter different rates of literacy. Consider now, with the rise of communication capabilities across the globe, why today's rhetoricians might see new possibilities—and needs—for rhetoric.

» Other Ways of Approaching Rhetoric

With multiple definitions of rhetoric and multiple means for persuading, rhetors have access to multiple rhetorical strategies. In 1995, Sonja K. Foss and Cindy L. Griffin explored an approach to rhetoric they termed "invitational." **Invitational rhetoric focuses less on persuasion and more on inviting the audience to share the rhetor's perspective. The scholars propose that ideally the audience members should listen to the rhetor and also have an opportunity to share their own perspective:** "When this happens rhetor and audience alike contribute to the thinking about an issue so that everyone involved gains a greater understanding of the issue in its subtlety, richness, and complexity" (5). Foss and Griffin acknowledge that invitational rhetoric may not always be a form of rhetoric "for which rhetors should strive or that it should or can be used in all situations" (17). But they offer this form to add to the available means of persuasion.

Similarly, twentieth-century psychologist Carl R. Rogers developed a communications system that led to what is known as **the Rogerian argument. Here, the rhetor introduces a problem and acknowledges the oppositional position.** The rhetor then first offers a description of the contexts in which the oppositional perspective may be valid, then describes the context in which the rhetor's perspective is valid. Finally, the rhetor states how the dissenter would benefit from adopting the rhetor's position; the rhetor may also identify how the two positions complement each other. (For more, see Ch. 18, "Thesis Statements" and Ch. 19, "Staking Your Claim.")

» What's Ahead

This chapter has provided a brief overview of a well-established field of study that has existed for over two millennia. Many more rhetorical concepts and theories exist. The remainder of this textbook will provide you with further information to broaden your understanding of rhetoric.

» Works Cited

Bitzer, Lloyd F. "The Rhetorical Situation." *Philosophy and Rhetoric*, vol. 1, no. 1, 1968, pp. 1–14.

Bizzell, Patricia and Bruce Herzberg, editors. *The Rhetorical Tradition: Readings from Classical Times to the Present.* 2nd ed. Bedford/St. Martin's, 2001.

Farris, Christine. "Where Rhetoric Meets the Road: First-Year Composition." *Enculturation*, vol. 5, no. 1, 2003.

Foss, Sonja K., et al. *Contemporary Perspectives on Rhetoric.* 30th Anniversary ed. Waveland Press, 2014.

Foss, Sonja K., and Cindy L. Griffin. "Beyond Persuasion: A Proposal for an Invitational Rhetoric." *Communication Monographs*, vol. 62, no. 1, 1995, pp. 2–18.

Glenn, Cheryl. *Rhetoric Retold: Regendering the Tradition from Antiquity Through the Renaissance.* Southern Illinois UP, 1997.

Gordon, Dexter B. *Black Identity: Rhetoric, Ideology, and Nineteenth-Century Black Nationalism.* Southern Illinois UP, 2006.

McCorkle, Ben. *Rhetorical Delivery As Technological Discourse: A Cross-Historical Study.* Southern Illinois UP, 2012.

Raphael. *The School of Athens.* Fresco. Ca. 1510–12. Stanza della Segnatura, Vatican Palace, Rome. *Wikimedia Commons.* Image source: Raphael [PD-art], via Wikimedia Commons: http://commons.wikimedia.org/wiki/File:Raphael_School_of_Athens.jpg.

Ratcliffe, Krista. "The Current State of Composition Scholar/Teachers: Is Rhetoric Gone or Just Hiding Out?" *Enculturation*, vol. 5, no. 1, 2003.

2. Rhetoric in Academic Settings

Brenta Blevins

In the previous chapter, you were introduced to some foundational concepts in rhetoric. In this chapter we'll explore how you might use rhetorical concepts in your academic courses.

Rhetoric is not just a tool for creating texts to respond to rhetorical situations, but also a means of understanding and talking about texts and rhetorical situations. Analyzing texts can help you identify how texts work and how you might or might not use some of the strategies that a particular text does.

The Rhetorical Triangle

Rhetoricians have long used a tool called the **rhetorical triangle** for thinking about how different aspects of communication relate to each other. Each time we communicate, there is someone who communicates, at least one person who receives that communication, and something that is communicated. The rhetorical triangle (see Fig. 1) helps us analyze others' rhetoric and create our own communication.

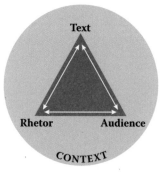

Figure 1. The Rhetorical Triangle

Rhetor. A rhetor is a person who uses rhetoric to communicate with an audience. Because communication can take place in writing, through images, in video, and in many other forms, a rhetor may be a writer, a speaker, an artist, a filmmaker, and so forth. Rhetors make a number of purposeful decisions about how to communicate their messages to audiences.

For example, you are a rhetor in a College Writing class. You will decide on **topics** to communicate about. Even when an instructor's assignment specifies your topic, you will choose particular ways of fulfilling that assignment. You will choose unique **evidence** to support your claims. You will decide the **arrangement** of what you choose to incorporate. Depending on the assignment, you may choose to incorporate images. If you are delivering a presentation, you may decide to include sound or video to convey claims and evidence. As Brenta Blevins's chapter "Rhetorical Delivery" shows, rhetors make more choices than what words to use. Even when they are composing an essay using a particular academic style, rhetors make decisions about how to conform to, say, the MLA format in designing their essay.

When making choices for words and other media, rhetors determine how to represent themselves not just through content, but also how to relate to the audience. For example, the rhetor can decide how much the audience already knows about a topic and how much is necessary to communicate to aid the audience's understanding. Whether the rhetor is speaking in person to an audience or communicating to a remote audience, rhetors make a number of decisions whenever they communicate that reveal much about them and their understanding of the audience.

To analyze the rhetor in communication, consider:

- Who is the rhetor? What is the rhetor's name (an individual, multiple individuals, or a company or other organization)? Is the rhetor a student? An expert via education or experience?

- In what manner has the rhetor chosen to represent himself or herself to the audience? Does the rhetor identify their[1] name and authority on the argument explicitly or implicitly?

- How credible does the rhetor seem about the topic?

- What does the rhetor's purpose seem to be? Their motivation? How enthusiastic or fervent does the rhetor seem in the argument? How believable are they?

---

1. Note the intentional usage here of the possessive pronoun "their" to refer to the rhetor. Although "rhetor" is singular, the gender of the rhetor is not specified, so the author has chosen to use "their" as an epicene pronoun (epicene being a word meaning gender is indeterminate or characteristic of both genders). Linguist and professor of English Dennis Baron has written extensively about pronouns and has noted that the singular they/their has been in use since 1365. For further information, see his website *The Web of Language*.

Audience. The audience is the recipient of communication, whether as a reader, viewer, or listener. The audience may have one intended recipient or it may hold multiple. We often use the term "audience" as singular, but the recipients of communication can be multiple. Many scholars view all communication, including writing, as a social act. This means that rhetoric is always social, whether you are in a class trying to make a claim in an essay or writing to yourself in a journal or blog. Even in the classroom context, you may be tempted to think of your instructor as the audience, but your instructor may ask you to imagine (or to construct) other audiences, so you will need to adjust your communication accordingly. Additionally, other students will be reading your drafts, so they too need to be considered recipients as you compose your communication.

Among the decisions a rhetor makes in creating a text includes first identifying an audience—or audiences. The rhetor then makes choices about how to make the message accessible to their audience. Such choices include the discourse—or language—of the text. For example, if the rhetor is writing an argument about a scientific topic, the rhetor may need to define technical terminology if communicating with a general audience. If the rhetor is writing to an audience of scientists, the rhetor will not need to define that language. Instead, the rhetor may choose to include scientific graphs or other numerical data representations familiar to scientists. (For more on considering audience in argumentation, see Ch. 19, "Staking Your Claim." For more about adjusting diction for different audiences, see Ch. 24, "Understanding Tone and Voice." For more on the connection between the canons and audience, see Ch. 3, "The Rhetorical Canons and the Writing Process.")

"Among the decisions a rhetor makes in creating a text includes first identifying an audience—or audiences."

As we will see, the rhetor can make decisions about how to approach the audience. The rhetor makes decisions to approach the audience in a friendly manner, in a serious method, or through an adversarial attitude. The rhetor may also anticipate the audience will initially react to the topic in a negative or positive manner and then subsequently make additional decisions.

To analyze the audience in communication, consider:

+ Who is the audience? Can you name the audience? What can we understand about the text by identifying the rhetor's intended audience?

+ How does the rhetor address the audience? Through particular language? By naming the audience? By identifying its concerns?

+ What motivates the rhetor to create the text? What purpose is the rhetor trying to fulfill?

+ What reaction have primary or secondary audiences already had to the text? As time has passed, have audiences changed the way they react to the text? Do you react to the text in a different manner than the intended audience?

Text. The communicative product that a rhetor delivers to an audience is the text. Because rhetoric pertains to forms of communication beyond writing, the text could be an essay, email, instant message, speech, presentation, film, piece of art, or even a building (see Fig. 2). Even body language is a form of text.

Figure 2.

As discussed earlier, the different aspects of the rhetorical triangle are relational. This means that when a rhetor writes, speaks, or otherwise communicates with an audience, they will adjust the text to best suit the audience. This may involve decisions about language, images, or following particular conventions to best fulfill the rhetor's purpose.

For example, if a rhetor needs to communicate a message to drivers—such as stopping at an intersection—they may choose to incorporate a sign. Because traffic signs have highly conventional forms, the rhetor may choose the usual red octagonal sign and use a familiar font that is easily read from a vehicle. If the sign is being posted in a location that has had a number of collisions or is located at the bottom of a hill, the rhetor may choose to have the word "STOP" painted on the road itself. The image of a stop sign may also be used outside the driving context, for example, as part of a smoking cessation campaign.

While it might seem that rhetoric is used in identical ways within such conventional texts as essays, letters, emails, brochures, and text messages, each of those texts differs based on their genres and purposes. If the letter is a job application letter, the text will be different from a letter to a grandparent. The text of an informative brochure will differ from a sales brochure. Even buildings involve rhetorical decisions beyond their functional purposes, such as to provide meeting or office spaces. For example, the U.S. Capitol Building is designed not merely to provide space for debates, hearings, and lawmaker meetings with citizens, but it is also a national symbol. Rather than a generic boxy construction, the U.S. Capitol is located on a hill with a towering center dome designed to impress viewers with its immense size and artistry.

To analyze a text, consider:

+ How would you summarize the text?

+ What language does the text use? Is its diction casual or professional? Accessible or complicated? Does the text use repetition? Metaphors or similes? Or other rhetorical/literary devices?

+ Does the text include images (still or moving) or sounds? Large or small, long or short? Or are those described instead of depicted?

+ What is the text's intention? Could you read other interpretations in addition to its intentional one?

Context. As shown in the rhetorical triangle image (see Fig. 1), **context surrounds any communication event.** The context is the situation or circumstance in which a rhetor communicates a text to an audience. The circumstances of context include a number of different components, such as time, space, and prior or concurrent communications related to or affecting the text. This chapter will expand on context in describing a rhetorical situation below.

The context may be acknowledged or unacknowledged, to different degrees of rhetorical effectiveness. (For more information on context, see Ch. 20, "Writing with the Rhetorical Appeals.")

Let's take a look at the different ways the classroom context shapes your rhetorical performance as a student. For example, even if they are on the same topic for the same class, an in-class discussion has a different context from an essay assignment. One of these calls for an immediate response—such as in response to an instructor's question, while the other usually involves weeks (or months) of work.

The context for writing in college is often an assignment created by an instructor. But that doesn't mean you, as a rhetor, can't think about context in the College Writing classroom. As we have previously discussed, communication is social. That means that others have talked about a topic before we write about it. You might consider, then, how to summarize prior conversations about the topic or otherwise indicate that you are aware of how the topic has been discussed previously.

One important aspect of context is kairos. **Kairos is the timely opportunity for offering input or responding to a particular context.** If you've ever thought of an intelligent answer two days after an in-class discussion, you have missed your kairotic opportunity.

To analyze context, consider:

+ What motivates this communication?

+ To what audience should the communication be addressed? How well does the text account for social or cultural expectations associated with the context?

+ What else is being communicated in this context? For example, is the text located in a magazine or website along with content that is similar or dissimilar? With similar speeches and presentations?

+ When is this text being communicated? A day after the motivating occurrence? A year after?

+ Where is the communication taking place? In a physical space with room for a small audience? In a large space with room for hundreds or thousands of audience members?

Rhetorical Appeals

Now that you have learned about the rhetorical triangle, this chapter will briefly introduce concepts that you will learn about throughout this textbook.

In *On Rhetoric*, Aristotle identifies three means by which rhetors may influence their audiences:

pathos	through the audience's emotions
ethos	through the rhetor's credibility
logos	through the logic of the rhetor's text

These three categories are the "rhetorical appeals," the means by which a rhetor can appeal to an audience's capacity to believe or act in a certain way.

Although this chapter and others discuss the rhetorical appeals separately, remember that only in the rarest of cases will texts use only one appeal at a time. In general, rhetors use the appeals in combinations, adjusting which are used to suit the audience and the intended purpose. (For more on the rhetorical appeals, see Ch. 20, "Writing with the Rhetorical Appeals" and Ch. 10, "Reading for the Rhetorical Appeals.")

Rhetorical Canons

A canon is a set of principles or a representative or model text, either as a single document or a collection of them. The rhetorical canons are principles that offer guidelines for describing and thinking about the ways we compose communication. Briefly, these strategies are:

Invention	The process for identifying and choosing the text's content.
Arrangement	The organization of a text's content.
Style	The artful communication of a text using, for example, figures of speech, such as repetition, comparison-contrast, or metaphors.
Memory	For a speech, this canon could represent memorizing a text. It also might represent the rhetor's capacity to memorize different rhetorical strategies for composing a text. It might also involve memorability for the rhetor and the audience.
Delivery	The choices for communicating content. These choices cover a range of decisions. For example, in a speech, the rhetor might choose a serious pronunciation or passionate tone. The rhetor might choose to convey an image using spoken words alone or with an accompanying slide presentation.

As with the rhetorical appeals, we may discuss these categories separately, but they each interact in a text in connected ways. Subsequent chapters will feature more information on the rhetorical canons. (For more on the canons, see Ch. 3, "The Rhetorical Canons and the Writing Process.")

Rhetorical Situation

Learning about rhetoric provides preparation for responding to rhetorical situations. **A rhetorical situation is an event, occasion, or occurrence in which rhetoric is provoked. Any time we write, speak, or otherwise create communication, we encounter a rhetorical situation.** A rhetorical situation includes specific in-class discussions, emails, class assignments, text messaging conversations, presentations, and more. Understanding the rhetorical situation can help us shape the content and form of our communication.

Lloyd F. Bitzer claims that all rhetoric is situational (3). To understand the characteristics in which speakers and writers create communication, Bitzer describes a **rhetorical situation** as being a combination of **exigence, audience,** and **constraints.**

Exigence. The exigence may be thought of as the motivation for the communication. For a rhetorical situation to occur, Bitzer says there must be the potential for "change to be effected" (6). A rhetorical situation must have at least one exigence that "strongly invites utterance" (5). In other words, a situation must possess the potential for change. If the situation—such as the current weather—cannot be changed through communication, Bitzer says that it is nonrhetorical.

Audience. We've already addressed in the rhetorical triangle how **the audience is the recipient of communication; Bitzer emphasizes the audience as a necessary component of rhetoric.** He claims that "rhetorical discourse produces change by influencing the decision and action of persons who function as mediators of change" (7). At the same time, though, rhetoric may call forth an audience as a "mediator of the change which the discourse functions to produce" (8). In other words, individuals may not know they care about, are affected by, or are capable of effecting a topic until after a rhetor creates a text.

Constraints. Constraints are limitations that affect the rhetorical response. Constraints include "persons, events, objects, and relations which are parts of the situation" because they can affect or limit the decision and action needed to modify the situation (8). Rhetors should consider the pre-existing "beliefs, attitudes, documents, facts, traditions, images, interests, motives and the like" that affect a rhetorical situation (8). The rhetor's decisions provide subsequent constraints by shaping the available choices for that situation.

Putting It Together

This chapter has introduced key terms related to rhetoric, ones that you will learn about in subsequent chapters. Keep in mind that although these terms are often presented in separate chapters, the concepts they represent are interconnected and interrelated.

» Works Cited

Baron, Dennis. *The Web of Language.* University of Illinois at Urbana-Champaign, 2016, illinois.edu/blog/view/25.

Bitzer, Lloyd F. "The Rhetorical Situation." *Philosophy and Rhetoric*, vol. 1, no. 1, 1968, pp. 1–14.

3. The Rhetorical Canons and the Writing Process

Beth Miller and Carl Schlachte

» Introduction

Cicero, the ancient Roman orator, created five canons, or categories, to divide the art of rhetoric. **These categories are invention, arrangement, style, memory, and delivery.** Though they were established for use in making speeches, we now apply them in speaking, writing, and other forms of argumentation. You can find chapters throughout this textbook addressing many of these concepts, but in this chapter, we'll introduce them, relate them to the writing process, and illustrate their use in analysis.

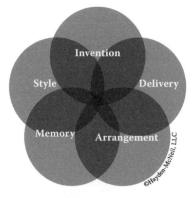

Figure 1. The canons of rhetoric have a recursive relationship, and each canon involves utilizing all the others.

One way to approach the canons is by thinking about the rhetorical situation and the rhetorical triangle. (For more on the triangle and canons, see Ch. 2, "Rhetoric in Academic Settings.") To compose any text, you will first want to consider who your audience will be, what they already know, how you need to address them, and what your message will be. If you can answer these questions, you have already begun using the canons. By thinking of ideas for your text, you have practiced the canon of **invention.** To do this, you probably considered what you know about your audience and what they know about your topic. This involves the canon of **memory.** To consider how you will convey your message, you may have imagined possible organization strategies (the canon of **arrangement**), the tone and method you'll use to address your audience (the canon of **style**), and how you'll ultimately present the message (the canon of **delivery**). And that's just in the brainstorming phase!

This example is intended to show that all five canons can be used simultaneously. This means they are functioning recursively; in other words, there is not a set order to the canons, and you can shift or change between them in any sequence. All five canons interrelate and affect each other. Much like dropping a stone into a pond, where one action causes ripples across the entire surface, if you work with one canon, you will influence the others as well.

"There is not a set order to the canons, and you can shift or change between them in any sequence."

In what follows, we will first discuss how you can incorporate the canons in your writing process—for essays, speeches, or other projects. Then we will examine how analyzing for the canons can give you greater insight into any text. This practice will allow you to more effectively recognize rhetors' choices. This in turn assists you in reflecting—formally or informally—on your own writing process and decision making.

» How Do We Incorporate the Canons in the Writing Process?

We can recognize the canons in the writing process by re-examining behaviors we are already familiar with. Let's pretend we are working on a research essay. We have already come up with a research question, found a few sources to cite, and started drafting. But, after writing the first several pages, we couldn't connect all our evidence, and, worse, we felt like we didn't know what else to say! So we may turn back to **invention**, asking ourselves:

+   What can we add to develop our idea?

+   What gaps exist in what we already have that need to be filled?

+   What connections can we draw between what we have?

+   Where can we look for new information?

(For more on invention, see Ch. 17, "Pre-Writing Strategies.")

If we find some of this material to add, we can simultaneously turn to both **memory** and **arrangement**. If we turn to **memory**, we ask:

+   How can we tap into what our audience already knows?

- How can we do our best to connect to what our audience finds familiar—to tap into their cultural and personal memories?

- What do our readers need to know to understand this new information, and how does that relate to what we've already written?

For **arrangement**, we might ask ourselves:

- Where does it make sense to include the new material we're offering our audience?

- What examples will help to fill out these details?

- How do we order these points to ensure they make sense to our audience?

(For more on arrangement, see Ch. 21, "Organization, from Beginning to End.")

We could repeat these questions at many times throughout the writing process. At some point, however, we may find ourselves needing to revise something we've already written. Here, too, the canons prove useful. For example, we may wish to consider the **style** choices we've made, asking:

- Are our tone and language choices appropriate to our message?

- Are we conveying our ideas as clearly as possible? Is our tone appealing and persuasive for an engaged but uninformed audience?

- Will our audience be excited by our word choice and transitions?

(For more on style, see Ch. 23, "Personalizing Academic Discourse.")

At this point we may return again to **memory**, where we might ask:

- Have we made our text accessible to our audience so that they can latch on to our message?

- Have we made our message seem important to them?

Or, we could turn to **delivery**, asking:

- Are we presenting this product in its most polished form?

- If we have a choice of form, have we considered what would be the most effective one for our message?

(For more, see Ch. 25, "Rhetorical Delivery.")

From this discussion, you can probably see that it doesn't make sense to talk about the canons *alongside* the writing process; the canons *are* the writing process. And because the writing process is recursive, we encourage you, as you write, to move from pre-writing, to drafting, to revision, and back and forth. Doing so can more fully develop your ideas and your assignments. (For more on revision, see Ch. 27, "Re-Seeing the Revision Process.")

"The canons *are* the writing process."

» How Do We Use the Canons in Analysis?

As with any time you are analyzing rhetoric, your first point of consideration should be the rhetorical triangle. This means that first, you should identify the context, the speaker, the message, and the audience. Recognizing these elements better allows you to understand everything else that is happening in whatever you are analyzing.

Once you have identified these aspects, the canons allow you to understand why the message is being **delivered** and **arranged** in a particular way, how it engages in **memory** through other existing texts, where its ideas come from, what commonplaces it draws on (**invention**), and the effectiveness of its **style**.

Recursiveness is at play here, too, because analyzing for the canons can lead to insights we might use in our own projects. For example, if we wanted to start a new social network, we might analyze the largest current one—Facebook. Once we did so, we would find that Facebook was not the first website to use the format of a social network; it was preceded by others such as MySpace and Friendster. Even though Facebook did not **invent** the format of the social network, it deserves credit for **arranging** and **delivering** it in a **style** that found great popularity with an ever-expanding audience. In fact, Facebook may remain popular because it is a storehouse for personal and cultural **memories** and delivers them to its users with great effectiveness.

"However, as you familiarize yourself with the canons and how they operate, through analysis, you become adept at locating them in any writing—including your own."

You may not intend to start your own social network. However, as you familiarize yourself with the canons and how they operate, through analysis, you become adept at locating them in any writing—including your own. When you are asked to reflect critically on your own writing or speaking, understanding the canons can help you see the choices you've made and be able to talk about them. It can also help you consider which areas of your writing you'd like to give more attention to when revising.

» Conclusion

As categories, the canons contain many of the activities that make up both rhetoric and the composing process. You can use them in any order you like *and* all at once. Because the canons are so intertwined, like a woven fabric, pulling on one strand causes tugs throughout the entire piece. We hope that you can become increasingly aware of what these canons involve, and how they are active in your work. Recognizing these choices in the work of others can also help you to better exercise them intentionally in your own compositions.

In writing this chapter, we started with the canons of **invention** and **arrangement** to determine what we wanted to say and in what order we wanted to say it. These involved considering our audience—you—and what we hoped to convey to you. We then turned to **memory**, considering existing scholarship about the canons, to see what we liked about aspects of it and wanted to imitate, but also what we wanted to do differently. We also considered what we expect you might know about the writing process, from your classes and other chapters in this textbook. We considered the **delivery** of this chapter as part of a textbook, where you could also find other chapters addressing specific canons in more detail. In terms of **style**, we opted for a tone that we hoped would be accessible and informative. As we revised this chapter, we turned back to **invention** to add some ideas about how the canons apply to speeches, adjusted the **style** to clarify our phrasings, and contemplated **rearranging** our conclusion to provide an effective ending. In our final edits, we returned to the rhetorical triangle to reexamine our choices, considering our audience and our message. In other words, we returned to our beginning, to recursively take up the canons once more.

What Can We Do with This?

+ Reconsider the order of steps in our writing process recursively

+ Employ memory to more persuasively engage with our audience by considering their experiences and expectations

+ Consider a wide variety of sources for invention

+ Be open to many possible arrangements for our ideas to find the most convincing order

+ Question how effective a draft is compared with our ideal delivery

+ Play with and vary style to address different audiences and situations

+ Utilize the canons in analysis to more fully understand the choices we've made in our own writing

4. Understanding Course Materials as Part of the Classroom Conversation

Alicia Beeson

A conversation in its most basic form is a verbal exchange of ideas between two or more people. With the development of recent technologies, our understanding of conversations has expanded to include mediums such as email, texting, or video chatting. Conversations in a classroom can include all forms of communication including lectures, emails, discussion board posts, and written student responses. Instructors' materials are often a continuation of classroom conversations that provide specific information about the course, an assignment, or an idea.

> "Instructors' materials are often a continuation of classroom conversations that provide specific information about the course, an assignment, or an idea."

The most important materials that you may receive, either in class or via Canvas, are likely the syllabus, assignment sheets, and rubrics. These documents provide information regarding your instructor's expectations for students in the class as a whole and for a particular assignment. **As part of an ongoing conversation, instructors' materials offer instructions, guidelines, and suggestions that you will respond to in the completion of the course and in the assignments.**

» Reading the Syllabus

Essentially, you can think of the syllabus as a document that establishes expectations about the course for you as a student. Some policies reflect agreements between the instructor, department, and university, such as the student learning outcomes that indicate the semester's educational goals. Other features of the syllabus, such as the technology policy, are chosen by the instructor but indicate to the university and to you as a student what students are expected to do in the course.

While an instructor may note that the course schedule may change during the semester, the policies generally will not be modified. Thus, when you receive a syllabus you should carefully read and consider the course's requirements and the expectations. By staying in a course, you are agreeing to the policies and parameters that the syllabus describes. **As part of the classroom conversation, the instructor is describing in the syllabus what is required to succeed in the course; by coming to class and completing the assignments, the student accepts the responsibility for meeting those expectations.** Below are some key components included in syllabi to consider.

The syllabus provides many pieces of necessary information for your success in the class. For example, the instructor includes their contact information and office hours so that students will know how to communicate with them. The syllabus also identifies the required texts (as well as any recommended texts) that you will need throughout the semester. In addition, the syllabus explains how the instructor assesses student performance in the course, including the weight or point value of each assignment or grading category. Typically found at the end of the syllabus, the course schedule will provide readings and assignments due for each day of class, which you should check regularly. Familiarizing yourself with these materials and returning to the syllabus when you have questions demonstrates your ability to use available resources and benefits your ethos more than approaching the instructor about basic questions that are explained in the syllabus.

> "The syllabus provides many pieces of necessary information for your success in the class."

Additionally, the syllabus includes student learning outcomes: the goals of the class. For example, the Student Learning Outcomes for English 102 indicate that at the completion of the course, students will be able to:

1. Locate and evaluate primary and/or secondary sources.

2. Employ sources to advance an informed, cogent argument.

3. Construct research-based writing projects that demonstrate focused, independent inquiry.

As you may notice, all of the course learning outcomes relate to research in some way, so it is apparent that research is a primary focus for English 102. However, the outcomes indicate that you should not only be able to find research, but that you should be able to use the research to produce your own original and focused argument. Understanding the main objectives of the course can help you understand the importance of individual discussions and assignments within the context of the course as a whole.

The syllabus also offers information regarding the instructor's policies, often related to attendance, participation, technology, late work, and peer review. These policies offer guidelines for being a successful student in the course. While the instructor will likely review these policies in class, you should also read the syllabus to familiarize yourself with these policies so that you can respond to them through your behavior and attentiveness in class. Carefully review all of these and any additional elements at the start of the course and refer to them throughout the semester when needed.

» Understanding Assignment Sheets

While the syllabus may contain an overview of the major assignments in the course, instructors often provide additional assignment sheets that contain more specific information regarding the focus and requirements of the assignments for the course. **The assignment sheet is part of a more focused conversation, providing information about a particular task within the course.** (For an example of an assignment sheet, see Appendix B.) When you receive an assignment sheet, it is helpful to read the assignment sheet and consider what is being asked of you. The following questions can help you break down and reflect on the assignment:

- What is the purpose of the assignment?

- What genre is the assignment, and what are the expectations of that genre?

- Who is my audience, what do they know about the topic, and what would be appealing to them?

- As an author, what am I interested in writing about, and what do I know about that topic?

- What are the requirements for the assignment?

Assignment descriptions often include words that are important to understand in order to completely comprehend what is being asked of you. As you read the example assignment description from an English 101 course below, underline any key action words—in other words, what you see as important to do and include for this assignment.

For this assignment you will choose an advocacy ad and thoroughly analyze how the organization uses rhetoric, including logos, ethos, and pathos, to convince their audience(s). You will also be required to research the context (such as the organization and related events and conversations) and consider how these elements affect the ad's rhetorical situation. Your essay must be thesis-driven, meaning that you should craft an argument regarding the rhetorical choices made in the advocacy ad, answering the questions "Is it effective for its audience? What makes it (or does not make it) effective?" You should clearly describe the organization's stylistic and rhetorical choices and organize your analysis with sophistication.

Some of the common keywords from the above assignment description are discussed below in relation to the example and to other assignments.

+ **Analyze.** Many assignments will ask you to analyze a text, such as an article, a speech, a song, or even a conversation on a particular topic. To analyze, break down a topic into smaller components, considering each part of the whole individually, as well as how it interacts with other parts. For this example assignment, you will rhetorically analyze the ad, meaning that you will consider individual parts of the ad and how they use the appeals, as well as how the ad as a whole has an effect on its particular audience. (See Ch. 9, "Strategies for Active Reading" for more.)

+ **Research.** Many assignments require that you research a topic, context, and/or author. When you learn that research is required, you will want to find out how many sources are necessary, as well as whether primary or secondary research and popular or scholarly sources are expected. Because the above assignment asks the student to analyze an advocacy ad, the student will likely research popular sources such as the organization's website or news articles, being careful to ensure those sources are credible. (See Ch. 14, "Research is a Process" for more.)

+ **Argue.** Most assignments in English 101 and English 102 will be argument-driven, meaning that you should articulate a thesis that communicates your stance on the topic or issue. The points that you offer in the project should support your thesis, and evidence should contribute to the persuasiveness of your argument. For example, in a rhetorical analysis of an advocacy ad, the argument could address whether and how the ad is effective for its audience. (See Ch. 19, "Staking Your Claim" for more.)

+ **Describe.** When an assignment asks you to describe, you will usually need to tell the reader about the text in detail. You will typically want to include the most important parts of the text and emphasize the elements that are most related to your argument. For the assignment above, this could involve what the ad looks like, what it contains, and what the organization chose to include. Remember that your audience may not have seen the ad (or whatever text you are describing), so your description should be detailed enough that they can visualize or understand it without seeing or reading it first-hand.

+ **Organize.** No matter what genre or length your assignment is, you will want to consider how to best order your ideas, as well as how to transition between them. Consider what information your audience needs to know before they can fully understand other parts of your argument. For the above assignment, you might consider organizing by rhetorical concept (logos, ethos, pathos) or by details in the ad (color, text, people, etc.). (See Ch. 21, "Organization from Beginning to End" for more.)

+ **Present.** While not included in the above assignment, sometimes assignments will require that you deliver the information via verbal presentation after submitting a written component. If this is a part of your assignment, consider how you can best communicate your ideas in the appropriate format to your particular audience through spoken delivery. For instance, if you presented your argument on the above prompt to your classmates, you would generally not need to explain what the rhetorical appeals are since you have all discussed them together, but would need to identify how the specific advocacy ad uses them to appeal to their audience. You can also consider what visual aids would be most useful for your presentation, if required or allowed by the instructor; for instance, for the above assignment, projecting the ad could be very helpful for your audience to better understand your analysis. (See Ch. 25, "Rhetorical Delivery" for more.)

In addition to the assignment description, instructors will often also include questions that you can consider or steps you should take to complete the assignment. These can be useful to help you stay on track as you move through the steps of invention, researching, drafting, and revising. If a professor does not include a list of steps, consider making some for the assignment yourself. Break the process down into small stages and indicate the order in which you should complete them. When making a list of the tasks you must accomplish to finish the project, it can also be helpful to look at your own calendar and establish deadlines for each step so that you have plenty of time to work on the project. Not only is this creation of steps helpful to understanding the individual tasks that you must complete, it also emphasizes the process of writing. For instance, your steps might include brainstorming potential topics, researching information, outlining your ideas, drafting the text, and revising.

» Participating in Discussion Boards

One common type of assignment in writing classes, especially if they are online, is a discussion board. Discussion boards are an opportunity for you to engage in conversation with other students through writing. Unlike conversations in person, when you contribute to a discussion board you have more time to collect your thoughts, articulate them in a clear manner, and revise as needed before posting. Take advantage of this opportunity by being deliberate and thorough in your discussion board responses. Often, you will not only be asked to write a post, but to respond to other students' posts. Just as you would in a physical classroom space, be sure to maintain a respectful tone in your posts, especially because readers do not have access to your tone of voice, facial expressions, or gestures to help them interpret your meaning. Just like all the other components discussed in this chapter, the discussion boards are an additional element of the conversation in the writing class.

» Considering Rubrics

Many instructors will provide a rubric that describes the categories they will use to assess a project or assignment. The rubric will usually describe what the assignment must accomplish in each category to be considered an A, B, C, D, or F submission in that category. Alternatively, a rubric might describe individual categories and the maximum points that can be earned in each area. Instructors will often use the rubrics to visually show the biggest strengths and areas for improvement, as well as to determine the overall grade. As a student, the rubric is a useful tool to use for self-evaluation of your work to determine ways that you can improve in various categories that will be assessed by your instructor. **When you receive a completed rubric with your graded essay, the comments and rubric serve as a continuation of the dialogue between you and the instructor.** Other assignments, such as presentations or discussion boards, also frequently include rubrics as part of the assessment and feedback.

In addition to rubrics for individual assignments in English 101, portfolio rubrics evaluate the portfolio as the summative assessment for the course. Such a rubric evaluates the effectiveness of all of your included projects, your revisions of them, and your ability to understand and apply the rhetorical concepts you have learned. Rubrics and assignment sheets often include similar terminology, including for example, "analyze," "argument," and "organize," and refer to research, all of which were discussed above. While the portfolio is essentially your final statement regarding your development as a writer in the course, this rubric allows the instructor to provide you one last form of feedback regarding strengths in your writing, as well as ways that you can continue to work on improving your writing in future courses.

» Reading Instructor Feedback

In addition to a rubric, many instructors will provide comments on projects when they are returned. Sometimes instructors will write marginal comments, which are written or typed in the assignment's margins and often ask questions or offer suggestions regarding a particular section of the project. Additionally, instructors may write a terminal comment, which typically can be found at the end of the assignment and provides feedback regarding the work as a whole.

Both marginal and terminal comments offer a response from your instructor about your unique composition style and approach to the project. These comments can be seen as an extension of the classroom conversation surrounding your project, but are more focused on your own particular work. Read over the instructor's comments carefully and ask for clarification if you cannot determine their meaning. If you are required to revise the project, these comments can be a starting point for revision. If you are not required to revise, you could still make changes to the assignment after receiving feedback to practice revision, or could intentionally reflect on the comments before starting the next project. (For an example of self-guided reflection, see Appendix H.)

» Connecting Materials to the Whole Course

When you receive materials from an instructor, whether the syllabus, an assignment sheet, a rubric, feedback, or other information, consider it one part of the conversation between you and your instructor. After reading and considering the material, if you have questions for your instructor, you should feel free to continue the conversation by inquiring further in class, via email, or in office hours. Understanding that all the textual interactions in a course operate within a bigger conversation helps connect ideas and assignment goals.

5. Personalizing Your Writing Practice

Beth Miller

» Adapting the Process

"Great ideas!" "Develop organization." "Interesting point!"
"Work on structure."

I'm sure I'm not alone in receiving confusing or contradictory feedback on an essay. How can someone tell that my ideas are good if the structure doesn't make any sense? It had to be easy enough to follow that they could tell I was saying something intriguing, right?

In these next few pages, I hope to give you a blueprint for understanding your own writing process. It took me years to piece mine together, but hopefully this chapter will show you some ways you can critically approach and understand your work and process. While this understanding will still take work and practice to develop, as anything worth having does, I propose that understanding *when* to look at persistent problems in your writing is just as important as knowing *where* to look.

Though there are many active debates among people who study writing, as in any field, almost all compositionists agree that:

1. Writing is a process.

2. Good writing is good thinking.

Putting these two ideas together, we can extrapolate that good thinking is a process we work through by writing. The reason we engage in the writing process, or even write things down in the first place, is to examine them more carefully and precisely once they are physically on the page. **When we organize our ideas with a specific reader in mind, we can see the holes in our logic or problems with our assumptions.** Giving the writing process more time and space also allows us

> "Good thinking is a process we work through by writing."

to find the gaps between what we thought we had written and what we actually composed.

The essay "Freewriting" by Peter Elbow explains that as writers, we need to separate our "editing selves" from our "creating selves." **When we try to edit and produce at the same time**, we may not only fix small mistakes, but **we also prevent ourselves from fully participating in the invention process** by editing out "unacceptable" ideas. This indecision, in turn, interrupts and stifles our natural voice.

Bringing out our personal voice and changing our writing process starts before we begin drafting. Regardless of how you feel about writing for a course assignment, viewing your essay as a finished product that will be graded probably creates some degree of nervousness, especially in the initial phases. You may imagine that you are expected to write in a certain way—one that often doesn't sound very much like *you*. **The problem with our voice and ideas being drowned out by what we think we are *supposed* to write versus how we actually express ourselves starts with who we picture as we write.**

What if, instead of your instructor, you imagined writing to someone who is easy for you to talk to? Someone with whom you do not struggle to be (and communicate like) yourself? **Shifting your target audience during the prewriting and drafting phases of the writing process allows your voice to come through and your ideas to come out more naturally.** (For more on style in academic discourse, see Ch. 23, "Personalizing Academic Discourse.")

Much of this textbook deals with helping you adjust your writing to address an academic audience. We also spend quite a bit of time encouraging you to approach writing as a process instead of a product. The goal of this chapter is to assist you in personalizing these two processes. **Academic writing can still include your personal opinions and voice, so I invite you to also experiment with *how* you write essays to find an efficient, effective practice.**

Before we go further, take a moment to reflect on your strengths as a writer, areas that you would like to improve in, and the feedback you most often receive. By feedback, I am not referring to surface-level errors like run-ons or sentence fragments. How have instructors responded to your ideas in the past? What types of changes have they asked you to make in your writing as a whole? Jot those suggestions down and put them to the side. Don't worry about those things while you're prewriting and drafting. Instead, when you get to the *revision* stage, you'll want to read for these issues. **Over time, you can adjust your writing process to bring out what you do well as a writer while you're creating and support your weaker areas when revising.**

Normalizing Writing

In the past, when I've asked students if the essays they submitted in high school sounded like them, the answer was overwhelmingly "no." I then asked if other examples of their writing—a text message, an email, a phone call (or other spoken text)—sound like them, and, as you might imagine, the answer was "yes." Why the disparity between academic and personal writing?

Elbow also helps to answer this question regarding difference in voice. In his book, *Writing Without Teachers*, he lays out the problem with much of our academic work—it is unnatural communication. **By unnatural, he and I do not mean that writing itself is strange or should be awkward, but that the challenge for much of our pre-collegiate academic writing was our audience.** When you wrote an essay about *Romeo and Juliet* for your high school English teacher, they most likely knew a lot more about the play and Shakespeare than you did at the time. This is the opposite of standard communication. **In most cases, when we communicate, we are telling someone else something new.**

For example, when you call a family member or text your best friend, you are telling them something they do not already know about your ideas, your experience, or your day. You would never call your mom and tell her how *her* day went. Along these same lines, much of our writing for instructors has been unnatural: we have been telling someone who knows more than we do about a particular subject something that they, very likely, already know.

"You would never call your mom and tell her how *her* day went."

You may be questioning, at this point, how this situation is any different in your College Writing course or other classes. The answer varies, but **an exciting aspect of college writing is increased freedom and choice.** Even if you cannot choose the *delivery* of your work, such as an assignment that specifies a researched essay with ten sources, you have a lot more control over *what* you write about. You can take projects in directions you find exciting, regardless of the prompt's specificity. **Your voice and ideas will come out more clearly if you write about something you're passionate about.** I cannot promise that everything you are asked to write will give you full freedom of subject and form, but each—given time, dedication, and curiosity—is **an opportunity for you to exercise creativity and individuality.**

Keep in mind that developing a personal voice in your writing and finding a process that works for you takes time and effort. Simply choosing what you want to write about, and then postponing that work to the last minute, will not greatly alter the personality of your writing. If you leave yourself a limited amount of time to write, you have no choice but to get it "right" the first time. Thus, when you approach a blank page, you end up expecting your work to be focused and perfect from the first sentence. Instead, taking time to engage the writing process alleviates this pressure.

College Writing, and writing in college in general, offers a vastly different opportunity for developing your writing. You will likely have several weeks, if not an entire semester, to create and polish your work. **Because writing is a *process*, giving yourself time (both for each assignment as well as over the course of your academic career) will result in a style that reflects your personal voice and ideas.**

My Own Practice

To explain a personalized process in more detail, I'll offer an example from my own practice. Beyond using it as a prompt for thinking about your own, remember that you will also have the opportunity to reflect on your writing— both the essays and how you made them—in your portfolio's critical reflection at the end of the year. (For more on reflecting critically, see Ch. 29, "Writing about Your Composing Process," and Ch. 30, "Reflecting Back.") Noting where you started and how you adapted throughout the semester is a great way to measure progress *and* reflect on changes you'd like to make in the future.

As a writer, my work is often creative or innovative; I can approach a topic in a new way. However, I struggle with organizing my ideas so that someone other than myself can understand them. These two things, a strength and a weakness, are interrelated. **The same different thinking pattern that allows me to say something unexpected makes it more difficult for my readers to follow my ideas.** I can arrive at my argument and conclusions in a surprising way, but my readers need more guidance to understand how I got there. Yet, because my thoughts make sense to me, it's hard for me to retrace my steps and carefully lay out the trail of breadcrumbs my readers need to follow my argument.

Recognizing this pattern, I had to adjust my writing process. **Because I struggle with organization, I ignore it entirely during the pre-writing and drafting phases.** Instead, I spend a lot of pre-writing time mulling the essay over in my head, and then freewrite. (For more, see Ch. 17, "Pre-Writing Strategies.") Once I have a page or two of brainstorming about my topic, I begin drafting my essay. I try to do this when I have a few hours dedicated to getting my ideas down on paper so I don't feel rushed and can make sure to keep my writer and editor selves separated. **At this point, I move in and out of freewriting and drafting, so I am both writing about *and* writing my essay.** I try to keep this up until I either run out of things to say or run out of time.

Next, ideally, I let my paper sit for at least 24 hours before returning to it for revision. **As I revise, I pay a lot of attention to organization** *because* **it's a challenge for me.** I use a few different strategies to determine the best organization for my paper: reverse outlining, checking topic sentences by pasting them into their own document, and reading the essay in reverse by paragraph. These methods help me move paragraphs around and think about how to communicate my ideas in a logical, focused order. I do not worry about editing the paragraphs or sentences until I have a reader-focused order that correlates to a working thesis. (For more on revision strategies, see Ch. 27, "Re-Seeing the Revision Process.")

Next, I ask someone in my writing group to look over my essay and help with the organization before I proceed to working on the paragraphs themselves. Collaborating with a writing group has become an essential part of my writing process. These groups work so well because everyone has different strengths when it comes to writing. We also bring new perspectives and ideas to one another's work. I encourage you to create a group of your own, with friends or classmates, to help everyone improve. In addition to joining a writing group, consider visiting the Writing Center to work with a consultant and reap similar benefits.

By honestly considering my strengths and weaknesses as a writer, I changed my writing process so that I can play to my strengths and, as much as possible, mitigate my weaknesses. **Because writing processes are as unique as the writers who engage in them, you should experiment with your own practice and find a method that works for you.** We improve as writers over the course of our lives, but the combination of small adjustments and time can inspire confidence and growth.

> "By honestly considering my strengths and weaknesses as a writer, I changed my writing process so that I can play to my strengths and, as much as possible, mitigate my weaknesses."

> **Ideas to consider trying out in your own practice:**
> - Experiment with *where* you write. Some people really enjoy writing alone at their desk, whereas others need noise, movement, and people to help themselves focus. Many writers prefer different locations for drafting versus revising and editing.
> - Seek help for areas you struggle with. For example, if you have a hard time coming up with enough things to say, have an inquisitive friend or family member ask you questions and challenge your ideas.
> - Remember that the writing process is recursive. You can't get it right the first time, so don't be afraid to return to prewriting or drafting. Save editing and proofreading until the very end.
> - Give yourself time to return to your essay so you can read over it, removed from its initial creation. You may *think* you've written something down only to discover that it is not actually on the page. This is especially important when you consider your ideal audience for writing in college: an engaged but uninformed reader. How will you fill in the gaps for them with your expertise and join those ideas to common knowledge?

» Work Cited

Peter Elbow. *Writing Without Teachers*. 2nd ed., Oxford University Press, 1998.

For further reference, see Donald Murray's "Teach Writing as a Process Not Product," and Charlotte Pence's *The Writer's Path: Creative Exercises for Meaningful Essays*.

» Teaching Text

Think, Pair, Share. Ask everyone in class to take a few moments to reflect on their own writing strengths and weaknesses. Are these connected in some way? Next, in pairs or small groups, share writing strengths with others and discuss how different writers can help each other. This would be particularly effective in peer review groups so that everyone can learn best practices.

Experiment. Pick a phase of the writing process and work through it in a different location than you normally would. What does it feel like to revise in a quiet environment but draft somewhere with ambient noise? Does prewriting outside keep your mind open and reduce your stress?

Reflect. Give yourself some time to think through some of the feedback you've received on your writing in the past. Removing any negativity from those comments, what constructive criticism can you gain from this reflection? Now, how might you change your writing process to take this issue into account in a way that doesn't affect the strengths of your writing or process?

6. Cultivating Your Ethos:
Class Participation, Written Communication, and Student-Instructor Conferences

Kayla Forrest

When we discuss our ethos as writers, we often consider the importance of recognizing and responding effectively to the various written rhetorical situations we might encounter. But when we talk about developing our ethos as students, what do we mean by that? And what kinds of rhetorical situations are we referring to?

While you may feel a little uncertain about how to answer these questions, it is important to keep in mind that when we discuss our ethos as students we are referring to qualities such as credibility and authority as members of the academic community. Class participation, student-instructor conferences, and written communication such as emails are all rhetorical situations, and to respond to them effectively, you should consider who you are writing or speaking to as well as the context and purpose for the communication. By effectively analyzing and responding to these various academic rhetorical situations, we position ourselves as credible members of the academic community. (For more on recognizing and using rhetorical concepts, see Ch. 20, "Writing with the Rhetorical Appeals.")

> "By effectively analyzing and responding to these various academic rhetorical situations, we position ourselves as credible members of the academic community."

» Your Ethos as a Student in the Classroom

Communicating with your peers and instructors in class is one of the main rhetorical situations in college. As a rhetor, you want to consider your persona as a student and how you can build your ethos. With this goal in mind, as you engage in class discussions and activities, consider how what you say and the way you say it comes across to your peers and your instructor. In order for there to be an environment of respect within the classroom, we have to do our part to show that we respect those around us, just as we would expect them to show respect to us.

Effective class participation does not just mean speaking up during class discussions or activities; active listening is also an important part of cultivating your credibility as a student. One way to get into the habit of active listening is through taking notes during class conversations and recording your thoughts and questions in response to your instructor's and peers' comments. Active listening also involves demonstrating through your body language that you are mentally present and intellectually engaged in the conversation around you. Your body language can do a lot to help or harm your ethos in the classroom; it is often easy for us to identify if someone is engaged based on interpersonal cues like posture and whether or not they are making eye contact.

"Active listening is an important part of cultivating your credibility as a student."

You can also cultivate your credibility by being prepared for class. It may seem simple, but even completing readings and assignments and bringing needed materials can contribute to your ethos in the classroom. Instructors assign homework or readings to enhance your understanding of the subject matter and provide information in advance of class discussion, so when students do not come to class prepared, it affects their ability to participate. Therefore, preparing for class and any related activities is another way of building your ethos as a student.

» Ethos and Written Communication

In addition to class participation, you should also consider how to establish your ethos in your written communication. One of the most common forms of written communication in which you will likely engage in college is email. Because we usually use the same device (such as a smartphone) to write an email and a text message, we may think of them as the same rhetorical situation, but they have important distinctions. We should consider how we can effectively communicate with our peers and instructors through email or Canvas. As you think about the email you have to send, consider how the rhetorical situation can help you make specific choices. In doing so, you might ask yourself these questions:

Who am I emailing and what is my relationship with that person?

If you are emailing an instructor, your tone and the structure of your email will likely need to be more formal than if you are emailing a peer. For instance, when addressing your instructor, you should use a greeting (i.e., "Dear Professor Smith") to start your email and a salutation with your signature (i.e., "Sincerely, Adam") to end it—much like if you were writing a letter. Some instructors do not mind receiving more informal emails, or if students refer to them using their first names, but it is a good idea to err on the side of formality unless your instructor has told you otherwise. Likewise, it is also important to show your respect for your peers in how you address them in your written communication. While emails to your peers may be less formal than those you send to your instructors, consider how you can still show that you value and respect them as individuals and fellow members of your academic community.

What is my purpose for emailing?

Are you writing to an instructor to schedule a meeting with them? Are you emailing your peers to collaborate on a group project? As you consider why you are writing, it is also important to consider your audience. If you are asking for clarification about an assignment, you can establish your ethos by letting your professor know that you have checked the syllabus or the assignment sheet for answers before emailing them. If you are asking a peer if they would look over a draft, think about how you can respectfully ask them to do so and provide specific questions that you want them to consider as they read. If you are communicating with a peer about a project, consider how you can clearly identify your questions, concerns, or ideas, and ask for specific feedback from them. Whatever your purpose is, it is important to be intentional about your rhetorical approach to emailing, always showing respect and professionalism in how you address your instructors and peers. Doing so helps you to establish your ethos as a member of the academic community.

"It is important to be intentional about your rhetorical approach to emailing."

When should I send my email and when might I expect a response?

In addition to the questions of your audience, purpose, and approach, it is also important to consider the timing of your email. Many instructors have an email policy in which they articulate when they check and respond to emails and how much time they typically take to respond to them. If your instructor does have an email policy, it is important to take that into account as you determine when you should email them and when you might hear back. Likewise, you might consider when it would be most effective to send your peers an email. If you are emailing to ask a question about an upcoming assignment, for example, you will want to give your peer enough time to get back to you about your question before the assignment deadline. Whether you are emailing a peer or an instructor, it always helps to allow plenty of time for a response, as it can be difficult for anyone to address last minute questions, requests, or concerns.

» Conferencing Rhetorically

Conferences are also rhetorical situations that you will encounter in your College Writing courses. As with classroom participation and emails, you can establish your ethos by thoughtfully considering each conference as a rhetorical situation and by making intentional choices which take the situation into account.

Considering the Purpose

Conferences are a great opportunity for students and instructors to communicate one-on-one, and instructors often have specific goals for conferences. For example, instructors may use conferences to discuss specific assignments, look over drafts, or discuss your grades in the course. In any case, conferences enable instructors to give individualized feedback to you on your work and performance in the course, but they also allow you, the student, an opportunity to ask questions and direct the conference in ways that will help you succeed.

"Conferences enable instructors to give individualized feedback to you on your work and performance in the course, but they also allow you, the student, an opportunity to ask questions and direct the conference in ways that will help you succeed."

Developing Your Ethos as a Rhetor and Engaging with Your Audience

As you anticipate and participate in your conference, it is important to keep in mind how you can develop your ethos as a student and a member of the academic community and recognize your instructor as your audience. Here are some things to keep in mind:

Consider the Format: Is it a face-to-face conference, or will you be conferencing through an electronic interface? In both cases, it helps to give yourself some extra time to either set up and test your technology or to find your instructor's office. Since your instructor is often conferencing with multiple students in a day, your promptness for your appointment will demonstrate that you respect your instructor's time as well as that of your peers who are scheduled after you. Failure to arrive on time may even mean that you miss your conference.

Come Prepared: Developing your ethos starts before your conference, as you understand and ask questions about your instructor's goals for the conference and prepare for your meeting. Often instructors will ask students to come prepared with materials, like drafts or pre-writing, or they might ask you to come prepared with questions you wish to ask. Coming prepared to your conference will show your instructor that you mean to make the best use of your time together.

Ask Questions: Whether or not your instructor asks you to bring certain things to your conference, it is always a good idea to come up with specific questions or parts of your paper that you wish to talk about. Asking questions during your conference shows you are taking responsibility for your education, and it can also help your instructor understand if they need to revisit or further discuss certain topics or activities.

Listen Actively: In any conversation, it is important that participants listen actively and respond thoughtfully to one another in order to promote clear communication; the same goes for conferences. Just as your instructor desires to listen to your ideas, concerns, and questions with respect, consider how you can listen to your instructor's feedback with an open mind, but not without critically examining it. Taking notes also shows that you are actively engaged in the discussion, and it can help you to recall what you talked about after your conference.

Think Critically: Remember that your instructor wants to help you succeed in the course, but they do not want to give you a list of things that you need to "fix" within your paper, as doing so would thwart the need for critical thought. Instructors often want to help you challenge yourself and think critically about your work, discuss strategies to work through issues like writer's block, and encourage your growth as a writer.

Develop Take-aways: Another way to demonstrate your ethos as a student and member of the academic community is to utilize what you have discussed in your conference through your future work and class involvement. That may mean you take the time to revise your draft further, or you consider a counter-argument in your paper. It could also mean that you take steps to be more active in your participation in class or in online discussion boards. Remember that conferences are an opportunity to show your instructor that you are a responsible student who is interested in improving and thinking critically about your work.

» Conclusion

Regardless of whether you are conferencing, participating in class, or sending an email to an instructor or classmate, remember that these moments are all rhetorical situations. As a student, taking the time to intentionally recognize the different parts of these rhetorical situations will help you actively prepare for and respond to each situation and develop your ethos as a student and member of the academic community.

» Teaching Text

After reading the chapter, consider the following email written from a student to a professor and answer the questions listed below.

> Hey!
>
> I don't really understand what we are supposed to be doing for our project. I remember in class that you said we needed to write a rhetorical analysis but I don't know what I am supposed to write about and where I should start. Can you please tell me what we are supposed to be doing?
>
> Thanks!
>
> A. Student

Questions

1. What seems to be the rhetorical situation for this email?

2. Given the rhetorical situation for the email, would you argue that A. Student is effectively responding to the rhetorical situation? Why or why not?

3. If you were going to advise A. Student to revise the email, what suggestions would you make?

7. Academic Integrity:
Promoting Intellectual Growth

Elysia Balavage

When you hear the word "integrity," what comes to mind? Maybe concepts like honesty, or reliability, or even moral uprightness? If someone has integrity, would you consider her an individual who behaves according to a strong ethical manner? If so, you probably have a good understanding of integrity. Now, what about when you hear the phrase "academic integrity"? Perhaps you think of the need to cite your sources correctly to avoid plagiarism, or of not cheating on a test. These instances speak to the facet of academic integrity that underlines the punitive "failure" or "violation" aspect of the concept. However, academic integrity holds a greater meaning than only breaking a university rule and being punished for that violation. **The idea of honest, productive, communal interaction and growth are also integral parts of academic integrity, and it is the responsibility of each of us to ensure that our university community continues to foster scholarly development for each of its members.** As a student, building your ethos within your university community is an important goal, and understanding the principles of academic integrity will help you achieve this; therefore, it is important to incorporate the values of academic integrity into all aspects of your academic career. Practicing habits that encourage academic integrity ensures that students grow intellectually.

> "Practicing habits that encourage academic integrity ensures that students grow intellectually."

Consider other communities you belong to: your group of friends, workplace, sports team, musical ensemble, or student activity group. No matter the community, there needs to be a measure of trust that all members share for the group to function well. For instance, if your roommate lied to you about eating your food out of the fridge, you would not trust him next time. Likewise, if your teammate lied to get out of practice, you might not feel like you could depend on her to perform her best in the big game. Without collective trust, a team cannot perform at its best, and relationships cannot function in a healthy, respectful way. If a similar situation occurs in a university community, the university's ability to foster scholarly growth is compromised, so it is essential that all members adhere to the principles of academic integrity.

43

As mentioned above, "integrity" refers to the characteristic of being truthful and having solid moral principles. In order to understand what academic integrity means, let us first think about these terms together. Colleges and universities all have academic policies that regulate academic standards and procedures, and these policies help students fulfill common responsibilities they will encounter in a university setting. An academic integrity policy helps students understand a university's expectations concerning their academic work. For example, the UNCG Academic Integrity Policy highlights the following five values as maintaining and promoting a high level of academic integrity: honesty, trust, fairness, respect, and responsibility.[1]

"'Academic integrity' is the moral and ethical code of academia as a whole, with 'academia' referring to a community of researchers, instructors, and students, often centered at a college or university, who participate in higher learning and inquiry."

Given those emphasized qualities, it is fair to say that academic integrity means more than breaking a university policy or using proper citations. In short, "academic integrity" is the moral and ethical code of academia as a whole, with "academia" referring to a community of researchers, instructors, and students, often centered at a college or university, who participate in higher learning and inquiry. So, by virtue of being a student, you are a part of the academic community as well as the process of intellectual inquiry. With that membership comes the moral responsibility to avoid engaging in dishonest behaviors, such as plagiarism and cheating, while promoting ethical qualities that facilitate a stimulating discussion that respects the sincere, ethical acquisition of knowledge. This is what academic integrity means.

» Academic Integrity vs. Academic Dishonesty

While the classroom is a space where academic integrity is fostered and nurtured, there are certain acts, as briefly mentioned above, that upset the atmosphere of effective scholarly discourse. It is important to be aware of these behaviors so that we may support our own as well as fellow students' endeavors to follow the guidelines of academic integrity. Furthermore, there may be a point when an act that may seem innocent actually breaks the principles of academic integrity and community trust. For instance, suppose your friend asks you to write a paper for her. She is falling behind on her assignments, and you feel that you would be helping her by agreeing to her request. However, this act violates academic integrity because the trust that each student crafts and submits his/her own work has been broken. While your intentions may

---

1. For more information, see the Office of Student Rights and Responsibilities website, osrr.uncg.edu/academic-integrity/.

be pure, community trust would still be damaged. Furthermore, your friend would not benefit in the long term for not completing her own assignments due to the missed opportunity to build and develop her academic skills. For a comparison between academic integrity and academic dishonesty, see the following chart:

Academic Integrity	Academic Dishonesty
Using the concepts of *honesty, trust, fairness, respect,* and *responsibility* in all areas of scholarly participation, like: taking exams; making oral presentations; writing assignments; and participating in classroom discussion.	Acts that disregard the concepts of *honesty, trust, fairness, respect,* and *responsibility* and disrupt the flow of intellectual conversation, like: plagiarising; cheating on exams; fabricating data; doing another student's work for him/her; submitting another person's work as your own; or using someone else's ideas/claims as your own.

» Academic Integrity and Ethos

In previous chapters, the rhetorical appeals of ethos, pathos, and logos were discussed in relation to successfully composing a holistic, argumentative essay. It is imperative to note, however, that the importance of the appeals extends beyond argumentative writing. To review, ethos, the "ethical appeal," refers to the quality, authority, and honesty of an individual's character. In order to portray effective ethos, you must acquire your audience's confidence by positioning yourself as a trustworthy, reasonable, principled individual. (See Ch. 20, "Writing with the Rhetorical Appeals" for more.) Like effective ethos, academic integrity promotes morality, honesty, and trust between individuals and a whole scholarly community.

Cultivating your ethos to reflect habits that demonstrate academic integrity also shows that you care about the process of learning and producing ideas in addition to the final product. That is, the way you learn is just as significant as what you learn and generate. For instance, showing respect for others' opinions even if you do not agree with them, just like you would do in an argumentative essay, fosters the learning community of a university and allows for an inclusive conversation in which intellectual growth can thrive. Furthermore, taking responsibility for your own work and studies contributes to the continued accomplishment of a scholarly conversation. By applying the strong ethos you cultivate in your College Writing courses to your participation in the university community, you uphold the values of academic integrity.

Likewise, engaging in academically dishonest behaviors diminishes one's ethos, and failure to participate in a university community in a way that reflects a mindfulness and value for the principles of academic integrity can compromise intellectual enrichment. If, for instance, a student plagiarizes a paper, his trustworthiness and credibility as a writer with unique ideas to contribute to an academic conversation is questioned and even challenged. Once that communal trust has been broken, it can be difficult to regain. Or, if a student uses confrontational language in a paper because she strongly disagrees with the opposing point of view, this demonstrates disrespect for alternate ideas and thus stifles a discussion that could yield scholarly growth. Since academic integrity and strong ethos equally depend on honesty, trust, fairness, respect, and responsibility, breaking those principles both demonstrates weak ethos and a disruption of the exchange of ideas.

» Academic Integrity and Rhetorical Position

It is important to understand that your words, whether spoken or written, can have a strong persuasive effect on your audience. Because of this, it is important to adhere to the rules of academic integrity so that your audience's trust in you is not misplaced. This can be accomplished by managing the information you include in an assignment as well as properly crediting the sources you use. By ethically and accurately representing the sources that you use to support your argument, you ensure that you present a fair, honest, and trustworthy project. Additionally, properly giving credit to the sources you consulted while crafting your project upholds the principles of academic integrity in multiple ways. First, it places your argument in conversation with other thinkers and specialists who have worked on your topic. Second, it allows you to avoid plagiarizing and claiming another person's work as your own. There are a variety of citation styles for academic disciplines, but here is a short list of the most common styles used in scholarly settings:

"By ethically and accurately representing the sources that you use to support your argument, you ensure that you present a fair, honest, and trustworthy project."

+ MLA (Modern Language Association): for English and the Humanities

+ APA (America Psychological Association): for Psychology and Social Sciences

+ CMS (Chicago Manual of Style): for History and some Humanities

+ CSE (Council of Science Editors): for the Sciences

Each style emphasizes the most important piece of information for the discipline that uses it. For instance, MLA style privileges names and page numbers to highlight particular examples from literary texts, while APA style focuses on names and publication dates to foreground the most recent scholarship published. (See Ch. 16, "Rhetorical Elements of Academic Citation" for further discussion of citation styles.)

» How to Prevent Circumstances that Could Result in Academic Dishonesty

There are many reasons why students might be tempted to violate the principles of academic integrity. You may be too busy to complete all assignments or you may think that your work is not good enough, but presenting plagiarized content to your instructor will end up hurting you more in the long term. Rather than turning to academically dishonest behavior to complete an assignment, consider the following points:

+   *Take the initiative*: If you are confused about an assignment, ask your instructor for clarification early in the process.

+   *Practice good time management*: Plan ahead to be sure that you will have ample time to effectively complete an assignment. Think about how much time your assignment will realistically take to complete and stick to your plan of action.

+   *Consult outside resources for help when necessary*: If you need extra help conceptualizing an assignment, visit the Writing Center for guidance, even to brainstorm ideas. You can also visit the library if you would like help locating appropriate sources for your assignment.

+   *Encourage your peers to promote academic integrity*: While you are not obligated to report a classmate for academic dishonesty, consider sharing the above tips with him/her if you notice a violation. A visit to the Writing Center or a meeting with the instructor are far better solutions than engaging in academically dishonest behavior.

By keeping these points in mind, you can play an active role in promoting an atmosphere of academic integrity in your university community that fosters the creative and intellectual growth of all members.

» Parting Considerations

The values of academic integrity are the principles essential to promoting an effective scholarly discussion in a college or university community. Without honesty, trust, fairness, respect, and responsibility, intellectual conversation and growth would be difficult, if not impossible, to achieve. As we write our papers, it is important to remember that academic integrity is about more than avoiding plagiarism or being disciplined for violating a university rule. Academic integrity asks us to ethically debate and challenge ideas in an environment that gives us the autonomy to grow both individually and collectively.

8. Collaboration in the Classroom:
Uncovering the Benefits of Group Assignments

Kayla Forrest and Marc Keith

When you think of collaboration in the classroom, what comes to mind? You might first think of the collaboration involved in peer reviews, but this is far from the only sort of collaboration you will encounter in a writing class. (For more on peer review, see Ch. 28, "De-Stressing the Peer Review Process.") You may also encounter formal group projects that need preparation outside of class time, informal group work in class, or even multimodal projects that require the expertise of several people. Each of these different types of group work comes with unique challenges, but collaboration can be an enjoyable and productive experience when approached with the right attitude. Below, we will discuss the benefits and opportunities of collaborative work, as well as offer troubleshooting strategies to help you navigate these types of work.

» Types of Group Work and the Benefits of Collaboration

It can be intimidating to be asked to work in groups, as it means you must depend on other people to get something done. But beyond meaning that you don't have to do all the work yourself, there are many benefits of collaboration and group work! **Collaboration enables you to combine your efforts and skills with those of your peers, to accomplish more than you could as individuals.** Without collaboration, we risk thinking in a vacuum, recognizing only our own ideas, and missing out on the valuable perspectives of others. Group collaboration also helps you to get to know your classmates better, which benefits the classroom community.

"Without collaboration, we risk thinking in a vacuum, recognizing only our own ideas, and missing out on the valuable perspectives of others."

Collaboration in the classroom can take many forms, including group presentations, informal group work, and group multimodal projects. These kinds of assignments vary widely in their scope and goals, even if they require the same skills. For group presentations, while instructors often focus on the importance of written communication, oral communication is also important. Sometimes it can be intimidating to speak in front of an audience, but doing so with peers provides support and solidarity that can help build confidence for communicating orally. Collaborating also allows you to develop your informal oral communication skills as you work *within your group*. (For more on written communication with peers, see Ch. 6, "Cultivating Your Ethos.")

Working in groups can benefit the development of your ideas in informal discussions as well. This structure provides **an environment for you to bounce ideas off of one another and work together to build something.** Ideally, the safety of small groups can help you feel more confident to share your ideas, vet them with peers, and ultimately contribute these ideas to the classroom community. By having conversations in small groups or pairs, you can compare your thoughts with those of your peers. By doing so, you challenge yourself to think through your own stances, listen to those of others, and practice synthesizing information.

More and more of our interactions are taking place in digital environments, and as a result, many of you will encounter multimodal projects. Oftentimes, instructors design these projects to be collaborative, because multimodal projects are diverse in nature and tend to require a wide skill set. The benefit of collaborating in this context is being able to draw on many people's expertise. For example, if your instructor assigns a project requiring your group to design a website, you may focus on editing the content, while another member of your group refines the website's visual appeal. In addition to splitting up the work, collaboration results in a type of cross-pollination where you pick up new information or skills from your peers, such as coming to a better understanding of how rhetoric functions visually as well as textually.

> "In addition to splitting up the work, collaboration results in a type of cross-pollination where you pick up new information or skills from your peers."

» Strategies for Successful Collaboration

Because collaboration allows you to join your ideas with the ideas of others to develop something more complex and multifaceted than the things you accomplish alone, you will be most successful if you approach it with a positive attitude. While it is understandable that you may feel apprehensive about collaboration, it's important to approach it professionally by practicing respect for those you collaborate with and doing your best to communicate clearly about common expectations for group work. **If everyone approaches collaboration with the goal of being respectful and communicating clearly, collaboration can be an immensely beneficial experience for all involved.**

In informal group work, you may have reservations about what happens when conflicting ideas arise. While this worry is understandable (no one wants to have their ideas shot down!), **differing perspectives and ideas are some of the greatest benefits of collaboration.** Remembering that you and your peers are all working toward a common goal will encourage everyone to behave mindfully and cooperatively. Respect must be the threshold for all group communication, even when disagreeing with a group member.

We also want to remember that communication involves listening as well as speaking, and **it is important to let all group members voice their ideas.** Making sure everyone's ideas and opinions are heard not only creates a more welcoming group atmosphere, but can lead to a wider variety of perspectives that fosters a more creative approach to your project. Finally, we must remember and acknowledge that compromise is an integral component of any collaborative enterprise.

"Compromise is an integral component of any collaborative enterprise."

Although it can be difficult to compromise, especially when a grade is at stake, all group work is going to require some degree of give-and-take. **Having clear expectations, fairly divided tasks, and a sense of how you interact with others can help make compromising, listening, and generally getting along with your group much easier.**

Working with others on complex multimodal projects can prevent you from feeling overwhelmed and will allow you to focus your energy where it is most useful. A multimodal project is, as Brenta Blevins says in her chapter "Rhetorical Delivery," a project or composition that "combine[s] a variety of communication modes including speaking, writing, and visual designs," so in collaborating on a multimodal project, you may want to consider establishing what strengths (and technological proficiencies) different members of your group have. You can also augment your group's strengths by consulting with the professionals in the Digital Media Commons and Digital ACT Studio.

» Practical Tips and Tools for Collaboration

In order to most effectively manage your collaboration, it is best to consider a number of practical strategies that will facilitate any group working together. These include actions like dividing the work and establishing deadlines, as well as digital tools designed to make collaboration even easier.

To collaborate effectively, it is important to **designate tasks for each group member to accomplish and to establish specific deadlines for when those tasks should be completed.** Dividing up work allows you to share responsibility and ensure that necessary tasks are taken care of. Deadlines allow you to check in with your collaborators in order to see what still needs to be done, how your group will move forward, and how individual tasks are coming together to accomplish the group's goals.

There are many tools you can use to help manage group work and deadlines. Through your university email account, you have access to all of the Google Suite software. This includes Google Docs, a word processing program, Google Slides, akin to PowerPoint, and Google Sheets, a spreadsheet program, among many other applications. The best part about the Google Suite is that **multiple people can simultaneously work on a single document, presentation, and/ or spreadsheet** from their own computers. This capability is a great way to work around the difficulty of finding a meeting time and place that works for your entire group.

If face-to-face meetings are helpful for your working style, or required, there are tools to help with that too. For example, rather than creating a long and confusing email chain or group text, try setting up a Doodle Poll. With Doodle Polls, you (or someone in your group) set up a calendar of dates and possible meeting times, and then each member simply checks when they are available. This is a quick and simple way to identify the best meeting time for your group. Finally, if a group member cannot physically be present at a face-to-face meeting, programs such as Skype, Facetime, and Google Hangouts allow the missing member to participate in the discussion, by video or voice-only.

» Collaboration in Context

While it's easy for us to tell you about collaboration, we think it's more beneficial to demonstrate what collaboration looks like. As co-authors of this chapter, we had to collaborate to develop a draft of the text you are reading. We set up a meeting to discuss our goals and ideas, and we worked together to create an outline in Google Docs of what we wanted our chapter to look like. We took turns sharing our ideas, asked each other questions, identified different problems and barriers, and suggested solutions. Both of us also took care to be aware of our tendencies in collaboration. For example, Kayla tends to talk through her ideas, whereas Marc tends to think them through before articulating them, so we both made sure to listen to each other and speak up when we had something we felt was valuable to contribute. After we developed our outline, we divided the tasks and set about completing them, once again using Google Docs to put our work together. We found that we needed more time to complete the tasks we assigned each other, so we communicated about that and worked until eventually we had a finished product.

Although this is just one instance of collaboration, it demonstrates the way group work can take individuals' ideas and join them together to develop a unified product. After reading this chapter, we hope that you will see collaboration

51

not as something to be feared or dreaded, but as **an opportunity to practice interpersonal communication, challenge your individual perspectives, synthesize the ideas of your group or partnership, learn in different ways, create new things, and build community.**

II

Analyzing and Acknowledging Others

9. Strategies for Active Reading

Meghan H. McGuire

Have you ever started a reading assignment and by the time you got to the end of the first page, you had completely forgotten everything that you just read? My guess is that this has happened to most of us at some point in our academic careers. Reading, processing, and interpreting written information is an essential part of academic work, but many of us try to read with too many distractions around us, which unfortunately prevents us from grasping the rhetor's argument and understanding the material in any substantive way. Whatever is causing our hurried and distracted reading experience, our inability to remember and comprehend the material means that we are not fully engaging with the text; we are not reading closely or critically. In instances like these, we are doing ourselves and the text a disservice by regarding reading as a passive activity that precedes writing. **Instead, we should recognize that reading is a dynamic and essential part of the writing process.**

> "We are doing ourselves and the text a disservice by regarding reading as a passive activity that precedes writing."

Many new scholars and novice writers approach writing assignments by adopting a linear process: read, think, and then write. This approach seems logical at first, **but it inaccurately implies that each activity occurs independently, at a separate stage, without overlap or recurrence.** Effective writing, however, begins with active critical reading, and critical reading involves careful and deliberate thought. **In order to become more effective at active reading, we need to learn to read with purpose and to approach reading as an ongoing dialogue with the text and its author.**

» Becoming an Active Reader

Throughout your college career, you will be asked to read a variety of written and visual texts, and many courses will require you to write about what you have read. In order to complete these tasks, it is important to read with intention, recognizing that different assignments require different reading strategies.

While all assignments will involve close reading skills, determining *why* you are reading a particular text increases your efficiency and effectiveness. While we may be accustomed to reading primarily for content, college-level assignments often require that we evaluate not only *what* is said, but *how* the author says it, and *why* it matters. Answering these more complex questions requires us to utilize active critical reading strategies. In order to move past reading for content alone, we need to approach the text as part of a larger conversation in which our voice matters. We should shift from passive absorption of information to an active engagement with the text. Consider the following questions when reading a text:

> * How is this text put together?
>
> * Who is the intended audience?
>
> * Do you agree or disagree with the opinions presented?
>
> * Can you relate to any of the author's points or experiences?
>
> * Is the rhetor's argument effective and persuasive? If so, how do they accomplish this?

As you can see, answering these questions requires an approach to reading that is far from passive or simple. It requires a significant amount of concentration and action from the reader, and it relies heavily on the practice of **annotation**.

» Strategies for Annotating and Responding to a Text

To annotate a text means that you add critical or explanatory comments to the text while you are reading. These comments are also referred to as **marginalia**, since they are usually placed in the margins of the text itself. It is impossible to overstate the value of annotating a text. As mentioned earlier, active reading requires approaching a text like a conversation. Annotation, therefore, becomes our way of participating in that larger conversation: speaking back to the text with our own ideas, questions, and responses. (For an example of an annotated text, see Appendix A.)

"Annotation, therefore, becomes our way of participating in that larger conversation: speaking back to the text with our own ideas, questions, and responses."

Some students are reluctant to annotate texts because they are concerned about being able to resell their expensive textbooks if they contain marginalia. One simple solution to this concern is to write in pencil rather than pen.

That way your annotations can still be utilized, and you can erase them later if necessary. Alternatively, you can take notes on a separate sheet of paper or use sticky notes and flags to mark passages and add comments without writing directly on the page. You can also take notes on a laptop, though recent studies have shown that taking notes by hand helps you understand and retain information more easily. **Regardless of the annotation method you choose, by making notes as you read, you are beginning the first draft of your written response, keeping yourself engaged with the material, and, ultimately, providing yourself with an indispensable record of your thinking process.**

Thoughtful annotation allows you to explore and record your reactions to a text, such as your observations, questions, and conclusions. As you annotate, consider the following questions:

- Does the text make you angry, sad, defensive, or empathetic?

- What assumptions and personal biases are contributing to this response, and how has the rhetor elicited these feelings?

- Do you agree with the arguments presented in the text? Are they persuasive?

- Do you find the author credible?

- What kinds of evidence and rhetorical strategies are present?

- How can you extend this rhetor's argument?

- How can you contextualize it within a larger conversation?

Although the process of annotation is essential to active critical reading, it is also important to remember that **there is no one correct way to annotate a text.** Your marginal notes may look very different from your classmates', but that is perfectly fine. Observations and interpretations of texts will vary because each person brings their own unique experiences and prior knowledge to their reading. We all learn and process information in different ways, so it is important to find a system that works for you. The following list is not exhaustive, but it does offer a few common strategies for annotation that may prove useful.

- **Underline or highlight important passages**

- **Include brief but specific comments in the margins**

- **Circle unfamiliar words**

- **Create a useful shorthand notation system**

- **Summarize each paragraph or section**

- **Ask questions in the margins**

- **Discuss the text with a peer**

- **Read the text again**

Close critical reading is not a quick or simple act, but it is an essential part of the writing process and a practice that will save you time in the long run. Instead of returning to a blank page with no memory of the material you read, you will have a record of your reading process: your reactions, observations, questions, and conclusions.

» Reading and Annotating Visual Texts

Although "reading a text" usually refers to something written like an essay, a news article, or a short story, we can also perform close, critical readings of visual and multimodal texts. Reading a visual text is actually very similar to reading a written piece. **We engage in a conversation with the text and the rhetor; we ask questions, make observations, draw connections to other texts and our own experiences, and then interpret our observations in order to form a strong analysis.**

In order to better understand how these close reading techniques can be applied to a visual text, let's look at the iconic American photograph, *Migrant Mother*, taken by Dorothea Lange in 1936.

Figure 1. Dorothea Lange's *Migrant Mother*.
Taken in Nipomo, California (1936).

This photograph may look familiar, but we will assume for a moment that you do not know much about its background. As we would with a written text, we should begin by reading and interrogating the context information provided.

+ **Title:** Why is the title *Migrant Mother*? Why not *Migrant Family*? Where is the father? Does the artist want to call attention to the woman instead of the children? Is Lange using the image of a mother to make an appeal to our emotions? Does it matter that the artist is also a woman?

+ **Date:** What is going on in America in 1936? Is it important that this was taken in California?

+ **Artist:** Who is Dorothea Lange? Why did she take this photo, and how did she use it?

Many of these questions can be answered through additional research, which can help us contextualize the image and its rhetorical intention and impact. (For more information on research techniques, see Ch. 14, "Research Is a Process.") Although this historical context can help us evaluate and analyze the image, it is not essential to our initial reading of the text. Without this information, we can still explore and critique the artist's rhetorical and creative choices through annotation. You can do this directly on the image, like you would a written text, or on a separate sheet of paper. Consider, for example, the following rhetorical choices:

+ **Subject Matter:** Even if we don't know anything about the background of this image, how does Lange call attention to the family's poverty? Which details suggest that the family is struggling? Also, why focus on one particular family? How does the artist appeal to the emotions of the reader?

+ **Composition and Arrangement:** Through the title and the composition of the photo, it is clear that Lange is focusing on the figure of the mother. She is placed in the center of the photo, and we only see her face. Her expression and furrowed brow tell us that she is deep in thought, possibly worried for herself and her three children. How would the image change if she were facing the camera, looking directly at the audience? Why are the children looking away? Are they scared or embarrassed, or is the mother trying to protect their privacy?

+ **Medium:** Is it important that this is a photograph? Would the emotional impact of the image change if it were a film or a painting, for example? Could a different medium reveal more details about the family's circumstances? Would it feel as personal and immediate as this photo?

As you can see, when we read a visual text, we are still engaging in a conversation. We are asking questions, making observations, and then drawing conclusions. We are analyzing rhetorical and creative choices and talking back to the text. This essential process allows us to move past a simple observation like, "The woman in this photo looks sad and poor," to a more complex analysis that interrogates the impact and purpose of the text: "By choosing to focus the viewer's attention on the mother, whose children lean on her for support, Lange creates an intimate and emotional image that conveys the dire reality of a family living in poverty."

» Conclusion

Whether dealing with a written or visual text, as active critical readers we need to participate with the material in an intentional and dynamic way. We need to read with purpose, to ask questions, underline passages, and leave notes in the margins. We need to remember that reading is an essential part of the writing process. It is a conversation we have with the text, and we want to leave our mark and make our voices heard.

» Works Cited

Lange, Dorothea. *Migrant Mother*. 1936, Library of Congress Prints and Photographs Division, Washington, DC. www.loc.gov/pictures/resource/fsa.8b29516/.

10. Reading for the Rhetorical Appeals

Lauren Shook

» Ethos

Ethos (ethical appeal) establishes the base of any text, so a rhetorical analysis should start with analyzing ethos. Essentially, you are looking for two components: 1) the rhetorical triangle—rhetor, audience, and text—and 2) the context of the text and how it establishes ethical standards and/or readers' expectations. These two components are intricately linked together. Ethos is rooted in the situation of the text (context) and in readers' ethical standards as based upon past experiences. Thus, a writer must define the context in order to gauge his or her readers' expectations and reception of his or her message. Let's use Sojourner Truth's speech "Ain't I a Woman?" to see how to identify and analyze ethos. Truth delivered "Ain't I a Woman?" at a women's rights convention in Akron, Ohio, in 1851 (the context). In her speech, she demands rights for African-American women.

First, when identifying the rhetorical triangle and its components, imagine that the message resides between the writer and audience and that the writer's goal is to communicate effectively his or her message to the reader. Once you identify the message of a text, ask yourself, "How is the writer relaying the message to the reader?" To answer that question, you need to pinpoint the writer—the person sending the message and his or her purpose or motivations for doing so—and the intended audience—the person or group of people receiving the writer's message and their expectations, beliefs, etc. Since a writer should always consider his or her audience, let's

"Once you identify the message of a text, ask yourself, 'How is the writer relaying the message to the reader?'"

begin with looking closely at what comprises an audience. Various factors influence an audience's reception of the writer's message, such as gender, ethnicity, class, education, etc. While these factors can be separated, writers usually combine them. Thus, a writer may address only women but he or she probably also considers the age range or class of women. Sometimes writers make their intended audiences easily identifiable, but oftentimes we must determine the audience from the textual clues provided by the writer, such as the writer's subject matter and use of language. We can also identify audience by considering the text's source—the place where the text originates (magazine, newspaper, academic journal, website blog). For instance, noting whether a magazine column on relationship advice comes from a men's or women's magazine will help determine the intended audience.

Let's see how Truth treats the concept of audience in "Ain't I a Woman?" In her speech, she immediately addresses her audience, moving from a general audience to a more specific one. "Well, children," she begins, "...I think that 'twixt the negroes of the South and the women at the North, all talking about rights, the white men will be in a fix pretty soon." That she calls her audience "children" indicates that she considers herself a mother or a teacher who has a lesson for her audience, children who have something to learn. Also, Truth names three groups of people with an eye to racial and geographical differ-ence—African-American Southerners, Northern women who are presumably white, and white males from the South and the North. Here, Truth identifies the audiences that her argument for African-American women's rights will affect, and her inclusion of such a wide array of people demonstrates that she considers her message invaluable for all to hear, which creates an atmosphere of importance. Truth also directly addresses the people present at the conven-tion: "That man over there says that women need to be helped into carriages," and "Then that little man in black there, he says women can't have as much as men, 'cause Christ wasn't a woman!" While we may not know at first exactly who she means by "that little man in black," we can deduce that he is a preacher because of her reference to his opinions about Christ and women.

Let's suppose momentarily that Truth does not directly name her audience. We could just as easily determine the audience from the context of the speech (1851—about ten years prior to the Civil War and in the midst of a women's movement promoting rights for women, particularly suffrage). We know that she delivers her speech at a women's convention; thereby, we know that the audience will mostly consist of women. Furthermore, we should anticipate that people who are against women's and African-Americans' rights will also be a part of the audience. In addition to Truth's identification of particular audiences, she also speaks to her audience's expectations about her as not only a woman but also as an African-American. Her use of informal language and her assertion that she does not know what intellect is—"Then they talk about this thing in the head; what's this they call it? [Intellect, someone whispers]"—plays to the contemporary conception in the 1800s of African-Americans and women as mental inferiors, a thought forwarded by some white men (and some white women as well). Yet while she meets these expectations of her audience, she also shatters the stereotypes simply by delivering such a pithy, rational speech.

The other crucial component of analyzing ethos is identifying the writer of the text and examining his or her credibility. Ask yourself, "Why do I trust the writer as the authority figure on the subject?" Perhaps the writer is well-known, or the writer's credentials or a short biography accompanies the text. If not, we must consult the text itself. Within the text, we should look closely at the writer's command of language, his or her appeal to higher authorities, and supporting evidence. These elements of a text will highlight the writer's credibility, proving that he or she knows enough about the subject in order to relay trustworthy information to the reader. Why do we accept Truth's authority as an advocate for African-American women's rights? First, we know she is credible because she is an African-American woman who was once a slave, as she tells us: "I have borne thirteen children, and seen them most all sold off to slavery, and when I cried out with my mother's grief, none but Jesus heard me! And ain't I a woman?" In addition to the emotional aspect (pathos) of this statement, she makes an ethical appeal to mothers and subtly identifies three more audiences—mothers, Christians, and Christian mothers—via her reference to "mother's grief" and to Christ. Furthermore, this statement most effectively proves her authority on the subject because she has firsthand experience as a suffering African-American woman, and audiences tend to value firsthand experience.

Of the three rhetorical appeals, ethos is relatively easy to detect and analyze in a text. You must always be aware of the rhetorical triangle—rhetor, text, and audience—and how these three components interact with each other. Finally, always consider the context of the piece of writing. The rhetorical triangle and its context are two crucial components of ethos, so keeping them in mind will ensure that you are thinking correctly about ethos.

» Pathos

Pathos (emotional appeal) refers to the emotions or moods that the writer hopes to incite from his or her audience. Because writers employ pathos as a way to get an emotional response from readers, pathos is easily linked to ethos; remember that part of a writer's ethos resides in his or her successful prediction of the audience's reaction to his or her message.

You may be wondering how one can identify emotion in a text. First, as with any analysis of a text, you must be able to name the message and audience. Imagine for a moment an army recruiter who is attempting to convince a group of male, high-school seniors (audience) to enlist in the army (message). He might use various references to well-known, respected patriotic men who have answered their call of duty to serve their country. Maybe he will also employ strong word choices such as "heroic," "bold," or "daring." Though it may not be obvious at first, a close analysis of the army recruiter's wording reveals that he purposefully uses pathos in order to spark an overwhelming sense of national pride in his male audience, prompting them to join the military. From this example, you should see that we identify a writer's pathos through his or her diction (one's wording according to the context).

As with the above example, employing pathos involves a conscious selection of specific word choices and emotionally charged language. Because words not only have denotations (the actual definition of a word) but also connotations (the negative or positive associations that accompany words), a crafty wordsmith knows which specific words will best elicit responses from readers. Another element of pathos is tone, the way a writer sounds on paper, which can be found by noting the connotations and emotionally charged language that the writer uses. Consider the difference between these two sentences:

1. You should vote because voting is a right given to all Americans.

2. You absolutely must vote; otherwise, you are unappreciative of your rights as an American citizen and are being unpatriotic.

In addition to the use of ethos that calls attention to American ethics regarding voting, these two sentences greatly depend on pathos—specific word choices, connotations, and emotionally charged language, all of which result in differing tones. The first encourages Americans to vote by implying that by not voting, one disregards his or her rights as an American citizen. The second sentence, however, forcefully accuses the reader of being "unappreciative" if he or she does not vote and goes so far as to label the reader "unpatriotic." The first sentence achieves its encouraging tone through the word "should," whereas the second sentence contains the word "must." Although the words are synonyms, the connotations of the words suggest a vast difference in how we respond to each word. We associate "should" with morals; one might vote because it is the proper thing to do. "Must," however, implies that one needs to vote because American citizenship requires and even demands it. The difference between "should" and "must" is an example of how specific word choices affect tone.

While specific word choices and emotionally charged language are perhaps the easiest ways to identify pathos in a text, another important tool of pathos is the use of references or allusions. When a writer references a particular person, place, or event, the purpose is to connect his or her audience's emotional reaction to that reference. To return to our previous example, if a writer wants to persuade an audience of college-aged women (18–22) to vote, she might reference the Suffragist movement and individual women who dedicated their lives to achieving suffrage for women. Similarly, if the writer is addressing an audience of young African-Americans for the same reason, he or she might allude to figures like Sojourner Truth, who, as we've seen, advocated for African-American women's equality and thus took a step in realizing women's vital role in voting. Martin Luther King, Jr., the influential Civil Rights leader, would also be an excellent historical person to use as an example of someone who worked to achieve African-Americans' right to vote. In either case, the writer alludes to either the Suffragist movement or the Civil Rights movement (or both) in order to motivate people to vote, illustrating that others have secured the freedom for them to do so while enduring hardship and persecution in the process.

To locate specific moments where one employs pathos, let's analyze Truth's "Ain't I a Woman?" to recognize Truth's manipulation of language and references and/or allusions to persuade her audience of the necessity of African-American women's rights. First, as Truth opens her speech, she calls attention to the "racket" or the noise surrounding the debate for women's and African-American men's rights that makes "something out of kilter." The use of "racket" and "kilter" connote a chaotic world that bars some humans from exercising their rights, which she intends to correct. In addition to specific word choices, Truth uses emotionally charged language to affect her audience when she laments, "I have borne thirteen children, and seen them most all sold to slavery, and when I cried out with my mother's grief, none but Jesus heard me! And ain't I a woman?" Truth wants her audience, especially her female audience, to recognize that she is not only a woman but a mother who has experienced heartache (a moment of building her ethos as well). The use of "cried" and "grief" emphasize the tone of heartache. Finally, Truth also makes allusions easily recognizable to her audience when she counters the erroneous claim that "women can't have as much rights as men, 'cause Christ wasn't a woman!" She asserts that Christ came "From God and a woman!" Thus, not only does she refer directly to Christ, a form of authority for the preachers in her audience, but Truth alludes to Christ's mother, Mary. She reminds preachers that if one is to believe the Bible, then Christ does indeed come only "from God and a woman," Mary. Moreover, Truth's choice to refer to Mary emphasizes her previous remark about a "mother's grief" because Mary, too, experiences a "mother's grief" when she watches Christ's crucifixion. We can see that Truth's meticulous word choice, emotional language, and allusions all reinforce the idea that she is a woman and should receive equal rights.

Truth's speech is full of pathos, so it becomes easy to analyze for pathos. Other texts may not contain such an easily identifiable use of pathos. If this is the case, just remember to look closely at word choices and emotionally charged language (and/or tone) and to keep an eye open for references and allusions.

» Logos

Logos (rational appeal) refers to the logical underpinning of an argument. By identifying an argument's logos, we can determine the argument's rationale and the validity of the argument. Just as with ethos and pathos, in order to identify logos in a text, you need to locate the message. Yet unlike ethos and pathos, logos involves checking whether the argument's supporting claims and evidence affirm the thesis. For instance, if you read a movie review of the newest summer blockbuster in which the reviewer asserts that this comic book-turned-movie has a gripping plot line along with amazing visual graphics, then she would need to support such a claim by clarifying what constitutes a gripping plot line and by providing evidence of the movie's stunning graphics. If you still need proof that her opinion of the movie is valid or if you are convinced that this is the movie for you, then you might actually venture out to see the movie. In either scenario, the writer has completed her job of persuading you to consider watching the movie.

Logos, however, involves much more than just verifying the validity of a writer's claims. Indeed, logos is associated with somewhat convoluted terminology, such as burden of proof (the obligation of the writer to prove his or her claims), fallacies (illogical or faulty reasoning), claims, grounds, warrants, and counter-arguments. While the task of analyzing logos in a text could seem daunting given the surrounding terminology, you should remember that logos is simply the sound construction of an argument, meaning that a writer clearly states his argument and leads the audience through it step by step. Along the way, he provides reliable and clear evidence for each step, demonstrating how each step leads to the next in a logical fashion. Sometimes a writer's evidence takes the form of statistics. In this section, for sake of brevity and clarity, we will not consider all of the above components in detail. Instead, we will return once again to Truth's "Ain't I a Woman?" as a concrete example of how logos functions in a text.

"Logos (rational appeal) refers to the logical underpinning of an argument. By identifying an argument's logos, we can determine the argument's rationale and the validity of the argument."

Logos, similar to pathos, is inextricably influenced by ethos and context, so we should first examine how Truth uses logos in order to construct a good ethos for herself. Truth, remember, is arguing for African-American women's rights in the midst of advocates and opponents of equal rights for women and African-American men. In her first point, Truth remarks,

> *That man over there says that women need to be helped into carriages, and lifted over ditches, and to have the best place everywhere. Nobody ever helps me into carriages, or over mud-puddles, or gives me any best place! And ain't I a woman? Look at me! Look at my arm! I have ploughed and planted, and gathered into barns, and no man could head me! And ain't I a woman? I could work as much and eat as much as a man—when I could get it—and bear the lash as well! And ain't I a woman? I have borne thirteen children, and seen them most all sold off to slavery, and when I cried out with my mother's grief, none but Jesus heard me! And ain't I a woman?*

Here, Truth carefully and logically draws attention to her role in society. She first identifies how society treats women with respect by placing them onto a pedestal, yet no one treats her as such. She then powerfully questions, "Ain't I a woman? Look at me!" Truth uses her physical body as proof (evidence) to persuade her audience that she is, indeed, a woman. After asserting her womanhood, she then juxtaposes herself and her abilities with those of a man, demonstrating that she is not a man but a woman who can outdo a man. Again she demands, "And ain't I a woman?". If her audience is still skeptical, she refers to her ability to give birth—something only women can do. The reference to motherhood serves as further proof of her womanhood as does the "mother's grief" that she feels at the loss of her children. Within the cited portion of her speech, Truth builds her ethos as a woman through three facts (evidence): she is a woman; she is not just a woman, but a black woman; and she is a mother. She thus uses logic to present herself as someone we can trust as an authority on the subject. As readers we can analyze her facts (the logic of an argument) to determine if she has provided enough evidence to prove her expertise on the subject of African-American women's rights. Here, logos helps construct ethos. As readers become distanced in time from Truth's argument, we might turn to articles and/or books on female slavery to test Truth's logos and ethos. In such academic texts, we would find statistics and historical proof for Truth's claims, which come from her own experience.[1]

After identifying how logos and ethos work together, we should then decide on the validity of Truth's argument by noting her steps of logic. As we've seen above, Truth first employs logos to establish her ethos as an African-American woman. She then addresses a counter-argument that women do not possess intellect and therefore should not be allowed equal rights: "Then they talk about this thing in the head; what's this they call it? [Intellect, someone whispers]. That's it, honey. What's that got to do with women's or negro's rights?" Truth's ironic, modest claim not to comprehend intellect, or to even know

---

1. See Deborah Gray White's *Ain't I a Woman?: Female Slaves in the Plantation South*, and specifically her chapter called "The Nature of Female Slavery." (Norton, 1985).

what it is called, belies her very use of intellect to construct her argument. Furthermore, Truth subtly connects her point about intellect to her previous point that she is a woman through her word choice. In her previous point (the above block quote), Truth declares that "no man could head me," and now she playfully refers to intellect as "this thing in the head." In the first instance, "head" means that no man could lead or control Truth, but this declaration reinforces the idea that she has intelligence—no man can outsmart ("out-head") Truth. She must overturn the belief that women are mentally inferior to men, and she covertly does so through her use of crafted logos.

Next, Truth addresses a religious counter-argument that women should be barred from rights because "Christ wasn't a woman!"—a claim that Truth refutes by simply reminding her audience that Christ was "From God and a woman!" and that man was not involved. Her reference to Christ also connects to her earlier statement that in her "mother's grief, none but Jesus heard" her. Finally, Truth ends her speech with a reference to Eve, who "was strong enough to turn the world upside down," and Truth insists that the women attending the convention should be able to "get it right side up again!" Thus, the women advocating for women's rights should succeed in restoring the world to a state of equality. In ending her speech, Truth effectively brings us back to her opening statement that "there must be something out of kilter," indicating a sense of chaos over the debate of women's and African-Americans' rights. What begins "out of kilter" at the start of her speech transforms into "right side up" at the end, and reaching this achievement, Truth casually concludes with "ain't got nothing more to say." In short, Truth carefully connects each of her arguments together through key words and repeated phrases (even the refrain, "ain't I a woman"). The steps of her argument follow one another logically in order to emphasize her belief in women's rights, specifically African-American women's rights.

While logos can seem daunting, remember that analyzing a text for logos simply involves first identifying the argument and then the particular evidence or support for that argument. Consider the writer's use of key words and repeated phrases. Finally, with logos, remember to examine the construction and structure of the argument.

11. Thinking Critically Using Rhetorical Analysis:
It's Not Just What You Say, But How You Say It

Kristie Ellison

Imagine a friend asks you: "How does this outfit look?" You might first consider whether you like the individual parts of the outfit, such as your friend's shirt. Then, you might examine the outfit as a whole by considering whether the pants match the shirt and whether the shoes coordinate with the rest of the outfit. **This skill, often practiced unconsciously, is analysis: breaking something into parts and closely examining those parts, including how they work in relationship to the whole.** A rhetorical analysis is simply a particular type of analysis, one that can help to cultivate your understanding of your own and others' arguments. Recall the rhetorical triangle—rhetor, audience, text. A rhetorical analysis is the examination of how a rhetor communicates a message to an audience through a text. It is done by looking at the rhetorical features of a text to consider the choices made by a rhetor. Here, a text is any product that delivers a message: it can be words on a page, but it can also take many other forms, such as images, videos, and speeches. **Conducting an analysis of something allows you to make connections between what it means and how that meaning is made.** Thus, no matter what form the product takes, the rhetor has made numerous choices, and you can analyze those choices to gain a more complex understanding of arguments, sources, and rhetoric.

> "A rhetorical analysis is the examination of how a rhetor communicates a message to an audience through a text."

» Critical Analyses

Examining how an argument is articulated requires you to think about not just what the rhetor is saying, but also the purposes and motivations behind their argument. When analyzing the rhetorical choices made in a text, it is important to begin by identifying the rhetorical situation—audience, purpose, and limitations. In other words, in order to make a claim about the rhetor's choices, such as whether or not they are effective, you must first ask yourself "effective for whom?" (audience), "effective for what?" (purpose), and "effective under what conditions?" (limitations). This means considering the context of the rhetorical situation.

Let's return to your analysis of your friend's outfit. To adequately assess the outfit, you would need to know where your friend intended to wear it. An appropriate outfit for a job interview would likely be very different from one for a party. Even a seemingly objective assessment, such as a belief that the outfit is very dated, might change if you learn that it is for "70s Day" during spirit week at school. Similarly, to make judgments about a rhetor's choices, you must first be clear about what they are trying to say and to whom they are trying to say it.

It is also important to consider the limitations of a text. **In his definition of rhetoric, Aristotle specifically notes the importance of the *available means* of persuasion.** (For more on this definition, see Ch. 1, "An Introduction to Rhetoric.") Whether or not you think your friend should wear a particular pair of shoes will likely depend on what other shoes are available. In addition, while it can sometimes be helpful to think broadly about possibilities, and can often be valuable to remain critical of problematic choices, you should be sure to acknowledge limitations, including historical or cultural limitations, to show that you understand your analysis and are arguing for change. For example, if you are analyzing an advertisement for cleaning products from the 1950s, you might observe that the rhetor seems to assume an audience of women. While you may suggest that such an assumption ignores that men also clean their homes, you should also acknowledge the difference in culturally-expected gender roles between the time the ad was published and today.

Once you've identified the rhetorical situation of your text, identify specific rhetorical features to examine. Remember that your goal is to analyze the *rhetorical* features of the source—how the argument is conveyed—not to evaluate the content of the argument itself. **This means that while you do not need to agree with the argument, it is important that you *understand* it.** (For more on the importance of understanding arguments, see Ch. 22, "Incorporating Evidence.") Also remember that *you* may not be the intended audience for the text. Even if you are, you are only one of many members. **Your analysis must go beyond merely considering whether or not you like something personally.**

If you are working on a specific assignment, your instructor may provide guidelines about the process of rhetorical analysis. You should always follow your instructor's guidelines first, but otherwise the rest of this chapter offers some strategies for approaching a rhetorical analysis.

» Analyzing for the Canons

One way to start is to consider the rhetorical canons as broad categories of rhetorical choices. Ask yourself:

> • What choices might the rhetor have made during the **invention** stage? Does the rhetor identify where any of their ideas come from—perhaps from research, or from experience? Are there any underlying assumptions that affect the communication? Has the rhetor made an unjustified assumption about the intended audience? Features may include the rhetor's ideas and how those ideas are presented.
>
> • What choices reflect the rhetor's understanding of the audience's collective **memory**? Does the rhetor provide enough background information? Does the rhetor make the audience care about the issue or assume they already do? Features may include documentation choice, or references to shared culture or experiences.
>
> • What choices has the rhetor made regarding **arrangement**? Is the text organized in a way that makes the argument understandable to the audience? Is it logical and compelling? Features may include organization, transitions, and visual layout.
>
> • How has the rhetor made **style** choices? Is the tone effective for the audience and appropriate for the subject matter? Is there too much jargon? Features may include word choice, tone, terminology, and use of subheadings.
>
> • How has the rhetor addressed **delivery**? Given limitations, is their choice of medium effective? Will the message reach the intended audience? Are other choices consistent with the selected method of delivery? Features may include medium, font, and color.

» Analyzing for the Appeals

An additional way to think about rhetorical choices is to consider how a rhetor employs the rhetorical appeals—ethos, pathos, and logos. (For more, see Ch. 10, "Reading for the Rhetorical Appeals.") Here, ask yourself how the rhetor has addressed a particular expectation of the audience. For **ethos**, you might ask how the rhetor establishes their credibility and trustworthiness. Notice how this question works with your examination of the canons. For instance, you might ask: How does the rhetor's **style** choice to use jargon establish their **ethos** on the subject matter? For **pathos**, the appeal to the emotions of the audience, you might consider how the choice to **deliver** a message as a video accompanied by a sad song persuades the audience to donate money to an animal shelter.

As you are thinking about how the rhetor appeals to the audience, you should also consider whether such an appeal is effective or appropriate given the purpose and audience. For example, a strong emotional appeal might be appropriate when asking people to donate money for animals, but if you are asking a bank to loan you money that you will repay, you would likely need to pay more attention to establishing your ethos as trustworthy by rationally demonstrating your plan for repayment. **Logos**—the appeal to rational, logical thought—is often the more significant appeal when analyzing how arguments are constructed, especially in academic contexts.

"Although in a rhetorical analysis you are analyzing the communication of an argument rather than the argument itself, you might consider *rhetorical* choices related to content."

Although in a rhetorical analysis you are analyzing the communication of an argument rather than the argument itself, you might consider *rhetorical* choices related to content. For example, you could examine whether certain information is included or excluded and what types of evidence are provided, such as anecdotes versus statistics. As noted in the discussion of the canons, you may assess whether the argument is arranged in a logical order.

When writing your own arguments, you should make sure your sources are supporting your ideas rather than speaking for you. That said, it is important to understand how these sources are working rhetorically to ensure they support you in the way you intend. Often, your argument will require you to borrow ethos from your sources, such as when you cite a scholar with academic credibility to support an idea. To borrow that ethos, you should understand how the rhetor in the source is establishing it. Similarly, you might want to use a personal narrative to appeal to pathos; understanding how a source is making such an appeal can help you craft your own. This may work by helping you create a similar story or by using the source to make the appeal. Finally, analyzing how your sources appeal to logos will help you structure your own evidence, both in making your argument and in responding to counter-arguments. (For more on argument, see Ch. 19, "Staking Your Claim.")

Logical Fallacies

A close consideration of logos can also help you identify problems with the reasoning in an argument, in your sources—so you can find a different source or perhaps respond to a counter-argument—and in your own writing.

Commonly encountered reasoning problems are known as **logical fallacies**; here are some of the most frequent ones:

- *Ad hominem* (Latin for "to the man") arguments attack the person making the argument rather than addressing the issue itself. Note, however, that if the issue is related to the person, such as their trustworthiness, an argument related to them, such as their history of telling the truth, could be significant. It is important to ask yourself whether the information presented is *relevant* to the issue being debated.

- **Begging the question** is a circular argument that attempts to prove the claim simply by restating it another way. Often these are framed as "one thing *because* another." Ask yourself if the statement after the "because" is just another way to say the statement before it.

- **Either-or arguments**, sometimes called *false dilemmas*, oversimply a complex situation and frame an argument as having only two alternatives, claiming that one is the better solution. This is problematic because it ignores all the other possibilities. When responding to a counter-argument that suggests one alternative is better than another in a way that seems hard to deny, ask yourself if the argument is wrong in its framing and ignoring other options.

- **Bandwagon appeals** argue that a claim is correct just because others agree with it or because it is the most popular opinion. Such appeals often assume that the audience wants to conform or go along with others. They also rely on the idea that popularity alone is a reason to agree with a given position.

- **Faulty causality** assumes that because one event comes after another, the first caused the second. For example, someone might argue that after the school started serving pizza in the cafeteria, fewer students left campus for lunch. However, there could be other reasons this occurred, such as a shorter lunch period. Ask yourself if there is any evidence that the second thing is caused by the first, such as evidence that the students who used to leave campus are now eating pizza.

- **Straw man arguments** mischaracterize an opposing view in a way that makes it seem extreme or otherwise different than it is so that it can be more easily refuted. It is important to make sure you are representing opposing ideas fairly so that you don't damage your own credibility.

- **Slippery slope arguments** suggest that one thing will lead to another and eventually end disastrously. Although sometimes one event leading to other events is an important element of an argument, ask yourself what evidence is presented to support the causal relationship. Also note that the further apart the beginning and ending events are—e.g., a relatively minor event leads to world destruction—the less likely it is that evidence supports the link.

- **Faulty analogies** try to connect a proposed idea to another idea that is already accepted but uses a comparison that is different in some crucial way. For example, arguing that a parent shouldn't make a child pack their own lunch because they wouldn't make the child get a job draws a false comparison between household chores and child labor.

- **Hasty generalizations** draw sweeping conclusions about broad groups based on little evidence. These generalizations often rely on stereotypes or too small a sample size. While some generalizations can be supported with evidence, it is important to qualify such instances based on how big of a group the evidence might support by using words like *some*, *many*, *often*, and *usually*.

» Considering Assignments

As with any analysis assignment, when writing a rhetorical analysis, it is important to keep in mind three components: **description**, **evidence**, and **insight**. Although you don't want mere summary to overtake your analysis, you should offer enough description of the text you are analyzing for your audience to understand what you are talking about. You will likely need to provide at least some detail about the overall text, as well as additional information about the specific parts you are focusing on. If you are analyzing a visual text or component, you may consider including the visual element in your text.

Next, be sure you are providing evidence for your points by including specific examples. Rather than simply saying the rhetor's tone is too casual for their audience, provide specific instances of casual tone, such as uses of slang. If you find yourself struggling to find specific examples, re-consider the claim you are making. Is the tone too casual, or is there something else going on?

Finally, consider what insight you have gained from your analysis. This might include the question of effectiveness, but will often involve more than this. Rather than simply arguing that a rhetor made effective choices, focus on *how* and *why* their choices work. For example, you might argue that a rhetor is effective *because of* their unique pairing of statistics and personal stories. Remember that **effectiveness is not an all-or-nothing question**. You might argue that the rhetor's use of statistics is persuasive but their argument is undercut by their failure to use inclusive language. Or that their use of statistics could have been more persuasive if they had made the style choice to include charts and graphs to make the data easier for the audience to understand.

As with any conclusion, consider the broader implications or next steps. Ask yourself why *your argument* matters to *your audience*. You've taken a text (or texts) apart and closely examined the pieces and how they relate to the whole; what have you discovered in the process? And what makes that discovery worth thinking more about? You won't be able to talk about every choice the rhetor made, so choose those that are most relevant to the argument you want to make based on the insight you've gained. Sharing your analysis of rhetorical choices is just one more way to add your voice to the ongoing conversation.

> "Sharing your analysis of rhetorical choices is just one more way to add your voice to the ongoing conversation."

» Critical Reflection

To think a bit more about how rhetorical choices can be analyzed, let's take a look back at some of the choices I made in writing this chapter:

+ How does my choice to use the example of analyzing a friend's outfit reflect my effort to tap into a shared cultural experience? What other examples do you notice and what do they say about my understanding of my audience?

+ How does my choice to use second-person point of view and contractions create a personal, accessible tone? How does my tone compare to other academic texts you have read?

+ How does my choice to use bold text for some words, phrases, and sentences indicate the importance of those points? What risk is involved in highlighting some points over others? What other design features do you notice?

» Teaching Text

1. Find 4–5 advertisements to analyze as a class. They could have a particular theme, such as ads for different types of drinks or ads for the same product from different time periods. Break the class into groups and assign each group an ad. Either assign common features to examine or allow each group to decide on 3–4 features, and have each group perform a rhetorical analysis of their ad, drawing insight from their observations. Then,

coming back together as a class, have each group present their findings and discuss comparisons of those findings.

2. Pick a current event and find 2–3 news articles from different types of sources. Discuss how the event is presented in different ways and what the implications of those choices are. For example, how does a differently phrased title reflect the intended audience? You can also discuss the implications of these differences with respect to news reporting.

3. Select a written text about a subject with visual components, such as a review of a movie or art exhibit. Discuss how the written text might work differently in another form, such as a picture or video.

12. Writing a Visual Analysis

Luciana Lilley and Jay Shelat

In this chapter, we will discuss a common College Writing assignment: the visual analysis. A visual analysis is an in-depth rhetorical examination of a visual image—including print and TV advertisements, comics, art, and more. **Like any rhetorical text, visuals make arguments and can work to persuade an audience.** (For more on rhetoric and persuasion, see Ch. 2, "Rhetoric in Academic Settings," and Ch. 3, "The Rhetorical Canons and the Writing Process.")

For this assignment, you are reading for rhetorical techniques such as the rhetorical triangle, appeals, and canons. The very word analysis communicates something important: this assignment is not an informative essay (meaning that it is not just a basic description of the visual image); rather, you are arguing for a particular and nuanced interpretation of the text.

> "The very word analysis communicates something important: this assignment is not an informative essay; rather, you are arguing for a particular and nuanced interpretation of the text."

Visual analysis essays break down an image to highlight the ways that a visual text—much like a written text—makes an argument. In light of this, when you pick an image to analyze, make sure you choose an arguable position, one that others could respond to with their own ideas and perspectives. **Your interpretation of the text, whether simple or complex, should represent your understanding of how it communicates its message, why, and how effectively.** Importantly, in order to be an argument, your interpretation should be debatable, meaning that a reasonable person could disagree with it. In your visual analysis, it's your job to convince your readers that your interpretation is correct!

Reading your image for its rhetorical qualities will help you better understand possible arguments. **When beginning your analysis, start by identifying its place in the rhetorical triangle; this starting point gives you a critical**

understanding of the image. While it may seem basic, or even obvious, this step is foundational. The rhetorical triangle provides crucial information, including:

- Who the creator of the image is (the rhetor)

- What the text is; what medium the rhetor is using to persuade their audience

- How the genre conventions of the text constrict or construct the image

- Who the rhetor's intended audience and sub-audiences might be, and how the rhetor appeals to these groups

  - Sub-audiences include audiences the rhetor may not have intended to reach but are communicating to regardless

- Whatever contextual information you have access to (either through what is provided or basic research)

  - What the history of the rhetor or text is

  - What information is surrounding the image (for example, a magazine ad might include where the ad was published, where it is located in the magazine, and what surrounds the ad)

All this information assists you in beginning your analysis, because it tells you who the text is speaking to, and in what contexts. (For more, see Ch. 11, "Thinking Critically Using Rhetorical Analysis.")

After establishing how the image aligns with the rhetorical triangle, gauge how it relates to the rhetorical canons and appeals. (For more, see Ch. 3, "The Rhetorical Canons and the Writing Process," and Ch. 10, "Reading for the Rhetorical Appeals.") You can approach your analysis through the appeals or canons, remembering that these concepts overlap with the rhetorical triangle. For example, the way that an image is logically presented to an audience appeals to *logos*, but perhaps its structure (*arrangement*) evokes nostalgia (*pathos*).

Below is a list of points to consider to get you started, based on the rhetorical canons:

- Invention

    - What words are they using in the image? What tone do they convey? Does the tone of the image provoke a particular emotion?

    - What kind of ethos does the rhetor seem to have? How do they communicate their reliability? What text, visual images, color choices, style, do they use?

    - What is the overall makeup of the image? Does it incorporate text, symbols, etc.?

- Arrangement

    - Are there humans, animals, objects? What are the faces or body language communicating?

    - How are the different elements of the image put together?

- Style

    - What colors are used in the image? Do they compliment each other or contrast? If the image is black and white, consider the *lack* of color. Which emotions are usually associated with those colors?

- Memory

    - Is there anything that triggers a shared collective memory in the audience such as referencing a familiar quote or childhood memory?

    - Does the rhetor use alliteration, rhyme, or visual images of the product/service to make the text more memorable?

- Delivery

    - How is the image drawn? If it is a film, what is its genre? How is the visual presented to the audience?

When analyzing a visual text, make sure to study every aspect of the piece so you can determine what's most important. Take a look at the vintage recruitment poster on the following page from 1917. What strikes you first about this image? Starting with what catches your attention is a great first step, because it allows you to then analyze *why* those aspects of the image jumped out at you. From there, you can develop an argument that ties all of these elements together.

We can begin prewriting our visual analysis by asking some questions about the image, using the rhetorical triangle, canons, and appeals.

+ Map the rhetorical triangle onto this ad. What does it reveal about the ad's purpose and context?

+ How does the text use viewers' expectations about who can serve in the Navy while still conforming to gendered stereotypes? Similarly, how does the ad present the young woman's thoughts?

+ The smaller caption under the photo states, "Be a Man and Do It." What does that caption express about the ad and its gendered aspects?

+ How is this image stylized? What do the color and design of the image tell us? Specifically, what do these style choices communicate about the target audience?

+ How does the young woman in the poster look? What message does her body language and expression send?

+ What is the Navy trying to convey in this ad? What was happening in America in 1917? How does the ad stand out from its contemporaries? How is this ad different than what you see in 2019?

Answering questions like these will help you write a visual analysis essay, but they're also useful for going about your other rhetorical and argumentative assignments. You'll notice that our questions are specific to the ad and keep the rhetor (the United States Navy) and keep their purpose (encouraging men to enlist) in mind. From there, we use detailed observations and contextual evidence to draw further conclusions about the other rhetorical elements involved.

Remember to use your knowledge of rhetoric when forming your interpretation and analysis. When you break down a visual using rhetorical techniques, the analysis becomes less overwhelming and answers questions about the triangle, canons, and appeals—questions the rhetor was likely asking themselves too! Additionally, questions are a great way to approach any essay. In this regard, a visual analysis essay can help concretize some of the skills necessary in a longer, more sustained essay such as a research paper.

> "When you break down a visual using rhetorical techniques, the analysis becomes less overwhelming and answers questions about the triangle, canons, and appeals— questions the rhetor was likely asking themselves too!"

» Teaching Text

Discussion questions about a visual analysis:

+ What is the purpose of a visual analysis?

+ How does it differ from a traditional rhetorical analysis essay? How are they similar?

In-Class or Small Assignment:

+ As a group activity, pick one company and have students bring in a print advertisement from a specific decade. Ask students to compare these ads in order to analyze how the company's use of rhetoric has changed (or not) as times and society have changed.

+ To scaffold this assignment, have students follow these activities by asking them to arrange the way they would present the information in an essay, and define what their argument might be.

13. Topic Selection:
Finding Your Foundation

Luke Huffman

For many students, an extensive project looms large in their view of the semester. Some students have pleasant memories of past engagement with research topics, while others feel less positively about their time spent researching and analyzing. The goal of this chapter is to help you find sure footing for embarking on your college-level projects, especially those requiring a lot of time or research.

Once you've been assigned a large-scale project, your first step should be choosing a topic. It may seem minor or straightforward, but carefully making this decision sets the stage for your success. **Your topic selection determines the depth and breadth of your research, and how many responsibilities you'll take on as a rhetor.** It also determines which ideas and questions will occupy your imagination for the duration of the assignment. If you feel overwhelmed by the options available to you, it may be comforting to know: *most* people struggle with topic selection. But so long as you begin with something workable—which this chapter aims to help you do—your topic can evolve and develop. Next, we will turn to some useful practices for determining a starting point.

» Start with the Assignment

First and foremost, start by closely reading any instructions or course materials you've received, to help you understand the assignment and expectations of your instructor. (For more on assignment prompts, see Ch. 4, "Understanding Course Materials as Part of the Classroom Conversation.") **Look for keywords.** For example, if a prompt asks you to discuss an "ongoing political debate," you might peruse the news for ideas. Conversely, researching a "historical event" might imply heading to the library or online library databases. **Make sure you are clear on what your assignment is asking for, and that you have asked your instructor any questions you have about the prompt before proceeding.** In doing so, you should get an idea of the kinds of topics within the general range and scope requested by the assignment. You can begin shaping your research question from there.

» Consider Your Own Interests

Instead of automatically choosing a topic because it seems "academic," or because it sounds like a typical essay topic, **consider how you could work within an assignment's parameters to connect to your own interests.** Take into account things that already interest you, in any aspect of your life. What in the world *actually* captures your imagination? What do you spend your free time thinking about, reading about, doing, watching, or listening to?

> "Consider how you could work within an assignment's parameters to connect to your own interests."

Don't discount one of your interests because you think of it as being more related to leisure time than academic concerns, in other words, because it doesn't seem "serious" enough. **Almost *any* hobby or pop-culture phenomenon can be suitable for academic work—if you investigate it with precision, depth, and rigor.**

» Elevating an Interest

One way to elevate any topic is to consider how it might be examined by an academic discipline you have experience studying, like history, psychology, biology, philosophy, or media studies. Then, imagine you are a scholar in that field. How might a historian study Kendrick Lamar? How might a sociologist look at makeup tutorials on YouTube? What might a philosopher find interesting about the video game Minecraft? **You can phrase your question along these disciplinary lines by linking the vocabulary they use to describe their work to the topic you'd like to examine.** For example, philosophers are interested in the question of free will, so you could think about how the non-player characters, or NPCs (a video gaming term), demonstrate autonomy (a philosophy term) in Minecraft gameplay. If you're not sure what concepts from your chosen academic discipline might be related, or which specialized terms to use in phrasing your research question, talk to a librarian or visit your instructor's office hours.

> "One way to elevate any topic is to consider how it might be examined by an academic discipline you have experience studying, like history, psychology, biology, philosophy, or media studies."

» Consider Debatability

Next, consider whether your topic is *open* or *closed*. A topic that is "open" means "open for debate." **Ask yourself: does your topic have an interrogative or argumentative angle?** Does your question ask *how* or *why*? Can you think of three or more possible perspectives, or a range of viewpoints, on the issue? If not, your topic is "closed," and you may find yourself writing an "all about" paper. These kinds of essays, which merely detail the ideas and analyses of others, can be limited because they don't leave enough room for you to offer *your* perspective. **In other words, writing a "report" doesn't allow you the space to develop new ideas, preventing you from accessing the excitement that can fuel further development of your ideas and argument.** You can avoid this issue by making sure your question digs into the significance of your topic by asking *why* or *how*. (For more on arguable claims, see Ch. 19, "Staking Your Claim.")

» Define Your Scope of Responsibility

One of the most important tasks in selecting a topic is honing the scope of your project. You may believe that choosing a general topic, like "Poverty," "Education," or "Mental Health," will make the research and writing process easier because there will be plenty to write about. But often, choosing such a broad topic makes writing an essay *more* difficult. With a broad topic, you become responsible for an almost infinite number of tasks as a researcher and rhetor. Because there's so much to learn and respond to, your research options can be overwhelming. You may feel as if you're in the middle of a room with a thousand different people talking about a thousand different ideas all at once, much like trying to join a conversation at a party you arrived late to. All that noise can make the research process feel incoherent. Then you're left to write the essay but have no idea where to start or what to include. To make your tasks more manageable, **give yourself a focused and limited area of responsibility**—then become master of that little patch. Rather than writing about "education" as a whole, you could examine *how changes in standardized test requirements for middle schoolers affects their preparedness for high school*. You could then narrow this further to address "standardized test requirements *in North Carolina*," taking place "*between 2010–2014*." This would be a much more focused and narrow place from which to begin your research.

How to Narrow

As in the example above, if you're struggling with narrowing your topic, **try using the Who? Where? When? strategy.** If your assignment instructions do not answer these questions for you, then you will need to take some time to conduct background research and identify the major outlines of your issue.

First, *who* has a role or a stake in your topic? Start by identifying groups of people who are parts of the conversation of your initial research. For example, if your topic is "education," as discussed above, you would find an array of voices, including different grade levels of students, teachers in different subject areas, administrators, and parents. All of these are possible groups you could focus on, so, as you can see, our "who" needs to be narrowed further. **Which group you decide to focus on determines key aspects of your research.** If you want to look at teachers, then your essay might focus on curriculum or classroom practice. Conversely, if you select administrators, then your essay might explore area-wide policies or issues related to funding. By narrowing the *who* that your essay addresses, you can better determine what aspects of these issues you'll need to discuss.

After you've identified a handful of groups who have a stake in your issue, consider the relationships between them. Are they at odds with one another? Working together? Is their relationship parasitic or symbiotic? Who is weak? Who is strong? Who depends on whom? By determining how these groups relate to one another, you can understand where debates and conflicts arise. By understanding where conflicts are, you can develop a topic with depth and complexity, and a deeper understanding of the ongoing conversation around it.

Next, you'll want to narrow the geographic scope of your research—*where* do you want the focus of your topic to be? Explicitly including geography in your research will help narrow later search results in databases. As before, winnow your topic down to a small area to make it more manageable. For example, let's continue working with education. Looking at educational issues across the entire nation could take years of work and pages and pages of analysis. But you're probably working with a limited amount of time and a limited number of pages. What if, instead, you looked at education on a state level, or even a city level? How does education in North Carolina look? What about when it's compared to another state? How does the education of children in Greensboro compare to Raleigh? Or Charlotte?

When you narrow your research by location and scale, you build a stronger foundation by eliminating sources no longer relevant to your topic. This leaves you with a more manageable number of sources to look through. As a result, you'll have more time to spend on all the details and complexities of your issue, which allows you to get to know your topic better and analyze it more closely.

Finally, define the *when*: what is the time period you primarily want to focus on? Tracing a topic's development since the beginning of time is an impossibly big task. Instead, decide which time period you'll investigate. As before, hone your area of responsibility. To return to our education example: examining how requirements for students entering high school have changed since the early 1900s, when high schools first were popularized, would be far too much information to possibly address with any depth. But what about examining how high school requirements changed in the years leading up to

World War II? Or since the establishment of the "Race to the Top" program in 2009? These are much narrower, and therefore it is much easier for you to become an expert in the issues they involve.

How to Broaden

Although a rare problem, it is still possible to whittle a topic down too narrowly. The danger you risk in this situation is finding yourself strapped for relevant, reliable source material to inform your arguments. You may be able to cross-reference the information that *is* available for a city or state with sources that talk about similar situations in other locations, and, in the process, come up with original research. **But if the topic is unworkably narrow, you may find yourself without the resources you need to make claims with sufficient confidence or evidence.** In such a situation, you'll need to run back through the questions above and choose a slightly bigger *Who, Where,* or *When.*

» Final Thoughts

Topic selection is a deceivingly complex task. It requires an honest appraisal of how much time you have and what can realistically be done in that amount of time. Carefully choosing a topic can lead you to a project where you feel like a dog chasing a squirrel. **The excitement of working with a fresh, original topic, one that has not been thoroughly investigated before or spoken about much—if ever—is an electric feeling that can invigorate your academic life.** I encourage you to pick something that energizes you, and to give yourself a focused area of responsibility.

"Topic selection requires an honest appraisal of how much time you have and what can realistically be done in that amount of time."

14. Research Is a Process

Jenny Dale and Maggie Murphy

In many of your courses—including College Writing—you will need to integrate research into essays, presentations, and other projects. **Research is critical in academic writing and speaking because it places your work in a larger conversation.** Research is a process that helps you expand on your ideas, discover new ones, and support arguments. When you integrate outside sources into your work, you build your credibility by showing that research supports your arguments and claims. **This chapter will provide a brief introduction to research and will cover the basics of finding, accessing, and using outside sources to build and support effective arguments.** For more detailed information about research as a process, visit the library research guides for English 101 (http://uncg.libguides.com/eng101) and English 102 (http://uncg.libguides.com/eng102).

> "Research is a process that helps you expand on your ideas, discover new ones, and support arguments."

» Types of Sources

When researching a topic, you are likely to come across a wide variety of published sources of information or evidence. Sources can be categorized in many different ways, and you may be asked by your instructor to use particular types of sources in your writing. **These include primary and/or secondary sources, and popular and/or scholarly sources.** However, it can be difficult to meet your instructor's requirements for sources if you're not sure how to identify or distinguish between these different types of sources.

Primary and Secondary Sources

You may have heard sources referred to as either primary or secondary when doing research in the past. The University of Maryland provides the following definition of primary sources:

> Primary sources are original materials. They are from the time period involved and have not been filtered through interpretation or evaluation. Primary sources are original materials on which other research is based. They are usually the first formal appearance of results in physical, print or electronic format. They present original thinking, report a discovery, or share new information. (University of Maryland Libraries)

While this definition is clear and succinct, you might notice that it does not provide any specific examples of primary sources. This is because what constitutes a primary source varies widely depending on the context or academic discipline. Here are a few examples:

+ For **historical** research on the Vietnam War, a primary source might be a letter or diary that provides a first-hand account of a soldier's experience, or a newspaper article from 1968 reporting on the war.

+ For a **psychology** topic like post-traumatic stress disorder (PTSD), a primary source might be an original research article about a study of treatment options for PTSD.

+ For research on the **visual rhetoric** of the anti-war movement during the Vietnam War, a primary source might be a photo of protesters.

Secondary sources are removed in some way from primary sources. Considering the examples in the last paragraph, a secondary source in history might be a book on the Vietnam War that relies on numerous primary sources like letters and newspaper articles to provide context. In psychology, secondary sources might be review articles that summarize and evaluate original research articles. In art, secondary sources might include a scholarly journal article or an in-depth review of an exhibition published in a newspaper or magazine. Like primary sources, secondary sources can take many forms. **Common types of secondary sources you are likely to come across in the process of doing research for a College Writing class include books, articles, and websites.**

Popular and Scholarly Sources

Many of your college research assignments will require certain types of secondary sources, like articles or books. **When you are doing research, you are likely to find a mix of popular sources, like newspaper and magazine articles, and scholarly sources, like books and journal articles.** Scholarly sources (also called academic, peer-reviewed, or refereed sources) are written both *by* and *for* scholars—people with education and expertise related to the topics they're covering. Scholarly sources also include formal citations and are published either in peer-reviewed journals or in books by academic publishers.

Popular sources, like magazines and newspapers, tend to be written by journalists for a more general audience, and they rarely include formal citations like footnotes or a Works Cited list.

Scholarly sources are not "better" than popular sources; the two serve different purposes. Scholarly sources will typically provide more in-depth analysis of a particular topic. They often cite primary and secondary sources, including other scholarly sources. However, if you are researching a recent event or a topic of current interest, popular articles are your best bet as they are much more likely to cover current events and news. Popular sources are also important because they can be read by anyone with access to the internet or a library, while many scholarly sources can only be accessed with specific credentials like a university ID. **With a general sense of the types of sources you are looking for, you can begin searching for sources that help support your argument.** The next few sections will help you get started with that process, but your research guides, linked on page 87, provide more detailed information about finding evidence, including tutorials on searching library resources like databases and catalogs.

> "Scholarly sources are not 'better' than popular sources; the two serve different purposes."

» Using Web Sources

Using the web for research is convenient and is second nature to many of us, but since most of what is available on the web has not been edited or reviewed, it is particularly important to carefully evaluate these sources before deciding to use them. At the time we're writing this, a Google search for *standardized testing* brings back 101 million results. There's a good chance that not all 101 million of those results would provide strong evidence for an academic assignment. There are many criteria to consider when you evaluate web sources—a Google search for evaluating web sources brings back more than 2 million results—but we recommend the ABCD framework.

A ...... Authority/Accuracy

B .... Bias

C .... Currency

D .... Documentation

A stands for authority, which requires you to consider the person, people, or organization responsible for the website. Look for "about us" or "contact us" links if the author is not immediately clear. Think about your context—a website on standardized testing by someone with a Master's degree in Education has more authority than a site written by a literature professor. When authors cannot be identified, authority is significantly compromised. That is one major issue with sources like Wikipedia. **Remember that you are using outside sources to build your own ethos as a writer, and sources with authority issues can negatively impact that ethos.**

Bias can be tricky to identify and might require a little extra research. Information creators have perspectives and agendas that affect the way they present information. Biased sources are often very one-sided or do not provide the full picture on a particular topic or issue. This can be very nuanced—it is often not as easy as finding a site entitled "Standardized Testing is the Worst" (the bias there is fairly clear) or a site written by the Educational Testing Service. Bias is a particularly sticky issue when we are dealing with controversial topics, as strong opinions are likely to be voiced. Just because an author makes an argument, it does not necessarily mean a source is biased. Balanced sources often present well-reasoned positions on one side of an issue, supported by a range of outside sources. For example, a magazine article about ocean pollution may have a strong argumentative thesis about eliminating the use of plastic straws in order to protect marine animals—a thesis that many people could reasonably disagree with for a number of reasons, including that some people with physical disabilities rely on straws for drinking. However, the author can create balance in their argument by offering multiple perspectives from scientific research alongside interviews with disability rights activists, public policy makers, and consumers. Similarly, just because a site has a clear bias does not mean that you should discard it as a source. Rather, you should consider seeking out additional sources that are more neutral. **You can help mitigate bias by seeking out multiple perspectives on a topic so that you have a fuller picture of the information available.**

> "Just because an author makes an argument, it does not necessarily mean a source is biased. Balanced sources often present well-reasoned positions on one side of an issue, supported by a range of outside sources."

Currency, or how up to date a source is, is relative to the topic at hand. **The first step in evaluating the currency of a source is to identify the date of publication, then consider whether the information in the source is up-to-date enough to serve as solid evidence for your argument.** Typically in a

90

College Writing course, you are going to be looking for the most recent information on a topic. It is important to remember, though, that the most recent information on standardized testing is likely to be newer than the most recent information about the Vietnam War. While older information can provide a useful historical perspective on a topic, a good rule of thumb is to look for sources published within the past five years when your topic is about current events, science, technology, or social issues. However, it is also important to read your assignment guidelines carefully, as some instructors will provide directions about how current your sources should be for research assignments.

Documentation is how an author or a publication indicates to readers that their assertions or arguments are backed up with evidence. The most common kind of documentation is the use of citations to outside sources. **Citations to other sources may be formal, such as the kind found in footnotes, endnotes, works cited lists, or bibliographies.** Formal citations are typically used in scholarly sources, such as academic journal articles or nonfiction books from academic publishers. **However, citations can also be informal, such as through the use of signal phrases ("According to researchers at Stanford, …") or even through hyperlinks to articles, reports, or other types of evidence in online sources.** Informal citations are common in newspaper and magazine articles, blog posts, and social media. If an author does not use formal or informal sources to document their work, you can also research the publication or platform in which the work appears. Is there documentation on a publication's website of an editorial process through which the author's arguments or assertions are reviewed before publication? For example, the website for the Associated Press news service outlines how their journalist's reports are fact-checked before publication. Similarly, the website for the *Journal of Social Media in Society* describes the peer review process scholarly article submissions to the journal must go through. Just as integrating and citing outside sources helps you build ethos as a writer, these forms of documentation can also help establish the credibility of the sources you find.

> "College and university libraries typically have many thousands or even *millions* of books and articles, representing original scholarship by experts as well as quality popular sources by journalists, critics, and other professional writers, that your tuition pays for."

» Using Library Resources

The web is always a great starting point for research, but when the research you are doing is academic, you almost always need to go beyond what is freely available. College and university libraries typically have many thousands or even *millions* of books and articles, representing original scholarship by experts as well as quality popular sources by journalists, critics, and other professional writers, that your tuition pays for. Next, we will cover some basics about using library resources, but you can find out more by using your research guides. If you need help with your research, you can always contact your College Writing Librarian or use the "Chat with a Librarian" link at http://library.uncg.edu.

As you use library resources, be aware that they do not "speak Google." In general, you cannot type in a question or a long phrase into a library database search box and expect to get useful results. **The best strategy is to do some brainstorming before you start searching to help you consider the terms you want to use.** If you are researching how well the SAT predicts college success, you should identify critical terms related to the topic: *SAT* and *college success*. You should also consider terms that are broader (like *standardized test* or *college admissions test* for *SAT*) and narrower (like *grade point average* for *college success*). Having a variety of search terms ready helps if you find that your initial search is not as successful as you would like it to be. When you have identified a handful of useful terms, you can use those to search for relevant sources in the library catalog or databases. To make your search as effective as possible, use connectors like *AND* and *OR* to help target your search. A search for "*SAT* AND *college success*" will bring back results that deal with both of these topics, which helps you narrow down your results to those that are likely to be relevant. A search for "*SAT* OR *college admissions test*" will bring back any results that deal with either of those concepts, so that broadens your results. These searches work in the UNCG Libraries catalog as well as in our databases.

+ The catalog (which you can find by visiting http://library.uncg.edu and clicking the "catalog" tab in the red search box) is your gateway to books, DVDs, CDs, and more at UNCG. For more in-depth information about searching the catalog, visit your research guide!

+ Library databases are searchable collections of subscription-based resources. Most of our databases at UNCG primarily contain articles (both popular and scholarly), but some also include citations to books, conference presentations, and other types of sources. We have hundreds of databases at UNCG, but you can find specific recommendations for databases, as well as video tutorials showing how to use them most effectively, on your research guides.

» Citing Sources

Citing sources is a critical part of the research process. Not only does it protect you from plagiarism, which is a violation of the Academic Integrity Policy, it also builds your credibility by indicating that your ideas are supported by research. In most English classes, you will be asked to cite sources in MLA style. Citations are meant to help your audience find the sources you have consulted, which is why they require so much detail; your readers need to have as much information as possible in case they want to find any of your sources. One thing to remember about citations is that they are somewhat like mathematical formulas. You never have to memorize the order of citation elements, you just need to be able to plug the information about your sources into the correct format. There are excellent citation resources online that you can use to double check the details of a citation. The OWL at Purdue is our personal favorite, but check your research guide for additional resources. (For more on citation and formatting, see Ch. 16, "Rhetorical Elements of Academic Citation.")

» Getting Help

This chapter only scratches the surface of the resources we have available and the strategies that can help you use them most effectively. If you need help with any part of the research process, from brainstorming search terms, to selecting the appropriate library resources, to citing your sources, you can always contact the UNCG Libraries. You can contact a librarian for research help by clicking "Chat with a librarian" on the Libraries' homepage.

"You can contact a librarian for research help by clicking 'Chat with a librarian' on the Libraries' homepage."

15. Managing Sources:
Finding Your Voice in an Academic Conversation

Kellyn Poole Luna

Acknowledging others' work is an essential part of writing a successful research essay, but keeping up with important content across multiple sources can be difficult. In this chapter, we will discuss how to manage sources for writing projects to help you avoid a mess of jumbled articles and lost notes. We will also discuss ideas for using multiple platforms to store sources.

Managing sources involves more than just saving a group of articles and revisiting them when you need to look up a quote or citation. **Managing your sources *well* means developing a method of keeping them together, determining how they work together, and understanding each source on its own.** A key aspect of using sources well and keeping information organized in your mind starts with how you collect and organize your sources in the physical world. (For more on gathering sources, see Ch. 14, "Research Is a Process.") For now, we'll turn to how to manage the sources you've found.

» Compiling Your Sources

Keep all of your sources for a project together in one place. That could mean keeping physical copies of everything in one folder or spot in your home or downloading everything into one folder on your computer. This simple step will allow you to return to your research again and again without requiring you to navigate multiple channels in search of one particular article.

"Keep all of your sources for a project together in one place."

One method of organization is to create a folder on your computer for each semester and each class. Having these folders will help you to organize all of your course readings, projects and assignments, or other electronic material in one place. Consider creating sub-folders for large projects to save your research articles. Place hard-copy sources together in a folder with a citation, brief description, and any corresponding notes attached.

When working with electronic copies of sources, you should name the files something that will let you know exactly what they are without having to open them. Once you have several sources, it will be difficult to remember which one `ahgjn1buirg23.pdf` is and why it was important. Instead, rename each document with the author's last name and the title. For example: `Berthoff_Composing is Forming.pdf`.

Finally, as you read and form ideas for incorporating each source into your work, consider making a "Notes" document or keeping a research journal. I like to keep one big document and put each source on its own page using page breaks so that all of my individual notes are in one compact place. We'll return to note-taking strategies a little later in this chapter.

» Weeding Out What You Do and Don't Need

Begin with an outline or a plan for your essay. If outlining is not a good pre-writing strategy for you, try freewriting, storyboarding, or brain mapping (For more, see Ch. 17, "Pre-Writing Strategies.") **Don't worry if your ideas change!** Outlines and plans for research essays tend to shift as you read through articles and books and develop your own ideas. Once you have a plan for your essay and are ready to incorporate sources, you'll need to determine which ones best fit your argument.

Keep in mind, the first few sources that come up in initial searches may not be the most helpful for your project. This means that you will need to find more than the specified minimum number of sources required by the assignment prompt. Also remember that you can look at the references and notes in each of the sources you find to direct you to more information and sources about particular topics. These pages can help you to better understand each author's engagement with the scholarly discussion around your topic and give you an idea of where you might add your voice. For your sanity and the sake of the essay, be honest about which sources work and resonate with you as you gather information.

First Things First: Read Closely and Annotate

Note-taking is a simple but incredibly helpful step. **Taking good notes will prevent you from having to re-read sources multiple times.** It will also help you keep track of ideas, interactions, and gaps in information between your sources. **If you've found a gap, you've found an excellent place to enter into a conversation about your chosen topic.** (For more, see Ch. 9, "Strategies for Active Reading.")

You might consider **annotating**, or **taking notes with a goal in mind.** Here, you are not merely copying information from a source but locating the most important and useful information in it to support your ideas, maintaining and strengthening your ethos as a writer. Taking clear and detailed notes helps you to remember important ideas or passages from a particular text, and it can be really useful for paraphrasing and summarizing as well.

Perhaps you've been assigned annotations, as part of an informal or formal annotated bibliography assignment. Whether or not this is the case, if you want to learn more about this more advanced method for keeping track of and using sources, see Appendix D.

☐ *Give yourself plenty of time to read.*

☐ *Re-read particularly interesting or confusing sections.*

☐ *Ask questions while reading and write them down.*

☐ *Formulate possible answers to your questions.*

☐ *Mark repeated or emphasized ideas.*

☐ *Identify the thesis and conclusion.*

☐ *Write down terms you are unfamiliar with.*

☐ *Tag pages and/or highlight important information.*

Be Honest about What's Working and What Isn't

"Remember, your sources should back up your work, not the other way around."

If you have a source that does not highlight your work and goals, it does not help you to force it into your essay. Remember, your sources should back up your work, not the other way around. This means that you will need to **give yourself plenty of time to find sources that are legitimately useful for your project, and to read them thoroughly.** This also means that you will, undoubtedly, find a source that looks great at first, but when you really get into it, seems utterly unhelpful. Take a moment to put down your reading or close your computer, curse the author, cry a little if you need to, but move on. It's not the one for you. (For more on re-visiting your sources during revision, see Ch. 27, "Re-Seeing the Revision Process.")

Remember, your goal is not to read every article or book ever written about a particular topic. Attempting such a feat is unhelpful and overwhelming. **Your goal is to familiarize yourself with scholarship concerning your topic.** Understanding how and why people are talking about a topic in a certain way will help you to understand the major arguments and viewpoints therein, giving you an opportunity to join the conversation.

The aim for any research essay is to know generally and speak briefly and narrowly about your topic. For example, let's say you're going to analyze Lois Lowry's *The Giver* and its engagement with genre and culture. Can you possibly know everything there is to know about dystopian literature, Lowry's writing style, her previous works, and all of the criticism about our society found in *The Giver*? No. Can you read enough about dystopian literature and Lois Lowry to be able to have a conversation about either? Yes. Can you then narrow your focus and research more heavily on the control of people's abilities to perceive and feel in *The Giver* and what our culture might look like if that happened? Definitely. Find sources that complement *your approach* to a topic, those that support your specific focus, and leave sources that are only minimally related for another time.

» Create a Draft Reference Page

A draft reference page is a working document that you can revise to keep your list of sources up-to-date and ready to use. As you find sources that work for you, go ahead and put them into a reference page using the appropriate citation style for the assignment. This page will expand and change as you continue working on your project. Now, not only are all of your working sources in one place, they are already formatted and ready for the final version of your essay. (For more, see Ch. 16, "Rhetorical Elements of Academic Citation.")

> *Pro tip:* Highlight the entry in your draft reference page as you incorporate that source into your essay, so you know what you've already used and what other sources you still have to work with.

» Conclusion

Managing your sources from the beginning of a project will help you more deeply understand your topic as you put your ideas into conversation with those of others. It might help to think of incorporating other authors' work into your own like you are introducing them at a dinner party. You'll start with the author's first and last name, the title of the source, and the key ideas of that source that you wish to bring out. Imagine that you are personally presenting this author and their work to your reader, explaining why their work is important for understanding your own work. (For more on synthesizing sources, see Ch. 21, "Organization, from Beginning to End," and Ch. 22, "Incorporating Evidence.") **Your source-tracking system will support you in writing more compelling and interesting essays.**

Maintaining sources throughout the writing process will help you move from brainstorming to final edits as smoothly as possible. My goal for this chapter was helping you consider a system of your own that will be informative, yet relaxed, like the writing process should be. There is so much information out there that putting the pieces together can be difficult, but I hope that finding sources, saving them, and note-taking will help keep you organized and aid you in writing clear and effective essays.

"Managing your sources from the beginning of a project will help you more deeply understand your topic as you put your ideas into conversation with those of others."

What Can We Do with This?

+ Reflect on your current writing process and how you could organize your research more effectively

+ Create (or improve) an information management system to organize your thoughts and sources

+ Consider which sources are most helpful for an individual project

+ Be open to the fact that ideas change as a project develops

+ Question sources and place them into conversation with each other

16. Rhetorical Elements of Academic Citation

Ben Compton

» A Brief Overview of Citation

Any time a student writes a research paper, lab report, or presentation during their college careers, they will have to cite their sources. The structure of these citations can feel confusing, rigid, and pointless. Why, for instance, do writers need to cite the names of the authors and page numbers parenthetically by use of in-text citations? Doesn't that just clog up the paper with needless trivia? Isn't putting something in quotes enough?

These are all valid questions that deserve to be answered. This chapter attempts to address these questions and explore how students and writers can see the citation process as a rhetorical act that brings further meaning and illumination to their work. This chapter will also look at a few citation styles, such as the Modern Language Association (MLA) and the American Psychological Association (APA), to see their essential differences and similarities.

» Why Do We Cite?

One of the most important reasons to use accurate citations is that they contribute to the ethos of the writer. For audiences who are familiar with the paper's topic, citations show that the writer has done research and that they know the tone, tenor, and content of the conversation into which they are entering. This is important because it establishes that the writer and his/her arguments are credible, informed, and relevant. This credibility lends weight to the writing and enhances the writer's standing as a voice in the field who has something to offer the ongoing academic discussion. For audiences who are not familiar with the topic, these citations will help to show that there is a larger discussion and that the argument is not simply a series of random assertions.

The eighth edition of the *MLA Handbook for Writers of Research Papers* begins with an important reminder: **"Academic writing is at its root a conversation about a topic or question"** (5). By considering research and writing as contributions to a larger community, it is easy to see that accurate citations are important because they show that the author is aware of the rules and conventions of the communities for whom they are writing. Writing within these conventions evens the playing field and allows the participants in the community to share a common language and communicate in a standardized way that maximizes clarity and minimizes ambiguity. By entering into the discussion in this way, students can take control of the conversation in the same ways the critics, scholars, and writers to whom they are responding do. In this way, students cease to be outsiders in the academic discourse; rather they are active participants in an ever-widening exploration of the ideas that will fuel the next generation of critical, academic, and scientific thought.

These citations also let the audience know where the writer's ideas come from, an essential element in academic integrity. (For more, see Ch. 7, "Academic Integrity: Promoting Intellectual Growth.") Of course, it is not the job of the writer to simply parrot back information, rather it is incumbent upon them to synthesize, transform, and further the seemingly disparate threads of the academic conversation into a coherent argument that both engages with the past and shapes the future.

> "Audiences should be able to look at a list of sources and follow them back to the original texts."

These citations can be like breadcrumbs that allow the audience to tag along with the author on the path to discovery. When audiences can follow this process, they gain a clearer and better idea of how the author arrived at his or her innovative and unique new thesis.

Because writers want their audiences to follow their argument and logic as closely as possible, they need to be clear and accurate with their citations. Audiences should be able to look at a list of sources and follow them back to the original texts. The ability of a reader to revisit these original sources allows them to gauge the accuracy of the information and to gain an understanding of the original context of the cited material. Additionally, this data may assist future scholars in their research.

» In-Text Citations vs. Bibliographic Citations

Before going any further, it is useful to delineate between *in-text citations* and *bibliographic citations* because they contain slightly different types of information and serve distinct purposes. In-text citations are, as their name implies, citations that appear within the body of the paper. These citations are contained within parentheses and serve to give the reader some basic information about the source and to point them to its bibliographic citation. These bibliographic citations appear at the end of the paper on either the Works Cited page (MLA) or References page (APA). These types of citations contain significantly more information about when, where, and by whom the original work was published. These citations aid readers and researchers in locating the source in case they want clarification or more information.

> *Note that a Bibliography is not the same thing as a Works Cited or References page. A Bibliography is a list of all relevant sources that a writer has consulted in their research process, regardless of whether or not they are directly cited in the paper. The Works Cited and References pages list only the works that have been actually cited in the paper.*

» Block Quotes

Sometimes, when writing a paper, students will find themselves needing to use longer quotes in order to fully explain and react to an idea. In both MLA and APA, these longer quotes will be set off from the rest of the text to ensure that the reader knows when the quote begins and ends. While both citation styles use block quotations, the rules for them are a little different.

In MLA style, a writer uses a block quote when the cited passage is four lines or longer. The writer will start the quote on a new line indented half an inch from the left margin. Because the quote is already set off, there is no need to use quotation marks. Immediately following the final punctuation mark, the writer will add the parenthetical citation.

In APA style, writers use block quotes when the cited passage is 40 words or longer. Like in MLA, APA block quotes start on their own line and are indented 1/2 an inch. Again, because it is already set off, there is no need to use quotation marks. As in the MLA style, the parenthetical citation should come immediately following the final punctuation mark. All block quotes should be double-spaced.

With these ideas in mind, it may be useful to explore some of the specific similarities and differences between MLA and APA style.

» Modern Language Association (MLA)

Many fields within the humanities, including English, Art, Music, and Comparative Literature, use MLA as a primary citation style. MLA style has a few distinct characteristics, but the most evident is the emphasis on the name of the individual or individuals who created the work. In order to understand why they provide this emphasis on individual author(s), it is helpful to stop and consider the implicit values of some of these fields. First, many of these disciplines are primarily concerned with the texts themselves and, as such, with their creators. To this end, MLA style puts the name of the creator front and center in both in-text citations (those that appear within the body of the paper) and bibliographic (those that appear at the end of the paper in the Works Cited page citations). Consider the following passage from an academic paper on W.B. Yeats:

> In addition to using imagery and language, Yeats also utilizes the dramatic and poetic structure of the poem to meditate on the futile, but necessary search for perfection in a fallen world. When *The Monthly Review* first published the poem in December of 1902, Yeats was embarking on more formal experimentations of the limits of both poetry and theatre. It was a time when many were questioning how the theatre of Ireland would develop. Thomas Sturge Moore, writing in *The Monthly Review* in the same year, opined that Ireland's theatre was in a critical phase of growth and that care needed to be taken in what types of plays to develop (103). Although Yeats had been interested in theatre since his youth, actively working on theatrical projects through the 1890s, it was at the beginning of the twentieth century that he began to commit himself to more readily exploring the boundaries of the theatre. His dramatic poem, *The Shadowy Waters*, first published in *The North American Review* in 1900 and first performed at the Irish National Theatre Society in 1904 is evidence of this transformation. (Ross 370)

In the above passage, there are two different ways of citing an author's work. First, there are direct references to an opinion piece that Thomas Sturge Moore wrote in *The Monthly Review*. Because these citations have a "lead-in" statement that introduces the author of the work, all the writer needs in the parenthetical citation is the page number(s). The second citation in the paragraph has no introductory "lead-in" and, as such, requires us to add the name of the author in the parenthetical citation.

If a work has more than two authors, a writer would cite both the authors' last names in an in-text citation [for example: (Zelda and Ender 42)]. If a work has three or more authors, a writer would use only the last name of the first author and follow it with and the phrase "et al." (this is a Latin phrase that means "and others") [for example: (Adams et al. 42)].

Some sources, especially those found online, may not list page numbers. If this is the case, simply put the author's last name into the parentheses. If you do not have the name of the author, list the article's title in quotes in the parentheses.

Let's also look at the way that a writer would cite these bibliographic entries on his or her Works Cited page:

Works Cited

Moore, Thomas Sturge. "The Renovation of the Theatre." *The Monthly Review*, vol. 7, April–June 1902, pp. 102–116. *Hathitrust Digital Library*, hdl.handle.net/2027/coo.31924065575676.

Ross, David. *The Critical Companion to William Butler Yeats: A Literary Reference to His Life and Work.* Facts On File, 2009. *eBook Collection (EBSCO)*, site.ebrary.com/id/10306178.

As is evident, the Works Cited page requires more information than the in-text citation. In addition to the name of the author, also required are the name of the text, where it was published, the name of the publisher, its year of publication and, if it is a web source, its URL or DOI (see below). These entries are arranged in alphabetical order with hanging indentations (the second line of the bibliographic entry is indented).

» American Psychological Association (APA)

Many disciplines, including the majority of sciences, social sciences, and psychology, use APA as their primary citation style. APA citation style differs from MLA in many ways, but the most obvious is that the year of publication features prominently in both in-text citations and bibliographic citations on the reference page. In order to understand why, it is helpful to consider the goals of writing in the disciplines that use APA as their primary citation method.

In these fields, more often than not, the most current information is considered the most relevant to the discussion. For example, research on quantum physics from 1985 may be illuminating, but may not reflect the most recent advancements in the field. For this reason, listing the year of publication serves to show the audience both the timeliness and relevance of the writer's work and the work they are referencing. Consider the following two paragraphs from the literature review of research study on the use of theatre in special needs classrooms:

Studies (Corbett et al., 2011; Trowsdale & Hayhow, 2013) have shown that activities that involve modeling and mirroring are effective intervention tools for self-awareness and social awareness because "most of human learning occurs by watching and imitating others. Children with autism who possess fundamental imitation ability are able to learn from observation, imitation, and modeling" (Corbett et al., 2011, p. 506).

---

or

Gessaroli, Andreini, Pellegri, and Frassinetti (2013) have noted, that "a number of studies suggest that the mental aspects of self-awareness are diminished and/or atypical in autism spectrum disorder (ASD). For instance, individuals with ASD have difficulty identifying and reflecting on their own mental states" (p.794). But, while many individuals with autism may have difficulty with certain elements of self-awareness, Gessaroli et al. contend, "not all aspects of self-awareness are impaired in ASD. Indeed, children with ASD are able to compare the currently perceived mirror or specular self-image with the mental representation of their bodily self-image" (p.794).

In both of these paragraphs, it is possible to see citations that privilege the year of publication along with the names of the authors, something that MLA citation style does not do. By referencing recent studies, the author of this work enhances their own credibility and the legitimacy of their research. Notice too that after the first reference to Gessaroli, Andreini, Pellegri and Frassinetti is made, the source is then simply referred to as "Gessaroli et al." In APA, writers can add the "et al." after the primary author's name when there are three or more authors of one text. This abbreviation helps to save space and increase clarity.

Let us also look at the bibliographic information for these sources as presented on the References page (the APA version of the Works Cited page).

References

Corbett, B. A., Gunther, J. R., Comins, D., Price, J., Ryan, N., Simon, D., …Rios, T. (2011). Brief report: Theatre as therapy for children with autism spectrum disorder. *Journal of Autism & Developmental Disorders, 41*(4), 505–511. doi:10.1007/s10803-010-1064-1

Gessaroli, E., Andreini, V., Pellegri, E., & Frassinetti, F. (2013). Self-face and self-body recognition in autism. *Research In Autism Spectrum Disorders, 7*(6), 793–800. doi: 10.1016/j.rasd.2013.02.014

Trowsdale, J., & Hayhow, R. (2013). Can mimetics, a theatre-based practice, open possibilities for young people with learning disabilities? A capability approach. *British Journal of Special Education, 40*(2), 72–79. doi:10.1111/1467-8578.12019

Notice that the year of publication is still featured prominently in these citations. This points to the fact that the timely relevance of the work is vital to understanding whether the research is still current. Note, too, that unlike MLA citations that list the author's full first and last names, APA citations only use the last names and first initials. One of the reasons for this is that work in fields done in the sciences, social sciences, and psychology are often done in groups, as opposed to many of the humanities where research can be more of a solo endeavor. Including only the last names and first initials both saves space and underscores the importance of collaboration over individual research.

» Some Practical Advice

While MLA and APA are two of the most common citation styles, there are many others that students may run into as they become familiar with their fields of study. Chicago, Turabian, and AMA (American Medical Association) styles are also used in academic disciplines such as philosophy, history, and medicine. It is important that students become familiar with conventions and expectations for work in their field, but how can one person possibly keep all of these rules in their head at once? It can be frustrating to try to remember the exact difference between how to cite a podcast and how to cite a lecture. Because there is so much information, rather than trying to remember *everything*, it is more useful to just remember where to look. With that in mind, here are four quick pieces of advice:

- Students should purchase an up-to-date style guide for the citation method of their particular field or discipline. These manuals are invaluable resources that students can always throw in their backpacks or keep beside their desks as a quick reference.

- Students should also familiarize themselves with online resources. There are many places to go online to get useful information about how and when to make citations. Two of the best of these resources are the OWL website at Purdue University (https://owl.english.purdue.edu/) and The MLA's Online Style Guide (https://style.mla.org/). These websites provide users advice on how to do a variety of different types of citations (multiple authors, songs, photographs, and so on).

- Be wary of "citation machine" websites that claim to do citation formatting. While these websites may simplify the citation process, they often provide inaccurate or poorly formatted results. One of the main reasons for this is that these websites often require the students to input the bibliographic information. Students who are not aware of what to look for in a bibliographic reference may forget to include specific pieces of information. So, even though these websites can offer shortcuts, students still need to know how the citation process works and how to check and make sure that their entries are accurate.

> ◆ Do not be shy about asking for help with questions or for clarification about citation and documentation. Your instructor may be able to help, but the library and the Writing Center are also great places to get assistance. The library has specific staff members who specialize in different fields and areas of research. These staff members are familiar with the accepted stylistic citation requirements for their fields and will be happy to provide assistance with research and accurate documentation. Along with the library, the Writing Center is an excellent resource for any questions that may come up about citations. The staff and consultants at the Writing Center are trained to work with students in one-on-one sessions to help them at all stages of the writing process, including citation.

Because this process can be confusing, we encourage you to look at one of the many reputable guides to citation in the format your course requires, available from the Library, or online. One particularly good resource is the Purdue OWL website, available at owl.purdue.edu. Lastly, because citation style guidelines are often updated, be sure you're using a current version of their guidelines. Follow these tips, and soon enough, you'll be citing effortlessly.

» Work Cited

Modern Language Association. *The MLA Handbook for Writers of Research Papers*. 8th ed., Modern Language Association, 2016.

III

Crafting
and Drafting

17. Pre-Writing Strategies:
Methods to Achieve a Successful Argument

Kristine Lee

One of the most challenging tasks we face is starting the work of writing. You may feel a sense of dread at the prospect of putting your thoughts down on paper, or you may be intimidated by the idea that writing must be perfect grammatically and syntactically. This may be your first college experience, and you may not be sure of the expectations from high school to this class. You may not yet have a structure in place that makes beginning less overwhelming. Thankfully, writing is always a learning process, and one of the best ways to develop your writing is to start the work with a blank slate. Polishing will come later in the writing process. (For more about revising and editing, see Ch. 27, "Re-Seeing the Revision Process.")

Although you may feel stressed about how to start an assignment, this chapter presents invention strategies you can employ to make the process more productive. You may even consider using some of the support available for you on campus, which can include meeting with the instructor or with a consultant at one of the Multiliteracy Centers to brainstorm ways to start.

> "As you get started, be flexible with trying a variety of strategies, be creative, and be sure to avoid procrastination."

In high school or previous writing classes, you may have used a traditional Roman numeral or lettered outline to begin the writing process, but College Writing courses will expose you to a number of other ways to get started in addition to this one. Every writer has their own rhetorical choices to make regarding how to begin, and each assignment might require a different strategy. As you get started, be flexible with trying a variety of strategies, be creative, and be sure to avoid procrastination. Here are a few helpful strategies to get you started:

- **Brainstorming:** Brainstorming is a low-stakes way of communicating ideas on paper or aloud to arrange them for an argument later. It often allows the writer to make connections between ideas before the formal writing process begins and provides an opportunity to think about what major topics should be covered. As you brainstorm, you may make connections between texts, find evidence for tentative claims, locate page numbers and references to back up these claims, or connect ideas to rhetorical purposes. As you integrate these brainstorming ideas, including transitions and ensuring logical arrangement of ideas is key. This way, the reader can see connections made between ideas and how these ideas build an argument throughout the text.

+ **Listing:** When you are assigned an essay or other writing assignment, making a list may be an effective starting place. For example, if you are assigned to write about a topic that you are passionate about while including naysayers and privileging your own ideas, you could start by making a list of possible issues you could write about well. This rhetorical choice can make writing more natural and strengthen the argument since you'll already have more to say and more evidence for claims. You may also be more confident writing about these topics. For example, if I were writing a list of potential topics for a paper, it may look like this:

1. Fair treatment of animals at shelters

2. Access to healthy food, regardless of financial status

3. The importance of acquiring education

4. Incorporating technology in the classroom

Then I may add both sides of the argument and where I stand regarding this issue to my list. As a final step, I would narrow down my topic by considering which one I could write about thoroughly and effectively. I could use the list to rank which topics would be most effective for me as a writer and especially emphasize the topics into which I could insert my voice easily.

+ **Questions:** Writing a list of questions can also help writers find a focused topic and/or ideas. The benefit of this practice is that it provides an opportunity to think about the answers to the questions posed and gives you a starting point for finding credible evidence and sources to back up your answers. Asking questions is often the starting point for forming an argument that addresses the conclusions in your thesis. For example:

+ What are three topics that relate to the assignment?

+ Of these three, which one could I write about confidently, following research or preparation?

+ What is my thesis and why is it significant?

+ What parts of the text support my claims?

+ What supporting resources do I need?

Of course, you may ask yourself a variety of additional questions to help jump-start your writing. You may also ask your peers, instructor, or Multiliteracy Center consultant to suggest some questions that could assist with starting the writing process. If your instructor does not provide a prompt and wants you to write about whatever you like, asking questions may be a helpful way to find a topic. Here are some potential questions you may consider asking:

+ What interests me?

+ Will I be making an argument in this paper or responding to something/someone?

+ Is there a topic related to my major that I would like to write about?

+ Who is involved in this topic I'm addressing? What is their stake in it?

(See Ch. 13, "Topic Selection: Finding Your Foundation" for additional examples.)

+ **Conversation:** Some writers benefit most from an oral conversation, and sometimes this is the most effective way to get ideas flowing. You may find that having a conversation about the topic assigned can help narrow down ideas, add other perspectives, and provide some additional points to consider. A few excellent resources for these kinds of conversations are peers during peer review, the consultants at one of the Multiliteracy Centers, and your instructor, though you are not limited to only these options. As you have a conversation about writing, you may find more direction, helping you make your argument more specific and refine points to support your argument. Conversations with others will provide an audience—a crucial aspect of the rhetorical triangle—for your argument and help you anticipate reactions and/or objections to your claims.

+ **Freewriting:** This method is very different from asking questions because freewriting helps the writer dive right into the writing process. The well-known scholar Peter Elbow came up with this method for beginning the writing process. Freewriting allows a writer to produce without the impediment of being too critical of their own work and without worrying about a polished product. With this strategy, the writer has the freedom to write constantly without stopping, gliding from one idea to the next. Elbow describes a process where editing and producing writing are separate: "The main thing about freewriting is that it is nonediting. It is an exercise in bringing together the process of producing words and putting them down on the page. Practiced regularly, it undoes the ingrained habit of editing at the same time you are trying to produce" (Elbow 69). As writers, we have the tendency to worry about our writing being perfect from the start, but Elbow's act of freewriting supports the idea that there is no perfect writing and that the most effective way to begin may be ignoring the lower-order concerns such as grammar and punctuation, at least initially. The polishing processes can occur in a later, more finalized draft. Following a free-writing exercise, you can go back and search for the useful ideas that support the argument and take out the information that isn't relevant to your claims. You may not use everything from your free-write; in fact, it's possible that you might use very little of it, but this exercise may point you to new ideas that may have been left out of a more structured pre-writing exercise.

> "Freewriting allows the writer to produce without impediment, and without worrying about a polished product."

- **Outlining:** While freewriting may be freeing for some writers who respond to arranging texts later, outlining could be helpful for those writers who appreciate structure from the beginning of the writing process. At this point as writers, you are likely familiar with outlining, but this tool can be changed to model an efficient, organized structure for your text that arranges your ideas in a logical order. You may recognize this model from high school, but for College Writing courses, we're moving away from the five-paragraph essay and into crafting a more detailed piece of writing. As a result, the outline should become much more detailed. Effective arrangement of your claims will make your points more clear and will build your argument cohesively. (See Appendix C for example outlines for a College Writing class.)

- **Webbing/Mapping/Clustering:** If you are a visual learner, this could be a strategy that provides a clear structure for you. Although an outline can provide organization for a writer, a web or map can provide you with the opportunity to place ideas in a specific order and build on them by connecting parts of the web visually and spatially. A web or map of your ideas aids the writing process by allowing you to develop ideas visually. Placing your ideas in a web or map can help you to make logical connections between claims, center ideas around the argument, and organize sub-topics. (See Appendix E for an example of a visual web/map.)

+ **Reverse Outlining:** Unlike regular outlines, reverse outlines involve outlining a draft that has already been completed. This method of outlining achieves a different aim since it happens after the writing process has occurred and not beforehand, and it relies on your choice of arrangement. Creating a reverse outline gives you an opportunity to examine structure, locate places that may require further development, and determine if your paper has been sufficiently argued and supported. This method supports the invention process after locating places to develop further and building ideas to strengthen your argument. Additionally, reverse outlining allows for practicing arrangement. Some questions that writers might ask themselves in this exercise may include: What is the best place for this paragraph to solidify my argument? How can placement of this paragraph make my claims more effective? Arrangement choices during this process of reverse outlining are flexible, in that you will be able to decide what will work best for your paper. Examining each paragraph critically also enables you to notice where logos, or the logical flow of your argument, may be improved. Here's how to start the process: look back through each paragraph of your paper and write a one-sentence summary of the main idea. Number the paragraphs on the draft to correspond with the numbers on your reverse outline for ease of use. Next, look back at each paragraph to determine the rhetorical function it serves in your broader paper. After you've completed these steps, consider looking at these areas for improvement:

  + Paragraphs that could be broken down into shorter paragraphs or combined into longer paragraphs for organizational purposes.

  + Paragraphs that include too many topics for one area of the paper. In these cases, you may break these down into a few paragraphs and develop your ideas further.

  + Places where an idea is repeated more than once, or reiterated in the exact same way. Consider omitting or rephrasing to avoid repetition.

  + Cohesion is an important element of crafting a persuasive paper. If you find that there are places where it isn't clear where your paper is going, consider re-ordering your ideas.

  + Ideally, each paragraph should support the main argument of your text. If you find one that seems off topic, revise it to fit the topic, or you may strike it.

One of the best aspects of writing is the ability to make it your own from beginning to end—there is no one correct way to get started. Many writers have said that getting started is the hardest part of writing, and using these methods or others of your own to begin the writing process takes the pressure off that first step to your final draft. You'll find that beginning writing, in one way or another, keeps you from procrastinating and gives you a head start on the draft you'll bring for peer review. You may also have a variety of other strategies that you use for getting started, and you may consider discussing these in class or mentioning what you've discovered works best for you when another assignment comes along. You are, by no means, limited to this list of suggestions. The most important thing is that you find a method that aids you in creating ideas for writing.

> "There is no one correct way to get started."

» Work Cited

Elbow, Peter. "Freewriting." *The Arlington Reader: Contexts and Connections*. 3rd ed. Edited by Lynn Z. Bloom and Louise Z. Smith. Bedford/St. Martin's, 2011, pp. 67–70.

» Teaching Text

1. Complete a short freewriting activity in class on a topic determined by your instructor. What were the benefits and challenges of this practice for you as a writer? Next, have the entire class discuss removing editing from the writing process. What was that experience like, and are you willing to try it again? Why or why not?

2. Examine the possible methods for pre-writing in this chapter. Write about one method you have not tried and why it might benefit your process. If you are familiar with each of these approaches, which one was most effective for you, and why? Which method would you be willing to attempt again?

3. Activity: Create a reverse outline of a completed draft from a recent assignment for this course. With a peer, look specifically at the arrangement of your essay and the main topic sentences for each section. Are there topics that seem better placed elsewhere in the paper? Why is this the case? Were there sections where the topic sentences were particularly difficult to produce? How could you revise to make these topics clearer? Are there areas that seem particularly persuasive? Discuss with your peer.

18. Thesis Statements:
Keeping the Beat in Written, Visual, and Spoken Arguments

Emily Dolive

Be sure you have a strong thesis. Check that all of your supporting points relate back to your thesis. Where is your thesis? These are just a few of the reminders you've probably heard instructors in many classes give. But what does it really mean to create and use a thesis statement in this way?

Every act of communication—written, spoken, and visual—has a driving purpose. This purpose is at the heart of the rhetorical triangle and it becomes the heart*beat* of your work if articulated clearly and regularly through a thesis. In other words, your thesis statement constantly pulses through your work like a heartbeat, giving life and force to all examples, evidence, and arrangement. In fact, the *Oxford English Dictionary* includes a definition of thesis as "The setting down of the foot or lowering of the hand in time" in music or verse. You can also think about a thesis as a drumbeat, a steady rhythm, when repeated throughout your work and when you explain your examples in relation to the thesis. Below I will discuss strategies for creating, reiterating, and connecting your thesis to the body of your work that will help you keep the beat.

> "Your thesis statement should share with your audience your exact purpose for communicating."

Your thesis statement should share with your audience your exact purpose for communicating; it announces what your contributions to the conversation are and why they are important. In fact, "statement" may be a bit misleading because a thesis is really a claim, conclusion, argument, interpretation, or resolution. We often associate thesis statements with written essays, but other media like speeches and visual presentations also present claims and support them using signposting and arrangement. In order to prove that thesis statements lend purpose to your written, spoken, and visual communications, this chapter will explore what constitutes strong arguments and how they can be created and revised.

The following chart defining thesis characteristics is adapted from Mary Lynn Rampolla's *A Pocket Guide to Writing in History*:

What a Thesis IS	What a Thesis Is NOT
• An answer to a question	• A question
• A debatable claim with which your audience can agree, disagree, or lie somewhere in between	• An informational, undebatable statement
• A claim that can be supported with evidence	• An opinion without sufficient reasoning or explanation
• An argument explaining the significance of the topic	• A description of your topic

» Examples of Effective and Ineffective Thesis Statements

Ineffective: TV shows today are ruining the morals of young viewers in order to get higher ratings.

Effective: With the rise of sex and violence in primetime TV shows, parents should consider limiting the time their children watch because excessive viewing can negatively impact social relationships, attention spans, and creativity.

Ineffective: David Foster Wallace's commencement speech, "This Is Water," uses logos, pathos, and ethos.

Effective: David Foster Wallace's commencement speech, "This Is Water," successfully convinces his audience that a liberal arts education can prepare one to decide how to view life's struggles through his use of humorous anecdotes, meaningful metaphors, and relevant experience.

How could you make these even stronger?

» Writing Your Way to a Thesis

Thesis statements like the more effective examples above do not suddenly appear, fully formed, to guide the rest of your work. As you begin pre-writing and drafting, try to stay flexible so you have room to fine-tune your thoughts and incorporate new research. It is often helpful to begin with a tentative claim that launches you into writing. Then, explore your key points, counter-arguments, and organization of evidence by writing some body paragraphs.

Once the body of the essay has been written, you can return to and refocus your tentative claim so that it reflects, in more definite terms, the argument you have proven in your body paragraphs. Thus, the body of your work will keep the beat of your thesis by steadily reminding readers what you are arguing and by demonstrating how your supporting points relate to that overarching claim. Acknowledging that your tentative thesis will change as you write and gather information frees you from being locked into a claim that your evidence does not quite fit and from having to develop a strong thesis statement at the beginning of the writing process. This way, you will continuously revise your thesis throughout the drafting process.

To get started, let your interests and inquiries be your starting point even if you have been assigned a topic. What unique approach can you bring to the topic? As you begin writing, gather some notes and questions about what particular aspect of the topic interests you. As shown previously in the chart, answering an open-ended question will give you a tentative thesis. Similarly, the more questions you ask and try to answer, the clearer and narrower your tentative thesis will become. Then, you can continue drafting, gathering support, organizing, and contextualizing until your main claims take a final shape. (For more, see Ch. 13, "Topic Selection: Finding Your Foundation.")

» Delivering Thesis Statements

Once you have a working thesis—a claim that alerts your audience to your purpose for communicating—you can then decide, within the guidelines of the course, if your ideas and evidence should play out in a written, visual, or spoken text. When you make such choices for optimal rhetorical effectiveness, you are taking into consideration the rhetorical canon of delivery. In addition to choosing a medium for your argument, successful delivery also hinges on your decisions about tone of voice and body language in spoken arguments, citations and formatting in written arguments, and color, spacing, and font in visual arguments. (For more discussion and examples of delivery choices, see Ch. 25, "Rhetorical Delivery.")

In class, you may analyze a visual text—a video, magazine ad, building, and so forth—for its rhetorical effectiveness. You may then have the opportunity to create a visual text of your own. All components of a visual presentation should point to its thesis, or claim, just the way paragraphs in an essay do. This can be achieved by careful arrangement and selection of meaningful details. With this in mind, let's consider some strategies for creating your own visual arguments in a poster, PowerPoint, podcast, or blog.

» Visual Thesis Statements

You can deliver the thesis of a poster in words and/or images, but you have limited space to do so. Therefore, the title and the most important evidence should typically come first and both should clearly express your thesis. The title or other prominent words and images should concisely convey what would be a longer, full sentence or two in an essay. A poster, PowerPoint, or blog might begin with "Standardized Testing Alternatives," or even stronger, "Portfolio Evaluation Sustains Student Achievement." Both titles alert readers to your specific plan to replace testing with something better, rather than simply beginning with "Standardized Testing Pros and Cons." The latter title does not suggest your argument, only an undebatable statement.

After the title that expresses your thesis, consider what colors, images, and arrangement choices will keep the beat of your argument. **All elements of the visual text should support, and not distract from, your thesis.** These elements include but are not limited to: a sleek color scheme, font size and style, balance, and the use of white space. Keep in mind that sometimes too much color or too many images might be jarring or distracting and thus detract from your thesis. The same goes for fonts that are too curly, thin, or bold to be easily read. Any written information you add to your poster or blog should be clearly related to the images you use and vice versa. White space can also be used strategically to pause viewers and to direct the flow of your poster's organization.

Posters and blogs can also be mapped out logically with transitions and images that keep the beat of your thesis. Check that your graphics or music accurately represent your purpose. While you may have an image that is symbolic of your in-depth understanding of the topic, be sure it will have the same meaning to an audience that is new to your ideas. Be creative, but not at the expense of clarity and exactness. Ultimately, ask yourself if all pieces of the visual composition—PowerPoint, blog, poster, and more—clearly support your thesis and do not mislead or distract your audience.

Creating an accessible and focused visual argument is often easier said than done, so you should spend some time translating your thesis into color and shape. For the sample thesis, "With the rise in sex and violence in primetime TV shows…" part of a poster may include an image of a TV divided in half or with an outline of a child in front of it. One side of the TV could be in black and white, with further images or keywords such as "fidelity" and "family" adorning it. The other side of the TV image, then, might be in a glaring red color, with representative images or keywords like "sex" and "violence." While you could translate your thesis almost word for word into a visual form, you have countless symbolic colors and images open to you. Consider your purpose and audience as you decide how your visual thesis delivery can best be arranged.

» Spoken Thesis Statements

In a speech, you can still rely on your written organizational and descriptive skills as you draft—and thereby alter and refine—the points you will orally deliver to an audience. However, in this format, you must cater to your audience's ear, especially with regards to your thesis. We have all been in a class or a meeting paying attention and taking notes, yet something has slipped past us unknowingly. In order to keep their audience and argument in rhythm, professors, musicians, writers—anyone working for a time in the verbal realm—repeat their primary claims. This act of signposting is vital in written, visual, and verbal arguments. But signposting is more than repetition and transitional phrases. **Signposting means indicating how a particular claim supports your overall argument.** To signpost, explicitly map out your goal and the steps or points which support it. You will want to explain *how* those steps or points support your overall argument. The phrases at the end of this section may help you achieve this.

With these guidelines in mind, be sure you share your thesis early and clearly in your speech. Be transparent with your language, rather than flowery or overly academic. Then, as you make new points and counterpoints, or bring in important evidence, remind readers of your argument and explain how these points support it. This signposting not only keeps the beat of your argument but helps you create smooth transitions to direct your audience. Additionally, your signposting during a speech will allow you to pause and reconnect with your audience and with your primary argument. Then, your audience will have more moments to digest and fully see the connections between your points. Phrases like the ones below will allow you to guide your audience through your presentation by making connections about your argument for them. In fact, this is good practice for writing as well. Try out signposting phrases like the following:

- *As I mentioned before…*
- *This connects to my earlier point…*
- *Next, I will explore…*
- *To return to my claim that…*
- *To further support this…*
- *In order to achieve this, let's look at…*

See Appendix F for more transitional and connecting phrases.

» Supporting and Revising Your Thesis

Another strategy to help explain and support your thesis is a Rogerian argument. **A Rogerian argument revolves around cooperation and common ground.** To employ Rogerian elements in your work, ask yourself: where and on what can you and your audience agree? What concerns do you share? After explaining this common ground, followed by a fair and objective description of each side of the issue, you would support your position in the following ways:

+ Present the benefits your audience would receive by moving toward your position.

+ Include strong evidence and clear explanations that support your thesis.

+ Additional support can come from offering compromises that would benefit both sides of the issue.

+ Conclude strongly by reinforcing your thesis and emphasizing its benefits.

(For more on argumentation, see Ch. 19, "Staking Your Claim.")

As with any text, you should repeat and clarify your thesis, but with a slight difference each time that makes your position stand out. For instance, the second example of an effective thesis statement above could be restated within a body paragraph as follows: Although Smart TVs offer parental controls, those controls must be fully utilized in order to limit the amount of harmful screen time that can negatively affect a child's development.

Remember to return to your tentative thesis once you have completed a solid draft and see if you ended where you began, so to speak. Once you have worked through a draft, then you can clarify, add to, and polish your initial thesis. That way, your thesis does not sit forgotten, but actually influences each new idea or piece of evidence you discuss. Remembering and revising your thesis during and after you write helps you restate and clarify it at key moments in your essay, PowerPoint, or speech, which keeps the beat going for your audience.

» Final Considerations

Another way to keep your audience attuned to the beat of your essay is to use your thesis to help you create a title. A thesis should present to you key words and themes you can use to formulate a compelling title. A title's purpose is twofold and similar to the purpose of a thesis: to keep the writer focused and to pique the reader's interest. Try out part of a quote, puns, colons, even italicizing important words for added emphasis. How can you catch your reader's eye by condensing and coloring your main themes? Just as your thesis will change and tighten as you draft, your writing may present to you a strong set of words for a better title. As we discussed with visual arguments like posters and blogs, all formal essays should have a focused and interesting title that previews the most important aspect of your work. The choice of a title is yet another way to enhance your overall argument.

As you probably gathered from the earlier sections, thesis statements do not come to us simply to be placed and forgotten in the first paragraph of draft one. They're gems that have to be mined out of dozens of possibilities; their final shape is waiting to be decided as you write, research, and revise. In the end, then, writing can help you discover and refine your exact thesis. Yet, having an early, tentative thesis can help you make important decisions about organizing and presenting your ideas. At every turn, your thesis should be a regular beat that guides you and your audience through written, visual, or spoken arguments.

> "Thesis statements do not come to us simply to be placed and forgotten in the first paragraph of draft one. They're gems that have to be mined out of dozens of possibilities."

» Works Cited

Rampolla, Mary Lynn. *A Pocket Guide to Writing in History.* 7th ed., Bedford/ St. Martin's, 2012.

"Thesis." *OED Online*, Oxford UP, December 2016, www.oed.com.

19. Staking Your Claim:
Strategies for Persuasive Argumentation

Kristie Ellison

What's the first thing that comes to mind when you hear the word argument? Perhaps a disagreement you had with your parents over curfew or a fight with a friend over which *Star Wars* movie is the best. While those are examples of one type of argument, arguments for College Writing and other courses represent another type, one that is not synonymous with fighting. At its core, **an argument in an academic context is a claim supported by reasons that are established with evidence.** This chapter will help you break down these three elements and develop strategies for effectively persuading your audience.

"An argument in an academic context is a claim supported by reasons that are established with evidence."

» Getting Started

The first step in developing your argument is setting forth your claim. **Your claim is the main point you are making that you want others to agree with.** For example, if you are trying to convince a group of people to go to a particular place for lunch, your claim would be something like, "We should go to Smith Street Diner for lunch." In academic terms, your claim is also referred to as a thesis statement. Because your claim may shift or narrow as you research and write, it is often referred to as a *tentative thesis statement* or a *working thesis* until your project is complete. (For more, see Ch. 18, "Thesis Statements.") It is important that you begin with a claim, even if it changes over time, so that you can narrowly focus your research and planning.

If you are just learning about a particular topic and aren't yet sure what your argument might be, you can focus on a specific research question that you are working to answer. For example, if you have recently moved to town, rather than starting with a specific claim about where your group should eat lunch and a plan to find evidence to support your claim, you would ask the question, "Where should we go to lunch?" Note, however, that it is still important for you to narrow your research, and, thus, you will want to be as specific as possible when forming your question. Here, you would consider what factors you already know, such as how big the group is and how much time you have to eat, and then ask a more specific question: "Where is the best place for a group of five students to get lunch in less than an hour?" As you do more research and learn more information, continue to refine your question.

Depending on your assignment, your instructor may provide you with a topic or you may be tasked with selecting one yourself. Either way, **one of the most important aspects of developing your claim within your topic is ensuring that it is *arguable*.** That is, make sure it is something about which someone could disagree, either in whole or in part. For example, stating that it is raining outside would not be an arguable claim if large drops of water are falling. However, if there are small, intermittent drops falling, you may be able to make a claim that it is sprinkling rather than raining. You may also be able to make a claim that a raincoat is a better way to stay dry in the rain than an umbrella.

Another important consideration when developing your claim is why it matters, both to you and to your audience. **Consider what's at stake.** Thus, while you might be able to make an arguable claim that it is sprinkling rather than raining, would it make any difference even if you convinced your audience that you are right? **A strong conclusion in an essay generally includes the broader implications of your argument—that is, other situations it may apply to—or next steps.** Considering these issues from the beginning, even if you're not yet sure of the answers, will help you make a stronger argument.

Counter-Arguments

While you are developing your own claim, you should consider other positions on the issue, also referred to as **counter-arguments**. Taking these other perspectives into account will not only demonstrate to your audience that you have thought through your position, but the process of that consideration will help you further develop your own ideas. One way to address a counter-argument is to refute it—that is, explain why it is wrong or why *your* argument is better.

Although your first instinct may be to refute all counter-arguments, you have another option: concede and limit. In this instance, you acknowledge the strength of the counter-argument, but explain how your own argument is different or limited in some way. For example, you could acknowledge that within the United States as a whole unsweetened tea is preferred to sweet tea, but then limit your argument to the South, where sweet tea is preferred. In either case, be sure that you are providing a fair representation of the counter-arguments you are addressing in order to increase your own credibility.

In addition, note that **you don't have to address every possible counter-argument; focus on those most related to your claim and reasons.** For example, if your claim is focused on the cultural implications of sweetening tea in the South, you may not need to address a potential counter-argument related to the cost of sugar. Instead, you could say something like, "It is beyond the scope of this essay to address rising sugar prices; however, cost is potentially a factor." Finally, if you find yourself unable to identify any counter-arguments at all, revisit your claim to make sure that it is arguable.

"If you find yourself unable to identify any counter-arguments at all, revisit your claim to make sure that it is arguable."

Try this 5-minute freewrite brainstorming activity to start thinking about how to build your own argument:

For 1 minute:

+   Write down what **specifically** you are **arguing.**

    Examples:

    +   X should/should not _____

    +   X is a problem because _____

    +   X is causing/caused by _____

For 2 minutes:

+   Write down as many reasons as you can think of for **why you are right.**

+   Do NOT evaluate or dismiss anything at this point.

For 2 minutes:

+   Write down as many reasons as you can think of **from the other side.**

+   Do NOT evaluate or dismiss anything at this point.

Be sure you SAVE your work so you can return to your ideas throughout the process!

This activity will allow you to think through all of the possibilities for supporting your claim and consider possible counter-arguments to address. **Once you have a list, you can choose the ones you find most compelling or that you are most able to find evidence to support.** You can also return to the lists you made during this activity if you find yourself stuck at any point in the research and writing process.

» The Role of Audience

Once you've figured out your claim, you'll want to start thinking about **what reasons justify that claim and what evidence will support those reasons.** An important consideration for both reasons and evidence is your audience. Because the goal of making an argument is to convince someone you're right, it is essential that you think about what reasons and evidence someone—your audience—will find persuasive.

Let's return to our example of making an argument about where to go to lunch. If you are trying to convince a group of your friends, your reasons for supporting a particular place may include that it is inexpensive and nearby. The **persuasive effect of these reasons would depend** on whether your friends are on a strict monthly budget and whether the group has access to transportation. Indeed, offering as a reason that a particular place accepts the campus meal plan would only be effective if at least one member of the group uses the meal plan. Similarly, if a member of the group is a vegetarian, you may offer as a reason that your choice has many such options. Consider, however, that instead you are home for a break and making the argument to your parent. In that case, you may offer completely different reasons, such as picking a place that is your shared favorite. In fact, if someone else is paying for the meal, you may have the opposite feelings about cost—even though you're unlikely to express them aloud.

Similarly, **you should consider what types of evidence your audience will find persuasive.** Sticking with our lunch example, you may offer your personal experience to support your assertion that the food is good. If you haven't been to the place you're suggesting, you might offer the experience of a friend or online reviews as evidence. Note, however, that again your choices are affected by audience. Your friends may be willing to accept the recommendation of another friend, while your parent may not find such evidence persuasive, instead preferring the recommendation of a trusted neighbor. Which online reviews are persuasive may also vary depending on audience.

"Having a clear understanding of your audience is essential to developing a persuasive argument."

As you can see, having a clear understanding of your audience is essential to developing a persuasive argument. In some cases, your instructor may give you a specific audience as part of the assignment prompt. But even if they don't, **you still must determine who you are trying to persuade and what reasons and evidence they are likely to find appealing.** To do this, you will want to **consider what values and beliefs your audience holds.** You should also think about the **existing conversation** about your issue as well as **what conventions are common.** The good news is there are clues to this information within the texts you read while gathering evidence. If you're reading a scholarly journal article on your topic, pay attention to the types of reasons offered and the sources cited. If you see a lot of statistical data, that's an indication that your field—or those who research your topic—find that type of evidence persuasive. Conversely, if you see mostly personal examples, then you may want to consider that type of evidence. Remember that writing is a process and don't worry if you're not entirely sure about what your audience wants. **Make the best, most thoughtful choices you can with the information you have, and if you learn new information, reconsider your choices.**

» Strategies

On the following page is a list of possible strategies to consider when developing your argument. Note that **the individual strategies are not mutually exclusive.** For example, you may choose to frame your overall argument as a problem/solution, and use analogy and example to further explain particular parts. **Having a clear understanding of how you are building your argument will help to ensure you effectively accomplish the things you set out to do.**

You may be wondering now about which specific strategies are the most effective for making an argument. The answer, like most answers in rhetoric, is "it depends." Which strategies will work depends on the type of argument you're making, your audience, and your own style and interests. Let's take humor as an example. Some arguments may appropriately be made funny, while others, such as trauma or tragedy, may not. Similarly, some audiences may be persuaded by humor, while some may find it to be disrespectful. Finally, even if your argument could be funny and your audience would enjoy humor, if your style is not funny or you're simply not interested in being funny, then you might want to consider a different strategy.

"Which strategies will work depends on the type of argument you're making, your audience, and your own style and interests."

Strategy	Description
Analogy	Comparisons that point out similarities in otherwise different things. This strategy can be effective to point out how your argument is similar to something your audience already agrees to.
Classification	Grouping together items based on similarities; often used to organize a topic.
Comparison/ Contrast	Focusing on the similarities or differences between things. Can be useful when explaining something that is unfamiliar to your audience. You may also use as part of your own argument; for example, your argument may involve comparing real estate prices in different cities.
Definition	Providing a clear explanation of a word or concept. This is important for terms your audience may not know as well as to establish how you are using particular terms.
Description	Explaining how something is perceived by your senses (i.e., how it looks, sounds, smells, feels, tastes). This strategy is useful to connect with your audience.
Example	Providing a concrete instance to explain an abstract idea. Examples are crucial to establishing your points clearly.
Humor	Can help you engage with the audience when appropriate. Examples include funny stories, jokes, parody, and satire.
Narration	Telling a story to illustrate your point. Personal experiences can be powerful evidence, but remember that one instance cannot represent the whole and be sure to include additional evidence.
Problem/ Solution	Establishing a specific issue and offering a way of addressing it. Note that your overall argument does not have to be evenly divided between problem and solution; you may want to focus more on one or the other depending on the current state of the conversation around your issue.
Reiteration	Repeating a word or phrase over and over for emphasis.

» A Word about Research

How much, if any, research you do in developing your argument will depend primarily on the expectations set forth by your instructor in your assignment prompt. However, if you are doing research, there are a few things to keep in mind. First and foremost, research is recursive. That means that rather than gathering a bunch of information then sitting down to write, **the processes of research and writing are intertwined and feed into each other, happening in any order and, often, repeatedly.** You may begin your research to figure out what the current conversation is on your issue, then write some on your own position, then conduct additional research to help you support that position. It is important to remain focused on *your argument* instead of letting others speak for you. **Use your research as evidence to support your own claim and reasons rather than merely reporting on what you find.** It may be helpful to first outline all of your own thoughts and then decide what evidence you will need to back up those thoughts. Finally, be sure to synthesize your sources—that is, put them in conversation with each other. Show how they work together to establish your ideas. This process will also help you see any holes in your research or ideas that aren't yet supported. (For more on research and synthesizing sources, see Ch. 14, "Research Is a Process," and Ch. 22, "Incorporating Evidence.")

The most important thing to remember about making an argument is that it is your chance to make your voice heard. If you take the time to consider what you want to say and what your audience already believes and values, you will be well on your way to making a persuasive argument.

» Work Consulted

Lunsford, Andrea, et al. *Everyone's an Author.* 1st ed., Norton, 2013.

20. Writing with the Rhetorical Appeals:
Opportunities to Persuade in Context

Amy Berrier

This chapter looks at the rhetorical appeals, which are methods rhetors use to persuade their audience. Knowledge of the appeals adds another layer to your understanding of rhetoric and its usefulness to you in writing for college and in your professional and civic lives. As with all aspects of rhetoric that you learn, the good news is that you already know how to use them, and you use them successfully every day. The key to being a truly successful rhetor, however, is to understand *how* you are successfully using rhetoric; understanding the how and why gives you a great deal more power and control over your words in future uses. This chapter examines the rhetorical appeals and how your ability to use them will strengthen your writing and allow you to succeed in new writing situations.

> "The key to being a truly successful rhetor, however, is to understand *how* you are successfully using rhetoric; understanding the how and why gives you a great deal more power and control over your words in future uses."

» It's All Greek to Me!

As with many concepts of rhetoric, the appeals come to us from the ancient Greek philosopher and rhetorician Aristotle. Aristotle defined rhetoric as the ability to identify in any given circumstance all of the available means of persuasion. The rhetorical appeals are a few of those available means by which a rhetor (writer, speaker, designer) shapes a text to persuade their audience. (For more on argumentation, see Ch. 19, "Staking Your Claim.") **The rhetorical appeals are generally called by their Greek names of logos, ethos, and pathos, and they refer to logical, ethical, and emotional components of arguments, as defined below.**

+ *Logos:* Strategy of reason, logic, or facts. Any type of argument that uses logic is appealing to logos.

+ *Ethos:* Strategy of credibility, authority, or character. Ethos demonstrates the author's trustworthiness, expertise, and honesty.

+ *Pathos:* Strategy of emotions and affect. Pathos appeals to an audience's sense of anger, sorrow, or excitement, among other emotions.

When you look at the definitions of the appeals a bit closer, you might wonder how you can build credibility, for example, with your audience. You might wonder how you can strategically appeal to emotion in your College Writing assignments; after all, isn't college and professional writing supposed to *avoid* using emotion? In the rest of this chapter we will examine each of the rhetorical appeals individually and look at examples of how students successfully use the appeals in their writing assignments. Although in describing the appeals Aristotle argued that logos was the strongest and most reliable form of persuasion, the most effective texts utilize all three appeals.

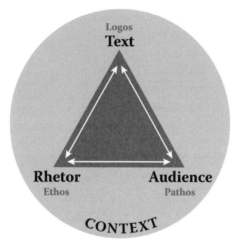

Figure 1. The Rhetorical Triangle and the Rhetorical Appeals

In your writing projects for college or professional work, you can use several tactics to appeal to your audience using logos or logic. **Since logos is the appeal to reason, any aspect of your writing that engages in logical argumentation will be using the rhetorical appeal of logos.**

Effective arguments include facts, statistics—if appropriate to the argument and other supporting details to back up the rhetor's claims/positions. They may contain researched information from scholarly sources and will demonstrate the writer's carefulness in choosing and considering evidence. By using carefully chosen quotations, facts, or figures from scholarly sources you are indicating to your reader that you have judiciously studied your subject and are giving your audience the information that you have found.

Not appealing to logos can seriously damage your argument and your relationship with the audience by causing them not to trust you. For example, if you are creating an argument that communicating via digital devices negatively affects our face-to-face communication and the only source you cite is the Facebook website, your audience will have a difficult time trusting your logic. If, however, in the same essay you offer your audience evidence from several scholarly sources that have conducted studies testing the effects of digital communication, you would be appealing to your audience's sense of logos. (For more on how research can strengthen your appeal to logos, see Ch. 14, "Research Is a Process.")

Effective arguments appealing to logos will also be well-organized and include a supportable and original thesis statement or research question. Let's use the student essay above for another example. Imagine the student's thesis statement was: **"I communicate with my family and friends using Facebook."** This argument would not appeal to an audience's logical reasoning for a few reasons:

1. The author offers no evaluation of Facebook communication as beneficial or detrimental, nor offers any recommendations or guidelines to others about what they should or should not do in their own digital communication habits.

2. Stating that the author communicates via Facebook is not an arguable thesis; it is simply an event that either did (or did not) occur.

3. The author might be able to prove that Facebook helps them communicate, but their argument would probably rely *solely* on personal examples rather than scholarly sources.

While some instructors allow the use of personal examples for particular assignments, you should always ask your instructor if you're not certain. (For more, see Ch. 18, "Thesis Statements.")

Questions to Consider While Evaluating Logos

Asking yourself the following questions will help you decide whether or not you are utilizing the logos appeal:

+ What evidence do I provide that will convince my audience that my argument is logical or that it makes sense? Is this evidence from a credible source?

+ What claim am I arguing? Is it relevant/original/specific?

+ Do I jump to conclusions or have logical fallacies (flaws in argumentative reasoning that invalidate a logical conclusion, such as making a broad claim but using a single personal experience instead of developing a reasoned argument using substantial evidence, assuming correlation equates to causation, or making an *ad hominem* attack on the arguer instead of addressing the argument, among others)?

+ Do I make appropriate comparisons to other people, places, or events to strengthen my position?

» Ethos

Ethos refers to a writer's "ethics," which means a writer's authority or character. Because the ethical appeal refers to a writer's credibility, consider what you can do to garner your audience's trust in you as a trustworthy rhetor. In writing projects for college or professional jobs, you have many choices for strengthening your ethos. One way to establish your trustworthiness is to demonstrate awareness that any issue is complex and accurately acknowledge other positions disagreeing with yours by summarizing their claims using clear, neutral language. Doing so indicates both your knowledge about the topic and, if you are fairly representing your opposition, that you are presenting your own argument in a fair-minded, principled, trustworthy manner.

"Because the ethical appeal refers to a writer's credibility, consider what you can do to garner your audience's trust in you as a trustworthy rhetor."

Another way to establish trust with your audience is to be very aware of the context in which you are communicating. You may remember from an earlier chapter—Brenta Blevins's "Rhetoric in Academic Settings"—that context surrounds the rhetorical triangle affecting all of its aspects (audience, text, writer). Context determines genre (that is, the form of a text determined by its purpose—such as a researched argument essay, an informative essay, a rhetorical analysis essay, and so forth), tone, choice of vocabulary, use and amount of evidence, and even misuse or lack of punctuation. So, what is the relationship between context and ethos? One aspect of your credibility, or ethos, as a writer is social; it is your ability to identify yourself as a member of a particular group. When a writer appears to be a member of a particular group, she can more easily gain credibility in that group. Let's look at a few examples to further our understanding of ethos and context and how your understanding of this relationship can make you a more powerful communicator.

Ethos and Context

As you've learned studying the rhetorical triangle, successful rhetors shift how they communicate depending on their context and audience; this shifting can also strengthen your ethos with the audience (social group) that you want to communicate with. For example, you told your friends you would be attending a party, but the night of the party you are sick. Within the context of this social group, you would probably text your friends something like this: "sick—can't come tonight—have fun!" You would probably even use emojis rather

> "Successful rhetors shift how they communicate depending on their context and audience"

than words to communicate your disappointment at not seeing your friends. Within this context, this text message would strengthen your credibility with your social group (friends); you are letting your friends know you aren't coming, why you won't be there, and ending with a wish that they have fun. Let's look at another example to uncover even more about the importance of ethos and its relationship to context.

Similar scenario: you are sick, but instead of missing a party, you miss a class. If you send an email to your professor that resembles the text to your friend, you would damage your credibility (ethos) with your professor because your professor is in a different social group. However, consider if you emailed your professor something like this:

Professor Williams,

I was not in class today due to an illness. I am continuing to follow the syllabus in regards to class assignments and readings, and I am also happy to make up any assignments I missed in class today. I hope to be feeling better by next class, and if not, I will email you my essay assignment that is due that day (or post it to Canvas if you have an assignment dropbox there).

Sincerely,
Simon Smith

This email might seem overly formal to you, but within the context it was written (missing class), it is appropriate for your professor in tone, genre, and language usage. Emailing a professor (or employer) in this way strengthens your ethos; you've used an acceptable medium, your professor knows that you just didn't skip class, and you've let the professor know you are keeping up with your assignments. All these qualities are ones that are necessary to build credibility and trustworthiness within this context and with this social group.

Effective Ethos

Successfully using ethos in your College Writing assignments often starts even before you begin writing; have you participated in class discussions and peer reviews; have you followed the assignment sheet? As we've seen with the previous examples, within the writing assignment itself, strengthening your ethos involves knowing the context and how to build ethos with this social group. If your writing assignment is an informal one that simply asks for your thoughts about a topic, you can probably pay more attention to content (your ideas) rather than spending a lot of time on correct punctuation and word choice. If, however, it is a formal writing assignment (context shift), then you would know your professor's expectations are likely more specific to correctness of form, tone, and vocabulary, and, of course, the quality of your ideas. By paying attention to the context, you will be more successful in building ethos with whichever audience you are communicating.

Questions to Consider While Working on Your Ethos

Asking yourself the following questions will help you know if you are using the appeal of ethos:

- Is my tone, genre, and word choice suitable for my audience and message?

- How am I communicating my trustworthiness to my audience (by using scholarly sources, crediting others through correct citation, choosing a suitable genre, word choice, etc.)?

- If I'm arguing a point, do I acknowledge the other side(s) of the issue?

- Do I use non-confrontational language when writing about scholars who disagree with my claim?

» Pathos

Pathos is the appeal to emotion; using this appeal can tap into an audience's sense of anger, happiness, excitement, fear, loyalty, and so forth. You may be thinking that in academic and professional writing we don't ever appeal to our audience's emotions, and you would be partially correct in thinking this. Academic and professional writing foregrounds ideas rather than emotions; we want our audience to focus on our writing rather than have a visceral reaction to our words. Appealing to emotions can be powerful and thus bring strength to your argument; however, overusing emotional appeals can damage a rhetor's ethos by exhausting the audience's feelings and weakening the argument's logic. Thus, appealing to emotions can be—and usually is in academic and professional writing—very subtle. Let's look at a few ways you can subtly appeal to your audience's emotions even within the context of formal writing.

Pathos in Action

Let's say you are unhappy with the food choices offered on campus and you want to write a letter (or essay or presentation) expressing your frustration at the lack of healthier options, as well as how much the food costs. You do research by comparing food options at nearby schools similar to the university and offer a plausible solution with specific, achievable suggestions to this issue because you know this will strengthen your logos. You also use correct genre, word choice, and tone to communicate with your audience because you understand how this strengthens your ethos. You know that you want your audience to act on your issue (provide healthier, less-expensive food options), and you know that appealing to emotion can often evoke change. But how, in this writing occasion, can you effectively appeal to an audience's pathos?

While pathos characterizes emotions, it can be considered more broadly to describe an audience's sense of identity or self-interest. To that end, in your letter you might try introducing yourself as a student at the university who lives on campus and also explaining why you chose to attend the university. By writing this you will help your reader see you as an individual and as someone who is happy to be a student at the school where your reader works. Subtle strategic choices such as this help the reader feel generous toward you as you continue talking about your issue. When you ask for healthier food options, you may mention how students with diabetes, food allergies, or other health issues are struggling to make healthy choices at the university. Notice the subtlety? You are evoking empathy—the ability to understand and feel the emotion of another—from your audience about students who have serious health issues. Some of these subtleties may seem, well, too subtle, but audiences respond to these strategies. By using strategies such as these to appeal to your audience's emotional responses, you are more likely to be successful at accomplishing your goal.

Questions to Consider While Evaluating Your Use of Pathos

To help determine if you are using the pathos appeal successfully, ask yourself the following questions:

- How will my audience feel when they read this? Will it make them want to do something (an action)?

- What specific places or words do I use that will evoke an emotional response from my audience? Should I add—or subtract—for better rhetorical effect?

- How can I help my audience identify with me as the rhetor, with my topic, or with the result?

» An Appealing Performance

It is important to remember that the appeals are not just used in writing. As you may remember, the ancient Greeks were a predominantly oral culture and rhetoric was originally used to guide speaking occasions. Even though in the 21st century we typically learn about rhetoric in writing classes, it is essential that you understand that these strategies serve you very well in both writing and speaking occasions both in school and in your professional lives. Let's look briefly at how the rhetorical appeals might work in a presentation or a speech.

To successfully employ logos in a speech or presentation, speakers can organize points and evidence using a logical arrangement. To do so, the speaker first introduces the audience to the topic and thesis, then they organize points and evidence to logically flow from one to the next, and to support each other and the thesis, and then they offer a conclusion that logically relates to the material that preceded it. To employ logos in a visual presentation, designers can, for example, ensure that information is arranged so it visually flows in a logical fashion for the audience.

Speakers can establish their ethos by demonstrating their knowledge about a particular topic. For a visual presentation, speakers are careful to credit others by offering citations of their sources on the appropriate slides and on the Works Cited page. Speakers also should provide oral citations of their sources. For example, if a speech refers to research from Sherry Turkle's *Alone Together*, the speaker would offer an oral citation that states, "According to Sherry Turkle's 2011 *Alone Together*..." and then state the referred-to material.

Finally, in much the same way that writers can use pathos, speakers can similarly employ pathos by establishing a common relationship with the audience. (For more on pathos and visual design and spoken delivery, see Ch. 25, "Rhetorical Delivery.")

» One Final Thought

It's necessary when first learning about the rhetorical appeals to learn them separately so as to get a good grasp on their intricate workings in writing or speaking. **However, it is important to remember that often a piece of writing will represent more than one aspect of these appeals.** For example, using scholarly rather than popular sources could be considered both logos and ethos since a credible source will help support your logical argument, but it also shows you as a reliable and responsible rhetor. Just as other elements of the rhetorical triangle work in tandem, the rhetorical appeals overlap with each other while working with the rhetorical triangle (see Fig. 1). Remember that while the appeals can be viewed as separate strategies, they most often work together to create effective writing.

21. Organization, from Beginning to End

Bryan McMillan

Have you ever felt uncertain about how to structure your introductions, body paragraphs, and conclusions to make them work together successfully? These components help readers engage with your topic, understand your argument, and appreciate your paper's importance. Indeed, clear organization is key for your rhetorical effectiveness because it highlights your supporting points and how they connect to your main argument. But, while most of us learned in high school that all our papers need these elements, it can often feel overwhelming when attempting to incorporate them effectively. This chapter focuses on how to do just that, offering approaches to writing and organizing introductions, body paragraphs, and conclusions. To illustrate important concepts we will imagine ourselves writing a blog entry encouraging our audience to reduce their social media usage. Since a blog is an informal genre, it employs various conventions—relaxed tone and style and incomplete sentences, for example—that you should avoid in other, more formal genres like academic papers. Nevertheless, the blog example will allow us to see these organizational methods in action.

> "Clear organization is key for your rhetorical effectiveness because it highlights your supporting points and how they connect to your main argument."

» Writing an Introduction

Introductions serve three main functions: they "hook" your readers, contextualize your argument, and propose your thesis statement. A "hook," which appears at the beginning of the introduction, is an interesting statement that entices the potential audience to read your work. The remainder of your introduction situates your argument (your thesis) within a given context. Context includes any necessary background information and helps readers not only see the significance of your writing, but also prepares them to hear what you have to say. Once you have hooked your readers and contextualized your paper, you can present your thesis, which states your claim and sometimes offers readers a roadmap. Your roadmap should mirror your writing's overall organization. (For more, see Ch. 18, "Thesis Statements.") The following chart provides an example of how we might consider writing the introduction of our hypothetical blog.

Introductions Provide	Blog Example
An interesting **hook**	Have you ever attempted to have a serious conversation with a friend while checking your Facebook feed, only to later discover that you missed out on some important information?
Context	Most of us have experienced not being able to pay attention to serious conversations while using social media. In fact, in December 2016 Facebook alone accounted for almost 12.5 million impressions and 3.5 million views ("Social Media Statistics"). We cannot seem to get enough of sites like Facebook, Twitter, and Instagram, and our relationships and mental health are paying the price.
A **thesis** statement	To help cultivate healthier relationships and increase our overall sense of happiness, we need to dramatically reduce our use of social media sites.

In our hypothetical blog example, we began by asking an engaging question about our readers' personal experiences. Since our blog is informal, asking a question is a great way to hook readers. However, while this kind of hook works well for some genres, like blogs or letters, you should generally avoid them in academic papers. This is because direct address evokes a relaxed, conversational tone that conflicts with the seriousness of your research and could inadvertently cause readers to take your work lightly. Alternatively, surprising statements, controversial facts, or thought-provoking quotes work well as hooks in academic papers.

After getting our readers' attention, we contextualized our blog entry by offering statistics that indicate the significant amount of time Americans spend using social media on a daily basis. This information eases our readers into our main argument (our thesis). Having read our hook, contextual information, and thesis statement, our readers are finally ready to read our supporting points.

When starting a writing project, our inclination is often to write the introduction first because we frequently want to write in the same order that we read: from beginning to end. However, when it comes to the writing process, this course of action can be unproductive. In fact, starting with the introduction frequently stops the writing process in its tracks. For many writers, it is easier and more beneficial to write the introduction last. By the time you have completed your body paragraphs and conclusion you will have a stronger grasp of your own argument. Consider beginning by drafting a tentative thesis statement, which will almost invariably change as you move through the drafting process. Then, write your body paragraphs and your conclusion. Once you have done all of this, begin working on your introduction. As counterintuitive as that might sound, writing the introduction last allows you to more precisely, and more effortlessly, establish context.

» The MEAL Plan: Paragraph Structure

When writing paragraphs, you can use the acronym MEAL to help you remember how to organize each paragraph. MEAL stands for: Main Idea, Evidence, Analysis, and Link. In many academic genres, your paragraphs (with the exception of introductions and conclusions) should include these elements in this order. Developing paragraphs this way allows you to effectively guide your readers from one idea to the next and to clearly demonstrate how each paragraph supports your thesis.

The first sentence of a paragraph, called the topic sentence, expresses the **main idea** you want the paragraph to convey; it supports your thesis statement. For example, in the sentence I just wrote, I presented to you what I will discuss in this paragraph, just as you will do for your readers in your own topic sentences. The topic sentence of a paragraph should give readers a complete sense of the paragraph's scope.

After you have written your topic sentence, you will need to support it with **evidence.** Evidence includes examples and outside source material, such as scholarly articles, interviews, or statistics. If you are analyzing a text such as a speech or novel, quotations and references to the primary text can also work as evidence. Take a look at my second and third sentences in this paragraph. They offer evidence of my main idea by describing types of evidence you can include in your arguments. As you select your evidence, consider what evidence both supports your position and persuades your audience. For example, a claim about fashion trends would require a different type of evidence than a claim about health care. Relevant evidence gives your argument a foundation by helping your readers make sense of your claims, and it boosts your ethos as a writer by demonstrating that you understand what evidence will best support your argument. (For more, see Ch. 22, "Incorporating Evidence.")

Before you move to a new idea, you must **analyze** your evidence. Too often we assume that our readers are already making the same connections we are, but what seems obvious to us is not always obvious to others. Think of evidence as what your source is saying and analysis as what *you* are saying. Analysis offers you the opportunity to demonstrate the relationship between your main idea and the evidence you provide in support of that idea. Notice that the third and fourth sentences of this paragraph analyze the evidence I offer in the second sentence. By analyzing evidence you help your readers understand how that evidence supports the claims you present in your topic sentences. As a general rule, avoid ending a paragraph with evidence; ending a paragraph with a quote, for example, is a red flag that you have not yet done the necessary analysis.

After you analyze your supporting evidence, you should conclude your paragraph with a **linking** statement. This is not the place to begin talking about new ideas or to reveal ideas coming in subsequent paragraphs. Your **linking** statement, usually one sentence or clause, should connect to the paragraph's main idea by tying up any loose ends, serving as the final element that fully unifies the paragraph. Alternatively, linking statements can bridge one piece of evidence to additional evidence within a single paragraph. If you would like to include more evidence to support your topic sentence, your linking statement will help you smoothly migrate to this new piece of evidence. In this case, your link can be as simple as a transition word. For example, note how I use the word "alternatively" in the middle of this paragraph to prepare readers for new information about linking statements (see more example transitions later in the chapter). Any time you add new evidence, you must also analyze it, and conclude the paragraph with a final linking statement, just as I have done here. The chart below provides an example of a paragraph we could use in our blog.

Main Idea	By weakening concentration and inhibiting our ability to enjoy our present experiences, social media addiction decreases our overall sense of well-being.
Evidence	A 2015 study published in *Stress and Health* indicates that social media addiction impairs people's ability to remain mindful of their present tasks "because of the distraction caused by the urge to access social media" (Kanokporn and Charoensukmongkol 428).
Analysis	Not only do the countless hours spent accessing social media sites provide abundant daily distractions, but the very desire to access these sites prevents us from fully engaging in the present moment. This means that we often struggle focusing our mental energy on conversations with friends and family, on our studies, on driving, or on anything because our minds are too preoccupied by our need to see the latest posts on our Facebook feed.
Link	As a result, social media addiction keeps us constantly feeling distracted and stressed.

In the previous example, we can see how following the MEAL plan enables us to form our paragraph as a complete thought. Our **main idea** (topic sentence) indicates our paragraph's entire purpose: to demonstrate how social media addiction inhibits our mindfulness, decreasing our sense of well-being. Our relevant scholarly **evidence** supports the topic sentence, illustrating the connection between social media usage and daily mindfulness. Our **analysis** of our scholarly evidence highlights how this connection results in impaired focus and damages relationships. Our **linking statement** articulates the ultimate problem that social-media addiction produces, fully bridging our analysis back to our topic sentence.

> "First, each paragraph should express one, and only one, main idea or purpose. Second, each paragraph should directly relate to your thesis statement."

There are two final points to consider when writing body paragraphs. First, each paragraph should express one, and only one, main idea or purpose. Second, each paragraph should directly relate to your thesis statement. Paragraphs with multiple purposes and tangents distract and even confuse readers. Fortunately, these are relatively easy to correct during the revision process. If your instructor tells you that there are too many ideas within one paragraph, it usually means that your paragraph is attempting to serve more than one purpose.

You can quickly determine if your paragraphs have tangents or multiple purposes by *reverse outlining*. Most of us have created outlines as part of the prewriting process, but reverse outlining gives us a snapshot of our work *after* we have completed it. It allows us to see our paragraphs' weak spots and helps us correct them. Here are the steps:

Reverse Outline Steps
1) On a sheet of paper create two columns.

| 2) In the left column: Read through your paper and summarize each paragraph in one sentence. Each paragraph should be represented by a single sentence; if you need more than one sentence to summarize the paragraph, it needs revision. | 3) In the right column: Notate how each paragraph advances or relates to your main argument. Look for any instances where a paragraph does not connect to your thesis. You must either rewrite these paragraphs, or, if you cannot connect them to your thesis, you must make the difficult decision to delete them. |

Transitions

Transitions are words and phrases that bind individual, and often diverging, ideas to each other. They help your readers seamlessly migrate from one paragraph, or one sentence, to the next by showing how your different ideas relate. If you get feedback that your writing is "choppy" or lacks "flow," missing transitions are often the culprit. Additionally, if you are experiencing difficulty with a particular transition, you might need to reexamine your overall organization, in which case, reverse outlines can help. The following chart will help you determine what kinds of transitions could be useful in different situations. (For additional examples of transitions, see Appendix F.)

Relationship	Transitions
Cause and Effect	therefore, consequently, thus
Comparison	likewise, similarly, as
Contrast	on the one hand ... on the other hand, but, however, nevertheless, yet, whereas
Conclusion	finally, ultimately, overall
Sequence	first, second, third, ..., next, afterward, subsequently
Addition	additionally, moreover, furthermore

Writing Conclusions

Conclusions are most effective when they highlight the significance of your argument while *reiterating* your main idea and supporting points, rather than simply restating them. In fact, conclusions that *only* restate the thesis essentially ignore, and encourage your readers to ignore, all the work you have done throughout your piece of writing. To prevent that from happening, use the conclusion as an opportunity to tell your audience why your argument matters. To illustrate, in our example blog, we could conclude by saying:

"Use the conclusion as an opportunity to tell your audience why your argument matters."

Reiterating Argument	Given the range of emotional health problems incurred by excessive social media use, we must begin actively making better choices about the frequency and duration of our activity on these sites.
Conclusive Remarks	There are several apps out there, like *Moment*, that can show us how much we actually use these sites, as well as when and where we are most likely to use them. With this self-knowledge in hand, we will know when we need to be most careful about pulling our phones from our pockets. More simply—but this is perhaps the most challenging option of all—we might try turning our tech devices off for a few hours a day.

In this example, we concluded our social media blog with a *call-to-action* (see question 4 as follows) in which we encouraged our audience to actively take steps to limit their social media usage. Why? For their own emotional and psychological health (see question 1 as follows). We could also conclude by offering contextualization or a discussion of the significance of our argument. Answering the following questions could help you generate ideas for your conclusive remarks.

Questions for Conclusions

1. So what?

2. Why is my argument important?

3. What do I want my readers to remember from my paper?

4. What do I want my readers to think/do after reading my paper?

5. Learning to effectively develop and organize introductions, paragraphs, and conclusions can be tricky, but the work is well worth the reward. Better organization inevitably leads to a stronger, clearer argument and allows your readers to follow your writing with greater ease.

» Works Cited

"Social Media Statistics Dashboard: December FY 2017 Summary." *U.S. National Archives, Office of Innovation, Social Media Team*, 2017, www.archives.gov/files/social-media/reports/social-media-stats-fy-2017-12.pdf.

Sriwilai, Kanokporn, and P. Charoensukmongkol. "Face It, Don't Facebook It: Impacts of Social Media Addiction on Mindfulness, Coping Strategies and the Consequence on Emotional Exhaustion." *Stress and Health*, vol. 32, no. 4, 2016, pp. 427–34.

22. Incorporating Evidence from Source Material to Make an Effective Argument

Erik Cofer

You will be required to incorporate source material to support your arguments for many assignments you are likely to encounter in College Writing. **By incorporating evidence, you establish your credibility and ground your argument in reason, thus enhancing the rhetorical effectiveness of your writing.** The particular guidelines and objectives of the essays you write for College Writing will vary by instructor, but the integration of relevant evidence through summarizing, paraphrasing, and quoting is critical to many projects. It is also important to understand how to use and combine sources within your writing; synthesizing, then, provides a meaningful tool for understanding and conveying how texts relate, or connect, to one another.

> "Make sure that there are always more of your own words and views than there are of those you cite."

While it can be tempting to allow the ideas of your sources to take over your paper, you should make sure that there are always more of your own words and views than there are of those you cite. **This chapter will provide an overview of when and how to summarize, paraphrase, and quote from sources in order to produce an effective piece of writing.** Although much of the information in this chapter can apply to all three forms of incorporating evidence, we will break them down individually to focus on particular considerations. Below is a chart demonstrating the basic use of each form.

Summarizing	Paraphrasing	Quoting
Useful as an overview of a source's argument and main points.	Useful when you need to relay specific information without preserving the original language of the source.	Useful when the evidence can best be conveyed by using the words of the source itself rather than summarizing the argument or explaining the specific ideas in your own words.

» Summarizing with Purpose

Summarizing provides context to your audience by describing the central argument or idea of a particular source. When constructed effectively, a summary offers the reader the necessary context to follow the argument without feeling confused, while also not being distracted by excess information. For instance, if a friend asks you about the plot of a movie you have seen recently, you would probably provide only enough information to give your friend some context, rather than describing the entire movie scene by scene. If you can relate to this example, you are already familiar with the benefits of summarizing concisely. Summarizing can be especially valuable in your own writing when only the main ideas from a source are relevant to your discussion, when the details could confuse your readers, or when the passage is too long to quote or paraphrase. However, excess summary can wear your audience down and detract from the more valuable analytical aspects of your writing.

Now let's take a more in-depth look at the practical advantages of summarizing in your writing. Imagine you are using Peter C. Baker's "The Tragic, Forgotten History of Black Military Veterans" as a popular source for an essay on the mistreatment of military veterans. Before launching into your analysis of the source and explanation of how it supports your claim, it would help to explain the article's central argument. Here are a few examples of what a summary for this article might look like:

1. In his article "The Tragic, Forgotten History of Black Military Veterans," Peter C. Baker chronicles the struggles of black veterans.

2. In his article "The Tragic, Forgotten History of Black Military Veterans," Peter C. Baker chronicles the brutal treatment of black veterans who fought in the Civil War, World War I, or World War II. Black men were only reluctantly allowed by the Union to fight in the Civil War, and many became targets of racial violence in the Reconstruction-era South. False rumors were spread about these soldiers, and some were even lynched. Then, during WWI, white individuals began to fear that black enlisted men would gain too great a sense of importance by fighting for the American cause, and they faced hostility upon their return. In WWII, many black men enlisted, but found themselves initially barred from combat and treated as second-class citizens. Unfortunately, even the G.I. Bill denied black veterans many of the benefits received by their fellow soldiers.

3. In his article "The Tragic, Forgotten History of Black Military Veterans," Peter C. Baker chronicles the brutal treatment of black veterans spanning from the Civil War to World War II, highlighting the hostility, racial violence, and inferior government benefits these soldiers experienced in this era.

From the previous examples, the third summary is the most apt for providing enough context to your audience about the source you are using without taking up too much space in your paper. By contrast, the first example is quite brief and leaves us with more questions than answers. What kinds of struggles? How were these different from the struggles of other veterans? What time period are we looking at? However, the second example provides too much summary because it provides specifics of Baker's article rather than simply describing the central argument or main idea. **Therefore, summarizing too much can detract from your own analysis and argument.**

» Paraphrasing Wisely

Summarizing is great for describing the big picture of a source, but communicating more specific information from a source can be better achieved through paraphrasing or quoting. Paraphrasing from a source means using your own words to describe a writer's specific point. **Solely relying on summary prevents you from addressing the particulars of an argument, whereas solely relying on quoting**—which will be discussed later this chapter—**can minimize your own voice.** Paraphrasing can be especially useful when you alter the language from the source to best accommodate your intended audience and more effectively advance your argument, or when the ideas but not the language presented in the source is needed.

> "Paraphrasing from a source means using your own words to describe a writer's specific point."

Although written in your own words, a paraphrase is a way of communicating evidence from a source to be analyzed, much like summarizing and quoting, rather than a substitute for your own ideas. Thus, as with summarizing and quoting, paraphrasing should be used moderately to leave room for your analysis.

Let's consider a short passage from Baker's "The Tragic, Forgotten History of Black Military Veterans":

> "The susceptibility of black ex-soldiers to extrajudicial murder and assault has long been recognized by historians, but the topic has never received such comprehensive standalone treatment."

Quoting this passage might be unnecessary because you may not need to preserve the original language or you may want to emphasize a particular aspect of the argument presented by your source. Here is a paraphrase of the sentence:

Baker suggests that while historians have acknowledged the excess of violent crimes against black veterans, the concept has generally been examined along with related topics rather than on its own.

As you can see, I have preserved the ideas from the text, but because the specific language or phrasing was not key to my own argument, I have rearranged and rephrased the information from the source using my own voice.

» Quoting Efficiently and Effectively

Summarizing or paraphrasing cannot always sufficiently capture the information from a source like a quote can. Certain sentences or passages may be written so eloquently that they seem to demand being quoted rather than paraphrased, or you may feel that the force of a particular statement can only be retained by quoting it. **Additionally, quoting allows the writer to engage in an analysis of the particular wording a source uses.** Quoting demonstrates that you are mindful of situations in which direct textual evidence can most effectively persuade your audience. Your instructor is likely to have their own specific guidelines on quoting properly, but the following are practical tips to keep in mind.

Contextualize Quoted Content

In the example below, I provide a formal mention of the author in the first sentence and I follow up with my own analysis of the quoted text. This combination of introducing a quote and elaborating on the meaning or significance of the quoted content to your argument is known as a **quote sandwich.** (See Figure 1 for a visual depiction.) Contextualizing quoted content helps ensure that you are connecting quotes to the ideas and arguments you wish to convey in your writing. Consider my use of a quote sandwich below that includes a scholarly source that discusses Lois Lowry's young adult dystopian novel *The Giver*:

> Literary scholar Michael Levy argues that because Jonas destroys his dysto-pian world, Sameness, he is successful in his dystopian goal, but unable to complete his quest and become a *Bildungsroman* hero because he has not been able to implement his newly acquired information. Although he has "gained new knowledge and has achieved a higher level of moral development...he has not had a chance to savor his success" (56). To Levy, Jonas's journey is a failure because by destroying his community, he leaves himself no community in which to establish himself and demonstrate his moral correctness.

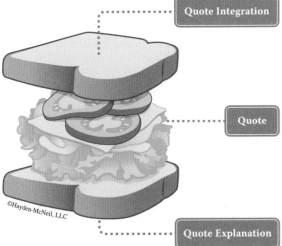

Figure 1. Visual depiction of a quote sandwich.

As you can see, I first introduce the author of the source, Michael Levy, then transition into the quotation. After directly quoting from Levy, I include some explanation that connects to the argument that I am making about *The Giver* and Jonas's community. In fact, the previous text box is itself the center of a quote sandwich, surrounded by my own writing, as I inform my audience that I will be using a scholarly source that discusses *The Giver* and then offer an explanation of how that example illustrates my point about contextualizing quoted content.

Use Colons to Set Up Lengthy Quotes

When quoting longer text, a practical solution is to lead into the quote with a colon. You may set up a lengthy quote with a colon if you fear that condensing it will compromise its meaning or effect. When using MLA style guidelines, quotations of more than four lines are considered **block quotations**. A block quotation is also introduced with a colon and should be set apart from the rest of your paragraph, with each line of the quote indented half an inch from the left margin and double-spaced. It is pivotal that you carefully assess whether or not a block quote is needed in each particular case so you avoid producing an essay with too few of your own words. Take a look at the formatting of the following block quotation.

Lois Lowry views her work not as political, but as moral and believes writers of young adult literature should present a protagonist who makes moral choices. Specifically, Lowry believes in the innocence of children:

> I do think young people have a very strong moral sense before they enter the adult world with its unfortunate compromises and trade-offs. I think as readers they relate to a protagonist faced with moral dilemmas and acting heroically. And who knows...if perhaps as young people, they identify with such heroes, even fictional ones...they will be more inclined to back off from moral compromise in the adult world they'll eventually enter. (qtd. in Hintz and Ostry 197)

Accordingly, given the distinct moral goal of young adult literature, its heroes are well situated to explore the morality of their choices and then return to the group with their newly learned lessons.

Just like the previous example of a quote sandwich, I introduce the author of the source, which in this case is Lois Lowry herself. I then transition into the quotation from Lowry's interview with a colon, and the block quotation is completely indented. Note that the block quote does not have quotation marks and the period is located before the parentheses, unlike normal MLA quotations. After a block quote, when you discuss and analyze the source that you have included, the paragraph should return to the left margin.

Condense Long Quotes When Practical to Do So

Often you will come across large chunks of text from which you wish to quote; you can select the most relevant parts of the quote as an alternative to paraphrasing. This can be accomplished through the use of **bracketing** and **ellipses**, as in the following example:

> When asked what she "hope[s] children will learn about utopian and political organization" from *The Giver* and *Gathering Blue*, Lowry replies, "[f]rom the response of readers, I know that both books have caused young people...to think, argue, debate, explore, and no longer take certain things for granted. I don't hope for young people to 'learn' from my books. I hope only that they learn to question" (qtd. in Hintz and Ostry 199).

Bracketing allows you to add or modify words to maintain proper grammatical structure, while ellipses allow you to bypass less relevant portions of the text. Anything that you include in the bracket symbols [ ] indicates what you have altered from the original source. For instance, in the above example I have altered the capitalized "F" to a lowercase "f" to reflect the word's placement in the middle of my sentence rather than at the beginning. When you include the ellipses …, you indicate to your reader that you have removed a portion of the original text, just as I have in the previous example. As you can see, though, the sentence still makes grammatical sense even with the removed portion. **However, it is critical to recognize that you bear an ethical responsibility to avoid intentionally misrepresenting the material you are quoting.**

Embed Quotes Within Sentences to Vary Your Sentence Structure Whenever Possible

You can also incorporate quotations by weaving specific quoted phrases from the source into your own sentences. Doing so allows you to quote while retaining a desirable flow. In addition, the practice of embedding allows you to extract the most relevant aspects of the quoted passage.

> Jonas reflects on a neighbor who often gets in trouble for small matters like misplaced schoolwork and believes that such a long list of transgressions, even where minor, "infringe[s] on the community's sense of order and success" (Lowry 58).

In this example, I start the sentence by paraphrasing in my own voice and seamlessly move into quoted text without a signal phrase or colon. **By embedding the quote, I emphasize the most important part of the quoted source.**

» Best Practices When Working with Outside Sources

Incorporating Evidence Accurately and Ethically

Your word choice and tone can greatly impact the way your audience regards a source. When incorporating evidence you must carefully consider the desired rhetorical effect of your diction. Furthermore, summarizing, paraphrasing, and quoting require a commitment to representing the words of others fairly. As a writer, you can adhere to this commitment by ensuring that you understand the argument your source presents. Ultimately, incorporating source material as accurately as possible is the best way to enhance your ethos as a writer entering into conversation with other writers. Let's take a look at the following passage from Hua Hsu's 2015 article, "The Year of the Imaginary College Student":

> "It was a rich year for even the casual observer of campus life. There were tales of students seeking 'trigger warnings' before being exposed to potentially upsetting class materials. There was a new interest in 'micro-aggressions,' or hurtful, everyday slights rarely uttered with the intention to offend. There was the Northwestern professor whose editorial against 'sexual paranoia' resulted in students filing a Title IX suit against her, and the University of Missouri students who sought to bar journalists from

a public plaza, which they claimed to be a 'safe space' protected from the media… Every week seemed to bring additional evidence for the emerging archetype of the hypersensitive college student."

One could very easily read this passage and come away with the belief that Hsu is criticizing, or even mocking, the current generation of college students. However, Hsu actually uses his article to critique the attitudes and assumptions of those who label the contemporary college student as too sensitive. Using the above quote without including the larger purpose of Hsu's argument misrepresents Hsu's position on these matters. This example demonstrates how critical it is to read sources fully and carefully before using them in your writing. Misrepresenting source material, whether intentional or not, often has serious repercussions.

Introducing the Author and the Source

"It can be disorienting to see a quote with a citation after it if the author has not been previously mentioned" (Cofer). As you can see, it can be confusing for a reader to come across a quote from a source that has yet to be addressed by the writer. Phrases that contextualize material you incorporate from outside sources are useful remedies in such situations. An introductory phrase provides information about the author and/or the source that contains the evidence you discuss. The phrase "Erik Cofer notes," for instance, could successfully lead into the quote that begins this paragraph.

"As convenient as it may seem to insert a quote and hope that it speaks for itself, it is your responsibility as a rhetor to demonstrate how the evidence you provide supports your argument."

When summarizing, quoting, or paraphrasing from a source that you have introduced previously, using last names will suffice. You should never refer to an author by their first name only because it is too informal and may send the wrong message about the seriousness with which you approach your writing. In the case of an oral presentation, you should identify the source of any quote to avoid confusion. Phrases such as "According to" or "And I quote" can be useful in these instances.

The MEAL Plan

Summarizing, paraphrasing, and quoting are important ways of communicating evidence in your writing, but evidence is only as valuable as how you use it. Recall the **MEAL** Plan, where M = main idea, E = evidence, A = analysis, and L = linking sentence. (For more information on organization and the MEAL plan, see Ch. 21, "Organization, from Beginning to End.") A summary, paraphrase, or quote should 1) relay evidence that supports your main idea, and 2) be followed up with an analysis. As convenient as it may seem to insert a quote and hope that it speaks for itself, it is your responsibility as a rhetor to demonstrate how the evidence you provide supports your argument. (For an example of summarizing, paraphrasing, and quoting using the MEAL plan, see Appendix G.)

When working with outside sources, it is important that you adhere to your instructor's particular requirements when incorporating evidence. Depending on your instructor and the assignment criteria, some of the types of sources cited in this chapter may not be applicable. Nonetheless, recognizing the benefits that summarizing, paraphrasing, and quoting from source material afford you, as well as the methods of doing so effectively, will prove useful regardless of the type of source you are working with.

» Synthesizing Sources

So far in this chapter we have examined practical ways to implement evidence from individual sources in order to support your thesis. However, many assignments in College Writing and other courses may require you to utilize several different sources. While you might feel good about the particular sources you have compiled for your research assignment, you will need to figure out how these sources fit together within the scope of your project. **Synthesizing sources describes how different texts or arguments relate, or connect, to one another.**

Being able to synthesize your research materials will serve you in several ways. In the prewriting stages, it helps to organize your research and assess *how* and *where* each text can prove useful. In the case of a research essay, you are more likely to feel confident getting started with the actual writing process if beforehand you have outlined the common themes, and differences, between your sources. (For more, see Ch. 17, "Pre-Writing Strategies.") **In the essay itself, revealing the connections between sources demonstrates your handle on the broader conversation surrounding your subject matter, and establishes the logical foundation for your particular argument.** In other words, synthesizing sources is an invaluable process for developing both ethos and logos in your work.

Beginning the synthesis process may seem like an overwhelming task, but there are a number of questions to consider that can help you determine the relationship between your sources.

- What is the main idea of the source?

- How are the ideas conveyed in this source similar to ideas found in your other sources?

- What ideas conveyed in this source *distinguish* it from your other sources?

- Is this source vital to understanding the subject matter of your work?

Depending on the specifics of your assignment, there may be other factors you will need to think about, such as the types of evidence you employ, but answering the above questions is essential in determining the value of your sources and how to best arrange them in your essay. For instance, if you meticulously study two of your sources but cannot find anything that meaningfully sets their ideas apart, it probably means that only one of them will add value to your essay. **When you utilize multiple texts that make the same point, you run the risk of being repetitive and weakening your ethos with your audience.** Along the same lines, if you conclude that a source is integral to understanding the subject matter of your work, you should consider incorporating that text early on so that your audience has the requisite information needed to follow your argument.

Synthesis at Work

In this section, we have discussed the practical benefits of synthesizing sources and some useful questions for doing so. Now let's look at a concrete example. Suppose a student is writing a research essay for their College Writing course on the role standardized test scores play in the college admissions process. The student compiles three sources:

- The first source examines the declining number of universities requiring SAT subject tests for admission and the emergence of schools allowing students to self-report SAT scores.

- The second source discusses potential flaws with "teaching to the test" in K–12.

- The third source argues for the importance of SAT scores, pointing out that students today are better prepared than ever for such tests due to the No Child Left Behind Act of 2001.

These seem like solid sources, but the writer must determine how they relate to one another. All three address standardized tests, but each with a different scope or viewpoint. The first and second sources concern an angst or disillusionment with standardized testing. However, the first source deals expressly with how institutions of higher education have deemphasized test scores, while the second source more generally takes issue with the practice of standardized testing in secondary education. Meanwhile, the third source provides a more favorable opinion of the significant weight historically placed on SAT scores in college admission decisions.

Determining the way your sources connect with each other allows you to narrow or clarify your stance. In the example cited above, the student would be able to review the relationship between their sources and decide where their argument fits in. Additionally, they would be able to outline where in their text to introduce each of their sources. In other words, synthesizing would help the student implement their sources in a logical manner.

It is probable that at some point in your college career you will encounter assignments such as annotated bibliographies, synthesis papers, or literature reviews that ask you to place texts in conversation with one another and/or identify gaps in existing research. (For more on annotated bibliographies, see Ch. 15, "Managing Sources," along with Appendix D.) The ability to synthesize sources will help you tremendously in such assignments, but more importantly, it is a skill that will serve you well in virtually *any* research assignment.

» Works Cited

Baker, Peter C. "The Tragic, Forgotten History of Black Military Veterans." *The New Yorker*, 27 Nov. 2016.

Hintz, Carrie, and Elaine Ostry. "Interview with Lois Lowry, Author of *The Giver*." *Utopian and Dystopian Writing for Children and Young Adults*, edited by Hintz and Ostry, Routledge, 2003, pp. 196–99.

Hsu, Hua. "The Year of the Imaginary College Student." *The New Yorker*, 31 Dec. 2015.

Levy, Michael M. "Lois Lowry's *The Giver*: Interrupted Bildungsroman or Ambiguous Dystopia?" *Foundation*, vol. 70, 1997, pp. 50–57.

Lowry, Lois. *The Giver*. 1993. Laurel Leaf Books, 2002.

23. Personalizing Academic Discourse:
Balancing Style and Academic Expectations

Gia Coturri Sorenson

When I started college, I was asked to write "academically." I wasn't sure what this meant, so I followed two seemingly self-evident guidelines I had heard in high school: I couldn't use contractions (like "don't" or "isn't") and I couldn't use the word "I." But my papers always came back with the same comments: "awkward," "confusing," "wordy," "missing your voice." I didn't understand what I was doing wrong, and therefore, I wasn't able to address my professors' concerns. Eventually, after a lot of practice and experimentation, I started learning how to cultivate my own style. **This chapter clarifies what "academic discourse" and "style" mean and shows how writers can personalize their academic writing.**

» Academic Discourse vs. Style

"Academic discourse" and "style" are not interchangeable. Instead, think of them as complementary or recursive: like the canons, "academic discourse" and "style" rely on and affect one another. (For more on the canons and their recursive nature, see Ch. 3, "The Rhetorical Canons and the Writing Process.") This recursive relationship is why style is so important: your writing style will be the difference between effective and ineffective academic discourse. Most instructors define "academic discourse" as the language a discipline uses to communicate its research. Each discipline, from biology to history, has its own discourse; you will learn about those in your major-specific classes. It is important to remember that various disciplines work in different ways and use unique discourses. This is why assignments written for an English class look so different from assignments written for a chemistry class. **Each discipline has different goals and expectations.**

> "Most instructors define 'academic discourse' as the language a discipline uses to communicate its research."

However, there are some conventions that almost all academic disciplines have in common. For instance, most every formal assignment you write during your college career will (implicitly or explicitly) ask you to display your intellectual curiosity and creativity. As Luke Huffman writes (Ch. 13, "Topic Selection: Finding Your Foundation"), many courses will have you select your own topic and you will always have an easier time if you select a topic you are passionate about. Once you have your topic, you will need to figure out how you can contribute new information to the conversation surrounding the topic. **As you are selecting a topic, ask yourself some questions: What issues related to your topic are researchers addressing or ignoring? What connections can you make between existing research and your own experience? What questions related to the topic still need answering?** Your answers to these questions will differ from other writers, which will help you establish your own style and find your own way to enter the academic conversation.

Furthermore, almost all your college writing assignments will ask that you conduct analysis, which means breaking down an idea and explaining why each part is important. Analysis is important because it shows that you understand a topic. **As you work to analyze a topic, consider all of its sides, support your claims with credible research, question the research, and draw conclusions that help you make recommendations to other researchers.**

A vital part of academic discourse is using credible sources. Academic writing builds on what others have written or said, so make sure you can discuss the important research surrounding your topic, but you will also want to practice writing and talking about your research in your own words. (For more on finding credible sources, see Ch. 14, "Research Is a Process.") When using research, you will want to think about whether or not you agree with a source, how you can blend your thoughts and research with what is published, and if you are citing your sources correctly. Writing in a particular discipline can require more nuanced discussions about conventions; your professors will often walk you through the various expected elements for presenting research. (For more on these expectations, see Ch. 22, "Incorporating Evidence," and for more on citing sources, see Ch. 16, "Rhetorical Elements of Academic Citation.") **While it can sometimes be difficult to talk about others' research without adopting their style, practicing your paraphrasing skills will make a huge difference and help you establish your own personal style.**

Finally, structure and clarity are vital aspects of academic discourse. Not only will you be expected to write clearly, make your thesis explicit, and organize your paragraphs effectively, you will want to make sure that your writing is clear and easy to understand. (For more, see Ch. 18, "Thesis Statements," and Ch. 21, "Organization, from Beginning to End.")

» Understanding Academic Style

If "academic discourse" can be roughly defined as "the way scholars write or speak," then "style" is how scholars make their work distinct. Many people have assumptions about academic writing: it is boring, complicated, only uses long words, and so on. But, honestly, these ideas don't have to be the case. **Academic writing should not be unnecessarily complicated or rely on difficult or inaccessible language.** Academic discourse does tend to incorporate jargon so that writers can make nuanced, careful arguments for specific audiences. The following table summarizes some other common "rules" about academic writing and covers how to identify and potentially "fix" these writing issues. However, these "rules" are more like guidelines that will help you mesh your own style with clear, engaging academic discourse. Keep in mind that you may need to ask your instructors about the expectations for academic discourse in your courses.

"If 'academic discourse' can be roughly defined as 'the way scholars write or speak,' then 'style' is how scholars make their work distinct."

Commonly Heard "Rules"			
Issue and Why	**Example**	**Identify and Adjustment**	**Revision**
Avoid -ly adverbs: Can seem insincere and unnecessary; often prop up boring verbs	Gardens are **really** cool because they make it **incredibly** easy to eat **healthily**.	Look for words that end in -ly Change how the subject is described	Gardens are important because they make healthy eating easier.
Limit prepositions: May overwhelm a sentence and can increase wordiness	Planting a garden **for** personal use **within** the boundaries **of** a city is legal **except** when the gardens make sidewalks **for** people **on** foot difficult **to** walk **on**.	Look for short words ("to," "in," etc.) and time or place words ("during," "before," etc.) or look for long sentences Reorganize and rephrase the sentence	While blocking pedestrian walkways is illegal, planting personal urban gardens is legal.
Avoid passive voice: Increases wordiness and makes it hard to see who is responsible for an action	When gardens **are planted**, a schoolyard **is made** beautiful.	If you can add the phrase "by someone," then you have passive voice Identify who is responsible	When students plant gardens, they make schoolyards beautiful.
Avoid contractions: Appears informal and conversational	Gardens **shouldn't** be planted next to roads.	Look for apostrophes (but do not eliminate possessives by mistake!) Replace the contraction with full words	Gardens should not be planted next to roads.
Never use "you": Sounds like a command, implies that we know how our audience is thinking, and can sound accusatory	**You** should plant a garden immediately because it will help **your** poor health.	Look for "you" or phrases that are commanding readers Rephrase the sentence	Planting a garden can improve poor health.
Before using "I," check with your professor; some do not want to see "I": Sounds conversational and can make you sound hesitant	**I** think that planting gardens can help alleviate global warming. **I** planted a garden, so **I** know this is true.	Look for uses of "I" that are unnecessary or that undermine your authority Phrase your argument more forcefully	Planting a garden helps alleviate global warming.
Avoid unnecessarily complicated word choices: Clouds meaning and can be confusing	When an **individual propagates** an **allotment**, he or she should keep **the time of year, meteorological** conditions, and **micro- and macroclimates** in **cognizance**.	Long words, lists of similar words, or unfamiliar words Try to use words that you commonly read in your discipline's publications	When a person plants a garden, they need to be aware of the season, the weather, and the climate.

Now for some examples. Think about what makes the two following quotations different. How can we tell that different people wrote the two pieces? How do the authors make academic language work for them?

> Modern environmentalists often take one of two equally problematic positions towards work. Most equate productive work in nature with destruction. They ignore the ways that work itself is a means of knowing nature while celebrating the virtues of play and recreation in nature. A smaller group takes a second position: certain kinds of archaic work, most typically the farming of peasants, provides a way of knowing nature. (White 171)

> The agrarian society of Thomas Jefferson's America has disappeared. Jefferson described a nation whose farmers constituted fully 90 percent of its citizenry; currently about 1.5 percent of the U.S. population engages in farm labor. Though 954 million acres remain in agricultural production, this number too has been shrinking (*Statistical Abstract*, 1999, pp. 426, 678). The remaining pastures, fields, and feedlots (which constitute 40% of all U.S. land) garner relatively little attention among either environmentalists or the public at large though ample room for concern exists. (Retzinger 45)

These are both dense passages of academic writing. But the two authors each have their own style. Richard White, who wrote the first excerpt, is more conversational; he has shorter sentences and fairly simple word choice. Jean P. Retzinger is more formal; her sentences tend to be longer, with more subordinate clauses, and she relies on statistics. However, both use precise, careful language that conveys their arguments clearly. Reading passages like these, and studying how they are crafted, helps us learn how to write effectively and presents us with more choices when we sit down to write. White and Retzinger balance personal style with the expectations of academic discourse. **Reading academic papers in your field will help you figure out what sorts of stylistic choices are expected.**

"When you are writing, make sure you appropriately identify and describe your audience, rather than relying on vague descriptions."

» Personalizing Your Style

While the rules for academic writing may seem prescriptive, notice that for each rule there are exceptions. For example, you might have noticed the use of "you" throughout this textbook (and this sentence!) and in your instructor's assignment sheets and syllabus. Instructors frequently use "you" when writing directly to their students to establish a friendly tone. This textbook's authors and editors use "you" because their purpose is to give advice and guidelines and to share their own experience as writers. When you are writing, make sure you appropriately identify and describe your audience ("people who overuse technology," "students," and so forth), rather than relying on vague descriptions ("you," "all people," and so on) to maintain specificity and clarity.

Similarly, notice my use of "I" at the beginning of this chapter. "I" is appropriate when we want to gain our readers' attention or when we have specialized knowledge. I started this chapter with a story about my experience with college writing because a short, relevant personal story in introductions can be an effective way to capture readers' attention and because I wanted to establish my credibility. When I discuss my struggles with style, I better develop my ethos by showing that I have firsthand experience. **When using personal anecdotes, always make sure that your stories are appropriate because using an inapplicable anecdote detracts from your ethos.** (Imagine if I had started this chapter by discussing tulips or adopting my cat!) Remember, some instructors do not want to see personal experience as evidence—either as a rule or for a particular assignment—so always check with them before writing, and consider your audience's expectations.

In many academic fields and disciplines, "I" is also used to differentiate our argument from others. In such cases, we can signal this by saying "I argue" or "I contend." These phrases help our readers understand what we are arguing and how it diverges from established discourse in the field. In contrast, writing "I think" or "I believe" repeatedly can distract readers or suggest a lack of confidence. **Academic discourse calls for us to make specific, nuanced claims.** Carefully choosing when to use "I" is often the difference between an effective argument and an ineffective one. Furthermore, "argue" and "contend" are strong, specific verbs whereas "think" and "believe" are more general and weaker. **You should rely on clear, precise verbs that help you make your point.**

Often, we think that wordier and more complicated papers are "more academic." **In fact, it is better to use accurate words that we (and our audience) understand, and that make our argument readable.** (This, of course, depends entirely on audience. If you are writing a subject-specific paper, be sure to use the typical jargon and vocabulary that your audience expects. If you are addressing a more general audience, you will want to use words that have broader appeal.) For most assignments, we are more successful when we pick words that are nuanced, precise, and clear, because these words help make our work easily readable. The most effective academic writing styles allow people to access our work in a pleasant way. In the chart above, I offered two example sentences that demonstrate this:

+ "When an individual propagates an allotment, he or she should keep the time of year, meteorological conditions, and micro- and macroclimates in cognizance."

+ "When a person plants a garden, they need to be aware of the season, the weather, and the climate."

While the first sentence is correct, it is not precise or clear. For instance, an allotment is a garden, but it is a British term and typically refers to a plot of land a person rents. Conversely, although "climate" is a broader category than "micro- and macroclimates," it is sufficient for most English 101 or 102 assignments. Furthermore, the first sentence is a little confusing because the verb appears at the end and is far away from its subject. The second sentence puts the subject and the verb right next to each other, helping readers more quickly understand what the writer is saying.

> "Incorporating personal style into academic writing is a skill, and all skills take practice."

While these guidelines about academic discourse apply to written assignments, spoken assignments present different expectations. For instance, the use of "I" is usually acceptable during presentations. Something new to consider, however, includes being careful to avoid filler words like "um" and "like." You also will want to keep your sentences simple, by making them shorter and ensuring the subjects and verbs are close together, so that they can be easily understood by listeners. When speaking, it is best to use clear transitions (such as, "first," "next," and so on), and to repeat your points periodically so that your audience will find them memorable. Nevertheless, each academic discipline has different expectations for communicating information. Observing experienced speakers and peers provides opportunities for learning these expectations.

Incorporating personal style into academic writing is a skill, and all skills take practice. It is impossible to practice a skill we do not understand. This chapter is a starting point; it offers guidelines and suggestions to help academic writing become more familiar and, therefore, less daunting. The next step is writing— a lot. Practice helps us hone our writing skills and personalize our academic discourse. **Writers, whether they write creatively or academically, are never finished working on their style.** Our academic writing evolves over time and varies from project to project. Every time we receive a new assignment, we need to think about what will work best—and then try it.

» Works Cited

Retzinger, Jean P. "Cultivating the Agrarian Myth in Hollywood Films." *Enviropop*, edited by Mark Meister and Phyllis M. Japp, Praeger, 2002, pp. 45–62.

White, Richard. "'Are You an Environmentalist or Do You Work for a Living?': Work and Nature." *Uncommon Ground*, edited by William Cronon, W.W. Norton and Company, 1995, pp. 171–185.

24. Understanding Tone and Voice

Lilly Berberyan

Whenever you write something, whether it is an essay for your history class about the Civil War or a casual email to a group of friends inviting them to dinner, you inevitably find yourself dealing with matters of tone and voice. As you consider how you would address the aforementioned scenarios, you are already making the kinds of choices that will lead to the most effective tone and voice in a given rhetorical situation, helping you strengthen your skills as a rhetor.

Even though tone and voice are often conflated in discussion, it might be helpful to think of tone as the kind of mood that a piece of writing might evoke, while voice is the set of specific characteristics that make your writing uniquely different from that of others. In other words, voice is *your personal arsenal* of diction, syntax, and grammar, while tone is *how you use this arsenal* to create a particular mood. Another way to think about tone and voice is through the analogy of attire: In the morning, one of the first decisions you make is what to wear based on an anticipated prognosis of your day and the contents of your wardrobe. Your chosen items of clothing constitute your voice as a dresser; the specific items you choose on a given day in response to the different situations you anticipate can be characterized as your tone. In other words, you are limited to what pieces of clothing you own (vocabulary and grammar skills). At the same time, how you utilize what you have—such as ending a sentence in an essay with a period as opposed to the exclamation mark you might use if you were sending a text message to a friend—becomes a matter of tone. Thus, you might wear a shirt with a pair of jeans when heading out to the movies to convey a casual dressing tone; however, you could also wear that same shirt with slacks to convey a more serious tone for an interview.

The analogy of clothing is quite apt in describing tone and voice when considering a specific writing assignment. After analyzing the assignment sheet, you and your classmates may choose to write about the same topic and decide that you will use a serious academic tone. While you might all use the same tone, your essays will be vastly different because your voices will differ. As you work to develop your tone and voice for a specific writing situation, consider the rhetorical triangle: knowing your audience's expectations for a given subject will help you tremendously in establishing your ethos as an author.

» Tone and Voice: A Rhetorical Situation

To better understand how your rhetorical situation influences your tone and voice, consider these examples from *Newsweek* and *Health Communication* discussing the correlation between the MMR vaccine and autism. As you read the following samples, be sure to assess the tone and voice in each by considering these questions:

+ What is the author's purpose?

+ What kind of vocabulary, syntax, and grammar are part and parcel of this author's lexicon?

+ Does the author use neutral or emotionally charged language?

+ What is the mood conveyed by the author?

+ How do I feel about the subject after reading a specific text?

+ How does the author's intended audience influence the tone and voice in a piece of writing?

First, let's look at a portion of an article from *Newsweek* about allegations of the MMR vaccine and supposed links with autism:

Andrew Wakefield, the sham scientist whose now-retracted 1998 paper led millions of parents to believe in a link between autism and the measles/mumps/rubella vaccine, has just lost his license to practice medicine in Britain. [...] If the first principle of medicine is "do no harm," Wakefield should have lost his license a long time ago. To say that his autism study was discredited isn't strong enough. Wakefield apparently lied about the young patients he reported on in his paper; his descriptions of their conditions didn't match up with records kept on file at his hospital. He also lied by omission, neglecting to reveal a huge conflict of interest: he had been paid about a million dollars to advise lawyers of parents who were worried their children had been injured by the vaccine. According to the *Guardian*, Wakefield "tried out Transfer Factor on one of the children in his research programme but failed to tell the child's GP. He took blood from children at a birthday party, paying them £5 a time." Ten of Wakefield's co-authors eventually renounced his study, and *The Lancet*, the journal that had published it, formally retracted it in February. Unsurprisingly, follow-up studies in 2002 and 2005 found no link between autism and the MMR vaccine. By then, though, it didn't matter: Wakefield's paper had gotten too much traction among the general public. Vaccination rates in Britain plummeted, and kids started to get sick. In 2006 a 13-year-old boy died of measles, the first victim in Britain since 1992. (Carmichael)

In analyzing the excerpt, you will note that the article's overall voice is geared towards the general public; names that could be confusing to readers are contextualized, examples are thoroughly explained, and diction that could possibly be confusing to the reader is eliminated. For example, rather than use the shorthand MMR that professionals in the medical community use to refer to the grouping of "measles/mumps/rubella," the author uses the full names of these diseases. Overall, the article seems to be focused on discussing the impact of Andrew Wakefield's study on public perception of vaccinations. While the author's voice is geared towards informing the magazine's readers about an issue that they might not be familiar with, the tone of the article has a more targeted role: that of discrediting the subject of the article—Andrew Wakefield. The author's use of the phrase "sham scientist" to describe Wakefield, her argument that Wakefield's work has caused harm to patients, and the examples of falsified data all work to discredit Wakefield. In this case, her tone changes in accordance to what she would like to convey to her readers—an attitude that would make her readers doubt Wakefield's credentials and his work.

By contrast, an article that originally appeared in *Health Communication* magazine discusses the same topic using a different tone and voice:

> Numerous epidemiologic studies subsequently failed to support an MMR-autism link (Gerber & Offit, 2009; Miller & Reynolds, 2009; see also Institute of Medicine, 2004), and criticisms of the study's methods, ethics, and conclusions remained prevalent. Notably, 10 of the study's 13 authors issued a retraction of the MMR-autism interpretation in 2004 (Murch et al., 2004). At the same time, allegations of Wakefield's professional misconduct were publicized by *Sunday Times* investigative reporter Brian Deer (2011a; 2001b). In June 2006, the UK General Medical Council (GMC) formally accused Wakefield of failing to attain ethical review board approval for the study and of failing to disclose that he had received compensation from a lawyer representing several children in the study whose families were involved in autism-related litigation against MMR manufacturers (Offit, 2008). In January 2010, the GMC found him guilty of these charges and revoked his British medical license (Whalen, 2010). One month later, *The Lancet* retracted the original 1998 article in its entirety. Finally, in January 2011, the *British Medical Journal* published a series of articles that summarized many of the prior accusations and demonstrated how Wakefield falsified data to strengthen the apparent MMR-autism link (Deer, 2011a, 2011b; Godlee, Smith, & Marcovitch, 2011). (Holton et al. 691)

The article is written by several authors and consequently captures a collective voice, which in this case is serious and academic. The general audience of the article knows enough about the subject matter that the authors do not have to spend time contextualizing who Wakefield is or how he relates to autism.

Right away, you'll notice that the second example seeks to demonstrate the lack of credibility of Wakefield's study, but does not ever resort to the ad hominem fallacy of attacking Wakefield personally. Rather, it argues that there has not been a clear link between the vaccinations and autism and supports its arguments by relying on studies rather than launching a personal attack against the author. The voice of the article follows the conventions of scientific writing. Unlike the first excerpt, the authors of this example are concerned with conveying a more formal tone and taking part in academic discourse following the conventions of scientific writing (e.g., the authors' explanation of abbreviations, such as the "GMC" shows that they are interested in educating their audience when applicable). You'll note the abundance of APA citations throughout the excerpt; these citations help support the authors' credibility while simultaneously enabling the article's audience to find out more about the presented evidence and further engaging in academic discourse. Following the conventions of academic writing, the authors of this article have abstained from making overtly biased statements regarding Wakefield and instead focus on the shortcomings of his study and the surmounting evidence against his credibility.

The two excerpts discuss the same topic, but the authors approach their subject matter from vastly different perspectives. The tonal and vocal differences between the two texts are partly motivated by the authors' perception of their audiences; while the first example is targeted towards a general audience, allowing for a casual tone/voice, the second example is meant for an academic one, necessitating a more formal tone/voice.

» Tone and Voice: Oral Communication

Throughout your college career, you'll be asked to deliver your work both orally and in writing. Oral communication takes various forms, including oral presentations, podcasts, feedback you deliver to your classmates during workshops, and class participation. Like written communication, oral communication is a skill that can be perfected with practice. Whenever you speak up in class, whether during an oral presentation or making a comment in class, you might find yourself elevating the tone of your language. You might find yourself enunciating for clarity, eliminating filler words, and expressing well-thought-out ideas.

Just as you will likely choose an outfit that is somewhat formal to deliver a presentation, you'll also want to adapt a more formal tone to deliver information to your instructor and your classmates. From the words you choose to the way you convey yourself while presenting in front of a class, you'll need to convey professionalism. The advantage of oral communication over written communication is that the former allows you to gauge your audience's reactions as you go through your presentation. Looking at your audience will allow you to determine if your audience is confused or bored and if so, you can adjust your delivery accordingly.

Another example of oral communication that you might engage in throughout your college career might be the conversations you have with your peers during workshops. Your peers might be your friends, but while you're discussing your writing with each other, you'll find yourself in a position where you have to generate thoughtful and helpful feedback. Thus, the comments you generate for your peers will have to be more formal in tone and go beyond qualitative statements like "this is good" or "this is bad."

» Tone and Voice: Written Communication

While you may not think of tone or voice during the initial stages of your composition process, you should take the time to consider how your writing comes across to your audience when revising your work. Mastering tone and voice and incorporating them into your writing process will help you control how your writing comes across to your audience, guiding the kinds of reactions that you want to elicit from your audience. As you work to develop your tone and voice for a specific writing situation, consider the rhetorical triangle: knowing your audience's expectations for a given subject will help you tremendously in establishing your ethos as an author. (For more on how to develop your credibility as an author, see Ch. 20, "Writing with the Rhetorical Appeals.")

Cultivating and fine-tuning your voice will instill a sense of continuity in your writing. Voice can be acquired and perfected through practice, but you will want to start out with the voice that comes to you naturally and proceed to fine-tune it in each writing project. For example, if you notice that your voice tends to be redundant, you will learn to take out unnecessary words and phrases in your editing process. In a typical week, you may be prompted to complete a number of writing tasks and knowing how to manipulate your voice to best fit the requirements of the assignment will help you become a more effective and proficient writer.

Tone varies from one writing project to the next. Tone captures a specific mood expressed through language, conveying the writer's attitude toward a specific subject. You can manipulate tone through the use of words or syntax. As evidenced in the first example from *Newsweek*, the simple addition of the word "sham" to "scientist" conveys the author's bias toward her subject and establishes a disparaging tone throughout the excerpt.

As you work to cultivate an effective tone or voice, be sure to keep in mind the various elements of the rhetorical triangle. (For more on the rhetorical triangle, see Ch. 2, "Rhetoric in Academic Settings.") Consider such questions shaped by the rhetorical triangle as:

+ What is your relationship with the text?

+ What would you like for your audience to learn about the text after reading your work?

+ How much detail do you need in order for the text to make sense to your audience?

Some additional questions you might want to ask yourself as you write include:

+ Do I need to address this topic in a specific tone or voice?

+ Will my audience easily detect what tone I'm using and is it important that they do?

+ To what purpose am I using a specific tone?

+ Does it achieve this purpose?

+ What do I want my readers to learn, understand, or think about as they read my work?

Your voice and tone can play a crucial role in getting your desired message across to your audience. As you work to develop and improve your writing abilities, it is important to keep in mind just how your writing comes across to your audience. Cultivating and improving your abilities to shape your tone and voice will help you deliver your message to your audience exactly as you want it to be understood.

» Works Cited

Carmichael, Mary. "The 'Autism Doctor' Isn't a Doctor Anymore. Does it Matter?" *Newsweek*, 23 May 2010, Newsweek, www.newsweek.com/autism-doctor-isnt-doctor-anymore-does-it-matter-222858.

Holton, Avery, et al. "The Blame Frame: Media Attribution of Culpability About the MMR-Autism Vaccination Scare." *Health Communication*, vol. 27, no. 7, 2012, pp. 690–701. *Taylor & Francis Online*, doi:10.1080/10410236.2011.633158.

25. Rhetorical Delivery

Brenta Blevins

» Defining Delivery

In antiquity, rhetoric focused on delivering—or sharing texts with an audience—through oral speech. In your writing-focused college classes it may be easier to think of rhetoric as primarily written. However, rhetoric isn't an either-or. Rhetoric encompasses the spoken, the written, and the visual—as well as the combination of these modes in compositions called "multimodal." Delivery is how we perform and speak, the medium and genre we choose, as well as stylistic considerations and more. The canon of delivery guides rhetorical decisions about how best to convey messages in specific rhetorical situations, whether delivered via spoken, written, visual, or multimodal compositions. (For more, see Ch. 3, "The Rhetorical Canons and the Writing Process.")

» Spoken Delivery

In speech, delivery is clearly spoken, but it can be so much more. For example, tone alone can convey much of a message. Even when using the exact same words, the tone in which those words are pronounced can convey very different meanings. Saying "I'm fine" with a testy pronunciation or a happy tone conveys whether the speaker intends the audience to receive the text as sarcastic or literal. Body language is another tool that can help deliver intended messages. Speaking with a smile or a serious expression affects the delivery of the text. Pausing or making gestures can elicit specific emotions from the audience to emphasize your point. And delivery is key for establishing ethos with the audience, building trust and rapport with them. If a speaker has innovative ideas but ineffective delivery, the message and the speaker's ethos get lost. (For more on tone and voice in relation to delivery, see Ch. 24, "Understanding Tone and Voice.")

» Written Delivery

Writing is also concerned with delivery. Determining whether to write up a bad day in the chemistry class in an email, an essay, or a lab report is a delivery decision, depending on your audience and their expectations. If the information is delivered in an email, the write-up might contain a few sentences, while a lab report requires a more structured format. An essay requires paragraphs and citations. An MLA-formatted essay, for instance, requires a particular format, with a recommended font and specific margin sizes, and specifications for in-text and Works Cited citations if the writer is to establish ethos with the audience. Even casual communication is affected by delivery. In a brief text message, for example, even the presence of punctuation is a delivery decision. Whether we write, for example, in an instant message that we are "okay," "okay.", or "okay!!!!" provides different messages for the audience.

» Visual Delivery

Information can be delivered through visual images like photographs, drawings, charts, tables, and more. The type of image conveys mood. For example, the use of cartoon figures conveys informality, while using graphs with numbers conveys a more serious tone. Color represents another delivery decision. Choosing black and white images might create a more formal environment, while choosing to use school colors can be an appeal to pathos. Spatial arrangement of the content is also a delivery decision, guiding the audience to look at some material first before looking at other material. This list is clearly not exhaustive. (For a more detailed discussion of rhetoric and visual media, see Ch. 12, "Writing a Visual Analysis.")

Let's take a closer look at visual delivery by examining the relationship between color choices and delivery. Consider the difference between the two text boxes:

I'm so happy

I'm so happy

The black and white image uses more traditional textual colors and thus may provoke an ironic response, while the pink block may catch the audience's attention and evoke an emotional reaction, like lightheartedness. Colors can suggest different moods; therefore, rhetors should ensure that the color usage of fonts or images aligns with the intended emotional impact to maximize the text's rhetorical effectiveness.

Designers should consider their audience in their visual decisions. The headings in this textbook, for example, are a different color than the body text to guide the audience's attention to major sections of the text. Similarly, this textbook's pages use color along their edges to help group like chapters together within similar content areas. While a means of gaining the audience's attention, color decisions should take into account that some color choices can make text less accessible. For example, it is much easier to read certain color combinations than others; consider the following example:

Yellow text on a white background

Or .

Blue text on white background

As this textbook and many other books demonstrate, readers are accustomed to and comfortable reading large amounts of dark text on light backgrounds.

Color and other visual choices should be carefully weighed to maximize the rhetorical effectiveness and thus should avoid an unintended audience response and/or undercutting one's rhetorical purpose. The content in a presentation, such as a PowerPoint or Prezi, may be excellent, for example, but the visual delivery can detract from the argument because of something as seemingly simple as the color of the font. Poor visual choices can make it challenging for the audience to receive the message. A font color that is difficult to read, crowding too many images or too much text on a slide, or not using standard MLA formatting for an essay can weaken the overall argument by detracting from the rhetor's ethos. Keeping the audience in mind when making visual choices can guide the rhetor toward effective rhetorical designs.

» Multimodal Delivery

Multimodal compositions combine a variety of communication modes including speaking, writing, and visual design. For example, multimodal compositions such as presentations, Web pages, wikis, videos, and even Facebook posts, may all call for authoring text, as well as audio, still images, moving images like animation and video, and much more. In making careful rhetorical decisions about font, color, image, music and even pacing, designers can take such compositions to a new level of "show, don't tell."

» Considering Delivery in Assignments

Let's take a look at some delivery decisions you may face in a College Writing class. One common assignment students receive is the linked assignment. In this assignment, students are responsible for writing an essay and then making a presentation related to that content while using a visual aid. For such an assignment, you need to make rhetorical decisions shaped by the delivery of each particular text. In this section, we'll examine some of the delivery decisions involved in a rhetorical analysis of *Narrative of the Life of Frederick Douglass* in both essay and presentation format.

For the essay, a student in a College Writing class will likely begin with an MLA-formatted essay (see Figure 1). While writing, the student considers the audience's expectations and visually establishes ethos through the arrangement of text, such as having appropriately formatted paragraphs and headings, and otherwise adhering to applicable MLA conventions. The student knows that each essay paragraph will develop a portion of the argument, starting with one point and including specific textual evidence in a logos-building move, as well as offering analysis of that evidence to support the argument. To enhance authorial ethos, the student will cite any use of textual evidence both in-text and on the Works Cited page at the end of the essay.

Christopher Smith

Prof. Moore

ENG 101

28 January 2013

    Conflicting Christianity: Arrangement, Logos and Pathos in *The Narrative of the Life of Frederick Douglass*

    In his landmark work *The Narrative of the Life of Frederick Douglass*, the author offers two conflicting forms of Christianity, each with its own purpose. Through personal recollections and thoughts, Douglass describes both real and false versions of religion and generally, the real or "true" form of Christianity he practiced as well as some whites opposed to slavery. The false form of religion, "the hypocritical Christianity of this land," is practiced by whites and is a complete bastardization of the true ideals behind genuine Christian thought (95). Douglass deliberately structures his narrative by interspersing discussions of religion that show slavery and true Christianity as opposing forces that cannot simultaneously exist. Further, he logically argues that if there is a "real" or "pure" Christianity, the existence and practice of slavery wholly and inevitably corrupts it. Through his careful, logical juxtapositions and appeals to pathos, Douglass' narrative moves beyond a traditional religious exposition of the evils of slavery to make an overt political statement about his current political and personal exigence.

Figure 1. A Written Essay Analyzing *Narrative of the Life of Frederick Douglass*

Once the essay is completed, the student then plans a speech to deliver in conjunction with a PowerPoint presentation. Because the audience will be listening, the student realizes they will not be able to remember the same level of detail found in the essay, when the reader can slow down, look up unfamiliar words, and re-read to ensure comprehension. To aid the audience's memory in the spoken presentation, the student decides to place the argument's key points visually on a presentation slide. In addition, the student considers the appropriate tone, volume, pitch and body language to deliver the speech given the subject matter, audience, time, space, and other constraints. Further, the student plans a speech that will provide good verbal cues to enhance the presentation by helping the audience follow the orally delivered text.

The student knows that rhetors can gain credibility by crediting the works used to develop a text's content. (See Ch. 7, "Academic Integrity: Promoting Intellectual Growth" and Ch. 16, "Rhetorical Elements of Academic Citation" for more on how student rhetors gain credibility through their citations.) While written texts use in-text and bibliographic citations to document their sources, the student delivering an oral speech names the authors, texts, and dates of texts, and also lists at the end of the presentation all citations on a Works Cited page. In the same way the student includes citations in the written text, he or she knows that material used within the presentation affects his/ her ethos. While most know that copying text off the Web is inappropriate, reusing images, music, and/or videos without giving credit is likewise unacceptable. Because of this, the student decides to locate an image freely available through Creative Commons, and cite the use of that image.

To take advantage of the multimodal format, the student decides to include a visual image of Frederick Douglass. The student conducts research to locate images of Douglass, paying careful attention to each potential text's overall composition and framing, noting Douglass's expression, body position and eye contact, clothing, and more. Because the slide's topic is focused on ethos, the student locates an image of Douglass that seems to represent the ethos that he is striving to invoke in his narrative.

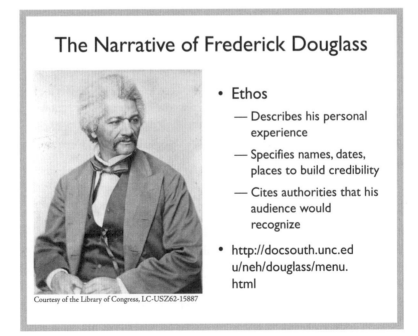

Figure 2. A PowerPoint Slide Analyzing *Narrative of the Life of Frederick Douglass*

Again taking advantage of the digital nature of the multimodal presentation, the student also decides to include a hyperlink for reference during the presentation and for later viewing through the class's discussion board. Including an authoritative website hyperlink both increases the delivery capabilities by linking to other electronic resources and affects the student's ethos by demonstrating credible research.

For optimum delivery, the student designs the multimodal compositions to utilize technological effects that augment rather than detract from the message, for example, making sure the images are an appropriate size in relation to text. Likewise, a good visual design in a multimodal composition recognizes that yellow text on a white background is hard to read, showing inadequate consideration of the audience. As another example, consider the differences between these fonts:

This is one font choice.

This is another font choice.

This is another font choice.

Which font adds the most ethos to a persuasive piece, suggesting a rhetor who respects his or her audience? The answer depends on the rhetorical situation and the rhetor's ability to respond to the audience. A whimsical font, as long as it is easily readable, may be appropriate for rhetorical purposes such as addressing a younger audience or to evoke a "fun" context. More traditional fonts appeal to more serious audiences and should be used in professional rhetorical situations. For this presentation, the student decides to use a font that treats the serious topic with a font that mirrors the text's tone, and thus uses the bottom font choice.

» Revision

The rhetorical canon of delivery can guide purposeful design decisions, choices that determine how a composition fulfills one's rhetorical purpose. These delivery decisions, which extend across the spoken, written, visual, and multimodal text, can all be used to show respect for the audience. As with traditionally written essays, texts using other delivery modes should be reviewed and revised upon completion of early drafts.

Revision of texts should account not just for content choices, but also for rhetorical effectiveness of the delivery. For example, in reviewing a spoken text, the author or reviewers should take into account the audience's short-term memory and whether verbal signposts guide the audience, whether sentences are accordingly concise, whether the verbal delivery is well-paced and appropriately pitched, and how body language enhances the presentation. Reviewing a visual text should take into account whether the design enhances or detracts based on color choice—which could include readability, whether clarity is maintained, and whether the spatial arrangement of materials is effective. Reviewers of multimodal compositions should take into account whether the thesis is supported throughout the *entire* composition, whether focus and a coherent organization are clear and maintained throughout the piece, and whether there is any feedback to provide based on spoken or visual delivery.

University resources can also provide feedback to improve the final delivery of all texts. The Writing Center can provide responses to written materials, while the Speaking Center can aid in refining the delivery of speeches. Students can take digital projects to the university's Digital ACT Studio to gain feedback for revision. The consultants in these locations serve as informed audiences, and by providing collaborative consultation they can help rhetors make rhetorically effective choices.

26. Exploring Alternative Genres:
Writing Outside the (Research) Box

Jessie Van Rheenen

Setting: College Writing classroom, week 3 of the semester. INSTRUCTOR enters through a door.

INSTRUCTOR

Good morning, everyone! Your first formal writing for this class is going to be a narrative assignment. I'd like you all to write a personal argument that draws on your own experience.

Murmurs from the class. STUDENT 1 raises hand.

STUDENT 1

So will this be a five-paragraph essay, then?

INSTRUCTOR

The personal story you tell is up to you, and so is the form this narrative takes. A five-paragraph essay will in all likelihood be too limiting for what you need to accomplish in this assignment. Feel free to get creative!

Students (half) display cautious excitement.

Students (other half) sit in nervous silence.

If this scene sounds familiar, you are certainly not alone. Many students walk into their first College Writing class expecting to tackle research papers and learn rhetorical terms, or maybe even to write a rhetorical analysis of a text. You might not be expecting, though, to have assignments that fall *outside* this more familiar type of research or academic work. Genres, narrative, personal essays, concrete writing—you may not recognize the vocabulary yet, but we will discuss all of these terms and how you can use many similar techniques across all kinds of writing.

In any writing course, college students will encounter a wide range of **genres**, meaning the types or forms communication can take. When we talk about genres of text, this could mean written products such as essays, letters, or fiction, as well as spoken genres like presentations. Each genre also has its own **conventions**—the standards or "rules" that usually apply to that particular genre. Notice that I've put "rules" in quotation marks because really, these characteristics are more *shared expectations* than hard-and-fast rules. **The expectations of your audience shape conventions in every genre**; for instance, someone receiving a handwritten letter from you would probably expect it to begin with some sort of salutation ("Hey!" or "Dear…") and end with a sign-off ("Sincerely," "Lots of Love," your name). (For more on style in academic discourse, see Ch. 23, "Personalizing Academic Discourse.")

This chapter will explore some alternative genres of writing, along with their specific conventions, which you might encounter during your College Writing career. As you read, though, keep in mind that assignments can vary across classes; you should always check with your individual instructor and follow the guidelines in their prompt.

» Narrative Genres

A **narrative** refers to a series of connected events that form some kind of unified whole. Narrative includes fictional forms like stories or novels, but also shapes nonfiction and spoken forms such as memoir, oral storytelling, and the personal essay. In addition, narrative can be used to take a stance on an issue or express an opinion. **Argumentative narrative**, for example, involves making an argument in the form of telling a story. In this case, you could weave together essential story elements—characters, plot, setting, details—so they support your main argument, or thesis. We might think of fairy tales or fables, like "Little Red Riding Hood" or "The Tortoise and the Hare," as narratives with a moral or "thesis" that becomes clear through the sequence of events. While these fables are fictional, they contain the type of argument-through-story you might develop in your own nonfiction personal narrative, discussed further below.

Personal Essay

A popular assignment in many College Writing classes is a personal essay, sometimes also called an **Autobiographical Argument** or a **Personal Narrative**. In this nonfiction genre, writers use their own story and memories—often in order to make a larger argument. Within the personal essay form, your firsthand experience becomes your evidence. As a result, this type of writing relies heavily on the first-person perspective, or the use of "I."

In "No Polenta, No Cry," a personal essay about unhealthy approaches to dieting, ZZ Packer writes, "I'm a normal-size woman who loves to eat out every chance I get, but who will leave the polenta behind in a Gorgonzola-trumpet-mushroom-watercress dish; who avoids mashed potatoes like the plague; and who has been known to toss perfectly good French fries down the garbage disposal." Notice how Packer puts the emphasis clearly on her own experience (*I'm* a normal-size woman") and next uses a detailed list of food choices she makes in her day-to-day life. Her examples are memorable, not generic; how many of us have eaten "a Gorgonzola-trumpet-mushroom-watercress dish" before?

Just because an instructor asks you to make an argument in a narrative or personal essay does not mean the tone must be combative, or that politics or personal conflict need to be directly addressed. Instead, **any narrative should convince your intended audience of your perspective.** (For more on argumentation strategies, see Ch. 19, "Staking Your Claim.") In choosing a topic, it's essential to select something you also believe you can write about objectively and clearly—and which doesn't feel too raw—given that your work will eventually be critiqued for a grade. When in doubt, always review your assignment sheet and check with your instructor.

"Any narrative should convince your intended audience of your perspective."

For many writers, a personal narrative can be an exciting opportunity to explore identity and past experience, or to construct an argument using autobiography. Yet some students may be less comfortable writing about themselves, at least initially. If this type of assignment feels daunting to you, keep in mind that **you have ultimate ownership over your work and its direction.** The prompt could be open-ended, or your instructor might give you some parameters for selecting a topic. In either case, brainstorm relevant ideas that you feel passionate about and would enjoy writing on—be that music, your hometown, or a relationship that has shaped who you've become. (For more, see Ch. 17, "Pre-Writing Strategies.") You might be surprised by how many avenues you can pursue in personal narratives, and applying the strategies below will help make any writing on your chosen topic as effective as possible.

Other Genres

Some assignments might include the option to choose your genre. Even if you do not find yourself writing in these alternative forms, you may come across them in your readings for College Writing or future courses. Other alternative genres include:

+ **Poems** (see the example from Amy Lowell below)
+ **Plays/Screenplays**, also known as scripts (as the opening of this chapter uses)
+ **Short Stories** or **Flash Fiction** (extremely short stories)
+ **Podcasts** or other forms of spoken delivery
+ **Journal and Blog entries**
+ **Comics/Graphic Novels**

» Strategies for Writing Alternative Genres

The possibilities for alternative genres may seem overwhelming at first, but as you get started, the good news is that skills you are developing for approaching argument, persuasive writing, and critical reading can be applied across countless genres in College Writing and beyond.

Tip 1: Choose Concrete Over Abstract

Understandably, students will sometimes try to explain ideas using only *abstract* language, or nonspecific terms. (Think of concepts like "love," "happiness," or "freedom.") While these abstractions might sound impressive and scholarly on the surface, writers who rely on them may find their arguments lacking in rhetorical power. These big, vague terms are often hard for readers to visualize or relate to, and therefore can make the rhetor's points come across as muddied and too broad. Instead, **consider how you can use *concrete* details, or specific, physical language that appeals to the senses.** Concrete words include objects I could drop on my foot—iPhones, cookies, soccer cleats—as well as descriptions that call on our sight, smell, hearing, taste, or touch.

To witness concrete language in action, let's look at part of a poem by Amy Lowell. In the opening of "A London Thoroughfare. 2 A.M.," Lowell describes the nighttime city outside her window:

> They have watered the street,
> It shines in the glare of lamps,
> Cold, white lamps,
> And lies
> Like a slow-moving river,
> Barred with silver and black.
> Cabs go down it,
> One,
> And then another,
> Between them I hear the shuffling of feet.

And later:

> Opposite my window,
> The moon cuts,
> Clear and round,
> Through the plum-coloured night.
> She cannot light the city:
> It is too bright.
> It has white lamps,
> And glitters coldly.

All of these images lead to the poem's final line, when Lowell reveals how alone and detached the speaker feels in this "alien city." Imagine if, instead of the lines above, Lowell had written, "I look at the street and feel sad." Without the "glare" of the "cold, white lamps," the "shuffling of feet," and the moon that "cuts" through "the plum-coloured night" of a city that "glitters coldly," what would be left for our imagination to conjure in this melancholy scene? We would lose the sensation and the suspense of *being* there. In the end, **imagery and use of the senses make our immersion possible.** By inviting readers more fully into this moment, Lowell helps us relate to the experience, and so reinforces her own ethos or authority within the text.

"Imagery and use of the senses make our immersion possible."

We are all guilty of glossing over certain ideas and relying on abstractions when we should go into greater detail. To work against this tendency, **look for abstract or vague language in your draft, and circle it.** If you have a line like "We fought about our different philosophies," the phrases "we fought" and "different philosophies" could be explained in more concrete terms by asking yourself questions like *how so* or *in what way?* See how you might "explode" or deepen those instances with specific examples and descriptions; just as Lowell does, you can ultimately use the senses to appeal to pathos and evoke your audience's emotions on new levels. In any writing during your academic career, such concrete examples will enliven your language and clarify your arguments.

Tip 2: Put in the Time and Work

"Creative writing" or "personal writing" may sound like a different category entirely, but these genres share a lot with what we think of as more traditional academic forms. Whenever students worry they are not "creative enough" or don't have "original ideas," I think it helps to call in the experts—people who do this type of writing for a living—and look at what they have to say about creativity.

In her 2009 TED Talk, "Your Elusive Creative Genius," author Elizabeth Gilbert focuses on harmful myths around the act of writing. In describing her own creative process, Gilbert says, "I'm a mule, and the way that I have to work is I have to get up at the same time every day, and sweat and labor and barrel through it really awkwardly." She makes it clear that, for her, writing is almost never a pretty or smooth process.

Are you worried that inspiration doesn't strike you and pour words onto the page as soon as you sit down to craft a narrative or write a poem? We've all been there. **But showing up and putting in the hours is a big part of *any* type of writing.**

Getting an early start and knowing your own writing process are also critical as you approach these alternative genres. Once you have something down on paper, put your draft aside for a few days. Return to it later with fresh eyes. Particularly if the topic you chose is more emotional or close to your heart, having a little distance can be a huge help in revising your work for the most effective organization, evidence, and language. (For more, see Ch. 5, "Personalizing Your Writing Practice.")

Tip 3: Seek Examples and Readers

Another excellent way to demystify alternative genres is to look at examples. Your instructor may give you samples to read and discuss; the authors of those texts can offer ideas about the genre conventions and example topics. Many more texts are a quick search away through the library and other online databases.

Just like any work you do for College Writing classes, alternative writing genres should be shaped with an audience in mind. Think of these projects as practice adapting your tone to different genres. (For a deeper exploration, see Ch. 24, "Understanding Tone and Voice.") If your audience is your instructor and classmates, for instance, you might have to supply more background about your family in a personal narrative essay than if your readers were your own siblings.

"Just like any work you do for College Writing classes, alternative writing genres should be shaped with an audience in mind."

Being aware of your intended audience can also help you to decide how much personal information to include, and what you are comfortable revealing to your peers or professors. When in doubt, always seek advice from trusted readers or visit The Writing Center to get input about your drafts in alternative genres.

» Final Thoughts: Why Bother with Alternative Genres?

As writers, cultivating our skills in different genres is a prime way to expand our persuasive capacities. For instance, I made a deliberate choice when I opened this chapter with the classroom scene; the screenplay is an example of putting an alternative form into practice as a way to (hopefully) pique my readers' curiosity. Though we might unfairly think of these types of writing as somehow less "serious" or "important" than research-based academic writing, alternative genres are a crucial part of representing the full range of our experience. **Mastering the approaches in this chapter will make your writing more adaptive to diverse rhetorical situations—and therefore empower your voice to resonate with any intended audience.**

» Works Cited

Gilbert, Elizabeth. "Your Elusive Creative Genius." TED. Feb. 2009. Lecture.

Lowell, Amy. "A London Thoroughfare. 2 A.M." *Academy of American Poets*, www.poets.org/poetsorg/poem/london-thoroughfare-2-am.

Packer, ZZ. "No Polenta, No Cry." *The New York Times Magazine*, 11 Oct. 2009, p. MM90.

» Teaching Text

Questions for Discussion

1. Think about a **genre** of communication you regularly come across or enjoy—poetry, graphic novels, blogs, emails, or even text messages. What would you describe as the **conventions** of that genre? What characteristics (in the format, word choices, visuals, etc.) do you tend to assume you'll encounter in this form of text?

2. When you come across an example that breaks or challenges those conventions, what effect does it have on you as a reader? Think of a time this has happened to you and describe how you reacted to the text and its rhetor.

3. How might these shared expectations be important in your own writing? What examples can you think of when it is especially important to *follow or stick to* conventions? What about times when it might be useful to *strategically depart from* some conventions?

» Class Activity: Developing Concrete Details

Materials

Assignment rough draft, paper/other writing surface, colored pens or highlighters

Instructions

Read through your own draft and choose a paragraph that you found difficult to write. Using one color, underline or highlight all of the **concrete** language you can locate in that section (physical objects, sensory details, and specific examples).

With a different color, circle a sentence that seems especially **abstract** or uses terms that feel broad and more difficult to picture. (For instance, in a personal essay, this could be a line like "Then one day I learned that I had to work really hard to make a difference.")

Write down that abstract sentence at the top of a fresh page.

Next, freewrite for 5 minutes to "explode" the sentence. What meaning are you trying to get at with each abstraction? Try to describe a scene or moment that your audience could visualize, whether it is about your own life, or about a music video you're analyzing rhetorically. When in doubt, draw on the senses—what we can see, smell, hear, taste, or touch.

Share your new "exploded" paragraph with a neighbor; see how you've each expanded upon your initial sentence.

IV

Revising and Reflecting

27. Re-Seeing the Revision Process

Carl Schlachte

Revision is like registering to vote. We're told to do it, often without being told how or why. Maybe we even have a sense that revision is something we "should be doing," but don't know exactly what steps to take to accomplish it. When we get comments on a project we're working on, the natural inclination is to do something with them. At best, this may lead us to decide that we're going to revise our work. But it still doesn't answer the question of how to revise.

The real answer as to how to revise depends on the project itself: there's no foolproof revision strategy that will work in every instance. Revision is also a lot like pre-writing; there are many different strategies to try, and different strategies may work better for different writers. Still, in approaching revision, it's important to keep several perspectives in mind: first, **revision is not the same as editing**, and second, while your instructor expects you to revise based on their feedback, **instructor feedback is only one way to consider revising**. Your own perspective is just as valuable when considering what to change.

> "Revision is also a lot like pre-writing; there are many different strategies to try, and different strategies may work better for different writers."

It's also important to remember that **revision takes effort**: it is writing just as much as the process of invention or drafting is. Working with text that exists may be easier than generating new text, but this doesn't mean revision is easy. Revision is a chance to take another look at our work and to improve it. It is literally a re-seeing. There is also rarely one right way forward; think of revision as an experiment.

Although this chapter focuses on revision as part of the *writing* process, **many of these revision strategies can apply just as well to a variety of multimodal projects.** No matter what you're working on—a speech, presentation, poster, t-shirt design, or anything else—keeping the principles of revision in mind supports the success of any text.

» Revision Is Not Editing

There's nothing wrong with editing, but it's important to point out that editing is different from revision. **Editing involves making minor changes to an essay, in order to clean it up, or polish it.** If you've ever asked someone to help look at your essay to pick out grammar mistakes, punctuation issues, or spelling errors, you've asked them to help you edit your essay. Making sure your essay's citations are properly formatted is also editing. These elements are helpful, and they make a difference in how your essay is read. Anyone reading an essay with persistent grammar inconsistencies or typos will doubt the credibility of its author. Similarly, if citations are missing important information, like the title of the book or website they come from, a reader may doubt the reliability of the information from that source. Editing aids an author's ethos by address-ing the format, citations, spelling, punctuation, mechanics, or other lower-order issues that could detract from their writing's effectiveness. But in comparison to revision, editing is a more surface-level task that should be saved for last. It doesn't make sense to correct small details in a section you're going to heavily rewrite or completely eliminate. Editing works best when the rest of the essay is solidly in place.

"While editing might be like filling a pothole in a road, revision might be analogous to rerouting the road entirely, to smooth it out over a larger distance."

If editing can be seen as "fixing" problems in an essay, revision can be seen as a larger process of "redesigning" the essay in significant ways. While editing might be like filling a pothole in a road, revision might be analogous to rerouting the road entirely, to smooth it out over a larger distance. While editing deals with issues like style and mechanics, revision addresses **higher-order concerns** like your thesis, analysis, support, research, and organization. Revision can even involve approaching an essay with a new thought process. **Anything about a piece of writing can be changed in revision; there's no limit to how far you can go.** The challenge to such a broad task is that it may involve changing, or even doing away with, portions of your writing that you worked very hard on. This often makes writers reluctant to revise; we have a natural inclination not to get rid of our hard work. However, just like every source you find while doing research may not ultimately make it into your essay, part of the writing effort involves selecting what actually does or doesn't belong in the text. Being open to revision means being able to look critically at our writing and feeling comfortable with taking out parts we labored over to make the writing better as a whole.

» Revising in Response to Instructor and Peer Feedback

Every instructor is different, which means that every instructor has different priorities when responding to essays. This means that any feedback you receive will be unique—it will reflect ideas about the assignment, your ideas about writing, your instructor's ideas about writing, and the rhetorical situation of the essay. When it comes to your peers, each of them will also bring a unique perspective to your work. This is one reason that peer review is so helpful, because of the wealth of ideas it allows you to draw on. It also means that you may receive a wide variety of suggestions. With so many factors affecting what feedback you receive, there will be many ways to respond to any comment. There are no inflexible rules. Thus, it may be helpful to ask yourself several questions about your essay and the comments about it:

+ **What patterns do I see in the feedback I've been given?** For example, maybe several comments are asking me to look at my organization, even if they say different things, like, "Does this paragraph belong here?" "How does this idea fit in with this argument?" or "Try adding a transition." Recognizing a pattern in the comments you receive can help you identify what areas of your essay you should focus on. Moreover, if you have noticed a trend in the feedback on one essay, it would be a good idea to look at your other essays to see if the same trend needs attention there, too.

+ **How successfully is my essay addressing the assignment?** Meeting the assignment requirements is always one of the key criteria by which any instructor evaluates an essay. You can try modeling the instructor's perspective for yourself by carefully and critically comparing your essay with the assignment and asking yourself, "What, specifically, is the prompt asking me to do?" Jot down the concrete things you think the assignment is asking for. Then ask yourself, "Where can I find these in my essay?" See if you can pinpoint concrete instances where you're meeting the concepts you've noted. Finally, you can ask yourself: "Am I meeting all of the criteria?" "Are there parts of my essay where I'm not meeting them?" and "What parts of my essay best meet these criteria?" Doing this can help you see your writing from a different perspective—as a *reader*. Often, as writers, we are too close to our work to be able to evaluate it fairly. Here, we are tasked with seeing through the eyes of the prompt.

+ **If my instructor is using a rubric, how successfully is my writing addressing it?** In this instance, you'll want to follow the same sort of method as before, but instead of modeling the perspective of the assignment, you'll try to identify the criteria the rubric is asking for and see how your essay is addressing those ideas. Prompts and rubrics are ways for instructors to communicate to you what they value in the assignment you're working on, so if you're wondering how your instructor is reading your essay, these documents may be a good indication.

A final word on instructor feedback: be careful about falling into the trap of thinking "if I fix everything my instructor commented on, I'll get an A." Note that the verb "fix" implies an editing approach, not a revisionary one. But beyond that, no instructor's comments are exhaustive; they may not account for everything you could change about an essay. Because we regard writing as a process, your instructor's feedback may be a good starting point to help spur your revisions, but addressing them doesn't represent an end goal in and of itself. Also keep in mind that your instructor's feedback, while valuable, represents just one perspective on your essay. Your peers' comments are others. Then, there is your own: in order to undertake revision successfully, you'll need to decide what you want to revise for yourself.

» Self-Guided Revision Strategies

One of the biggest hurdles we face when attempting self-guided revision is knowing what to change. We did the best work we could the first time around; if we didn't know how to make it better then, how will we know how to make it better now? This is why instructor or peer feedback can be a helpful starting point to show us some places we might wish to focus on in revision. In fact, **any outside perspective might help us see things about our essay we had trouble seeing for ourselves,** and so we might wish to take our essay to the Writing Center or ask a trusted friend or colleague to give us feedback. These perspectives, too, can help give us an idea of what to focus on.

Outside perspectives are helpful, but they aren't a complete solution. One important tactic to try is letting some time pass before returning to an essay to change it. If we wait and gain some distance, we can return to our work with a fresh set of eyes. I let a few months pass between first writing this chapter and starting to revise it, and that helped me see lots that I wanted to change (including adding this paragraph). I also sought advice from the editors of this textbook, and used their comments and questions to hone my thoughts.

Once we've sought out other perspectives and addressed their feedback, if we feel like we're not ready to show our work to someone else, or if we are somehow still unsatisfied with our essay, we also need strategies to approach our work in new ways, for ourselves. This is, after all, our writing, and we ought to be able to meet our own high standards for our work, too. In light of that, here are some strategies by which you can try to revise different major aspects of an essay. Some of these strategies are questions you can ask yourself, while others can be seen as experiments to see if the result is better. Some of these strategies may create effective results, and some may not. **It's important to try different strategies to see what works for you, which may depend on the context in which you're writing.**

Revising Thesis Statements

+ Look at your thesis statement. **Write down every possible way in which your thesis could be proven wrong. Does your argument account for these possibilities?** You don't need to address all of them directly in your essay, but consider whether any of them could represent a fatal flaw that undoes your argument. If so, try changing your thesis so that it addresses this idea. Doing this will also mean that the rest of your essay should follow suit: a revised argument will require revised support and analysis.

+ This method is similar to the last, except this time, **try breaking down your thesis into its smallest parts: what has to be true in order for your thesis to be true?** For example, let's say my argument is that paper books are more readable than e-books. I first need to establish what "readable" means in this context. Then I need to examine how both paper books and e-books meet or don't meet this criteria, being specific about the ways they do that. Does my essay address all of these points? Covering them will make the foundation of an argument stronger.

+ **Imagine what if, having made the argument you have already made, you had to argue for its opposite?** How would you do so, given what you've established in your original position? Considering your own argument as a person who opposes it allows you to see it in a more objective way and gives you a perspective on where its weaknesses may lie. (For more on arguments and counter-arguments, see Ch. 18, "Thesis Statements," and Ch. 19, "Staking Your Claim.")

Revising Supporting Evidence

+ Here's an arbitrary change you could make to test the quality of your sources: **if you had to drop one source entirely, which would you choose, and why?** What is your weakest source? What is adding the least to your argument? What is your strongest source? Which one is so crucial that you'd never give it up? What is that source doing for your argument? Considering questions like these allows you to see what work your sources are doing for you—and what they're not.

+ This one's pretty simple: **find a new source and weave it into an existing paragraph.** This method is more effective if you know, from the previous point, what sources aren't helping you as much as they could be, or if, from before that, you know what part of your argument needs bolstering. Adding a new source can help build your credibility, in addition to supporting your claims more fully.

◆ **Consider if there's a different kind of support you could incorporate into your essay** that hasn't been used before. If your essay relies on analytical sources, could you find data/statistics that go along with them? If you've got lots of statistics, is there more narrative information you could use to demonstrate how this data takes effect? If you're only drawing on personal experience, what about more objective, secondary sources—or vice versa? Your instructor may have specified what kinds of support are appropriate for your assignment, so remember to follow those guidelines. Supporting evidence can take many different forms, and each one fits a slightly different goal. Having multiple kinds of support adds depth to your evidence.

Revising Organization

◆ **Consider each paragraph individually,** first by summarizing it to yourself in a sentence or two. What do you think this paragraph is about? You might write this summary in the document's margin. Once you have that down, consider: are there parts of this paragraph that aren't about what I thought this paragraph was about? If so, they should be moved elsewhere, or cut out completely. Is what I said the paragraph is about what the paragraph says it is about? This means taking a look at the topic sentence. Maybe I wrote that the paragraph claimed that paper books are appealing because we can physically interact with them, but the topic sentence says it's arguing that paper books are more engaging. These are slightly, but importantly, different claims. Since your topic sentence should clearly address what the paragraph is about, if you notice a discrepancy between your idea of the paragraph and what the paragraph says, find a way to reconcile them. Consider using a reverse outline to identify discrepancies and sites for revision. (For more, see the reverse outlining section in Ch. 17, "Pre-Writing Strategies.")

◆ Once you've ensured that what the paragraphs say they're about is actually what they're addressing, **look at the topic sentences of each of your paragraphs together. Does their order make sense?** It's easier to see, without the buffers of detail and analysis that make up our paragraphs, if the connections between our ideas are logical. Maybe I have three paragraphs that say that paper books give physical feedback, that e-books can be more visually complex, and that people have been writing in books for centuries. By putting them side by side, I can see that it would make much more sense to switch the places of the first and second paragraphs, because the first and third are both developing a thought about the ways people physically use books.

♦   Another way to see where your argument is strongest is similar to the first bullet point about supporting evidence: **if you had to drop your weakest paragraph, which one would you choose?** Forcing yourself to make this hard choice leads you to examine your paragraphs critically, to see where they are stronger and weaker. Equally revealing would be your rationale: if you had to explain why you chose to drop one, you might start to see what its weaknesses are, on its own, or for your argument. Maybe you dropped it because, even though it's crucial to proving your thesis, it wasn't doing a very good job. Or maybe you dropped it because it wasn't as related to your argument as you initially thought. Your reasons will tell you something important about how your paragraphs and your argument relate.

» Conclusion

Writing is a process, and revision is an important part of that process. In many cases, revision may be the majority of that process. While it takes time to get the initial words on a page, once they're there, we can continue working with them forever. For that reason, it may be helpful to regard revision as a process of experimentation. The goal, of course, is to make our writing better, but in order to do so we may have to try strategies that don't work out. At the same time, **if we aren't willing to occasionally attempt drastic changes, we may not ever see significant results.** The invention of the airplane got people into the air, but it took a drastic rethinking of how flight worked in order to send astronauts into space. Really strong revision requires this kind of departure from our normal modes of writing; that's what makes it hard. It's also what makes it, when taken seriously, so effective.

> "The invention of the airplane got people into the air, but it took a drastic rethinking of how flight worked in order to send astronauts into space. Really strong revision requires this kind of departure from our normal modes of writing; that's what makes it hard."

Quick Revision Checklist

☐ Read your work aloud

☐ Wait before revising to gain perspective

☐ Ask others for feedback

☐ Imagine your work from the perspective of the audience

☐ Consider the fit between your work and the assignment

☐ Look for patterns in your feedback

☐ Critically examine your thesis, support, and organization

28. De-Stressing the Peer Review Process

Marc Keith

Sharing our writing with others can make us feel vulnerable, but it also enables us to engage with the rhetorical component of *audience* on a deeper level. Each time we sit down to compose a text, we imagine our audiences and their expectations, but the opportunity to *be* the audience is an entirely different experience. Peer review also highlights that any text can have multiple audiences, such as your peers and your instructor, and it is important to keep all of these audiences in mind. Being mindful of multiple audiences while reading a text reasserts the rhetorical nature of peer review and helps us develop a deeper understanding of how rhetoric influences the writing process. Frequently, students believe the purpose of peer review is to find every single mistake in their classmates' papers. As this chapter argues, however, this kind of mentality leads to a confrontational and judgmental situation that leaves both rhetor and reviewer lacking confidence and results in comments that are ultimately not helpful. Instead, you should think of peer review as an opportunity to improve your writing through friendly and constructive conversation.

> "Being mindful of multiple audiences while reading a text reasserts the rhetorical nature of peer review and helps us develop a deeper understanding of how rhetoric influences the writing process."

» Reconceptualizing Peer Review

Peer review is a helpful part of the writing process because it allows you to see how a peer interpreted and executed an assignment and gives you feedback on your own writing. Some students approach peer review nervous about sharing their writing with classmates or insecure about their own ability to provide helpful feedback. These feelings may arise from past peer review experiences in which students felt pressured to find all of their classmates' mistakes, both to preserve their reputation and to help their classmates. Unfortunately, this model of peer review inevitably leads to a mindset of *judgment* rather than *constructive criticism*, which then inhibits the flow of conversation. Judgment is a pronouncement, a conclusion that is not meant to be challenged, whereas constructive criticism leaves room for questions, comments, and revision. Peer review is not a competition where you try to appear smarter than your peers. Rather, peer review should be thought of as a conversation amongst friends or colleagues where you offer each other advice and suggestions on how to improve your writing.

Reframing peer review as a conversation rather than a competition relieves both the sense of vulnerability and the pressure to provide "smart" and "impressive" feedback. Just as in a conversation, however, you want to make sure you stay on topic and provide relevant comments. When it comes to peer review, this means gearing your feedback towards *revision* rather than *editing*. (For more, see Ch. 27, "Re-Seeing the Revision Process.") While editing and proofreading are important steps in the writing process, and can certainly play a role in peer review, your comments should help the rhetor address larger concerns. While participating in peer review, consider providing feedback on aspects such as the strength of the thesis, the overall organization and flow of the paper, and the clarity of the writer's logic. Unlike smaller editing issues such as typos, which writers can often identify on their own, these larger issues of organization, logic, and clarity can be much more difficult to spot and are more vital to an effective argument. In our own minds, our ideas seem clear, and it frequently takes an outside audience to identify what gets lost when transferring these ideas from our thoughts to the page.

Not only does peer review provide a real audience, it also provides an audience of equals. Aside from relieving the pressures mentioned above, working with peers rather than your instructor opens avenues for different types of feedback. For example, while your instructor will likely focus his or her assessment on the guidelines laid out in the prompt after the assignment is completed, your peers offer suggestions during the writing process. Remember, you are working with other students who, like you, are taking several classes and are feeling many of the same strains and stresses that you are. Collaborating with other students through peer review can help you figure out the writing process and more quickly identify strengths and areas for improvement in your own writing.

» Useful Issues to Consider in Peer Review

You should always pay attention to your instructor's guidelines for an assignment. But, if you and a peer have created drastically different projects based on the same prompt, do not assume that one of you did the assignment wrong; check with your instructor for clarification. During peer review, your instructor may ask you to look for very specific issues related to the assignment prompt (i.e., the prompt requires five outside sources, so your instructor specifically asks you to look for that), or may have a certain process they want you to follow. Frequently, your instructor will make a concrete assignment for the peer review, and in this case you should be sure to do what the instructor asks. This does not mean you cannot informally provide feedback for your peers. **Just getting together and talking about your writing and ideas with friends can be a highly productive and relaxing activity that can help prepare you for the tasks set up by your instructor.** The following list provides some general questions to consider when providing feedback for a peer that applies to most of the assignments you will encounter in College Writing courses:

+ The thesis: Does the thesis make an arguable claim? Is the thesis clearly identifiable and located in a logical place? Is the thesis too vague/too narrow?

+ Paragraph organization: Does each paragraph have a clear topic sentence? Does the topic relate to the rhetor's main argument/point? Does the material in each paragraph relate back to the topic sentence?

+ Use of outside material: Does the rhetor include relevant examples from trustworthy sources? Are outside quotes successfully integrated into the text and properly cited?

+ Overall structure/organization: Does the paper progress from one point to another in a manner that makes sense? Does the rhetor offer sufficient analysis and commentary to explain how his/her outside examples support his/her claims?

+ Ethos: Is the rhetor using an appropriate tone for his/her audience? Does the rhetor handle alternate or opposing views in a respectful way that will not alienate the audience?

+ Relevance to Prompt: Does the assignment meet the requirements laid out in the assignment prompt?

» Reviewing Different Types of Assignments

The suggestions above are applicable to most assignments you will encounter in your College Writing courses, but what about projects that require more than just a written text, such as a presentation? Or what if part of the project involves creative writing in addition to analytical writing? What if the assignment is a written project, but something other than a typical essay, such as an annotated bibliography? **When it comes to dealing with multimodal projects and alternative written genres, the key to providing a useful peer review is to remember that rhetoric applies to *all texts*, not just written texts.** (See

Ch. 26, "Exploring Alternative Genres" for examples of other genres of written texts and Ch. 12, "Writing a Visual Analysis" for on how to analyze rhetorical choices in visual texts.)

Let's take a look at some concrete examples of different types of projects you may encounter and the types of comments you can make to help your fellow rhetors.

Example 1

Your instructor has given you a rhetorical analysis assignment with the following prompt:

> For this project, choose a conflict with two clear sides. You are a participant in this conflict, and have chosen to abandon your current side in favor of the opposition (ex. Harry Potter choosing to join Voldemort). You must compose two creative texts explaining your actions to members of each side of the conflict (ex. A video message left behind for Ron and Hermoine, and a letter to Voldemort). In addition to the two creative texts, you will then write a 3–4 page analysis that explains your rhetorical decisions in each text. The purpose of this project is to emphasize the importance of audience awareness. You should also discuss all three appeals and at least two of the canons in your analysis.

While you may be comfortable offering feedback on the analysis portion of this project, dealing with the creative texts could be more difficult. Remembering that the project needs to function as a whole is helpful. If the rhetor claims in his/her analysis that "Creative Text 1" makes a lot of credible claims but you see the emotional appeal being used more, that indicates a weakness either in the analysis or the creative text that must be addressed. Peer review creates an opportunity to interrogate this disconnect, not by calling out the rhetor and saying "this is wrong" or "doesn't make sense," but by asking the rhetor to explain what they meant. By giving the rhetor time to talk through their ideas, the complexity of the argument can flourish and grow as the rhetor becomes more self consciously aware of their thought processes. This interrogative and exploratory approach also helps to ensure a balanced review that takes into account all the separate parts of the project and emphasizes how these different parts work together.

Another strategy for dealing with unusual projects is to pay close attention to all the materials your instructor provides. In the above example, the prompt explicitly identifies a key goal of the project: developing an awareness of who the audience is. Do the creative texts and the analysis achieve this purpose? If not, how could the project be improved to better meet this goal? Also notice that the instructor has asked for a discussion of all three appeals and at least two canons in the analysis. As a logistical matter, you should check to see if your peer has mentioned the required elements, but you should not let your analysis stop there. Remember, you want your feedback to be probing and thoughtful, so even if a paper meets all the guidelines laid out by the instructor, ask yourself how successfully it meets those guidelines, and where it could it be improved.

Example 2

Perhaps towards the end of the semester your instructor asks you to expand your rhetorical awareness to multimodal texts, or texts that incorporate visual, aural, and written components. A prompt for such an assignment may go something like this:

> For this project, you need to choose one specific issue that is related to our class theme (environmental rhetoric). Your job is to convince your classmates to take action on whatever issue you have chosen by composing some sort of visual component (infographic, short film, powerpoint, etc.) and a final five minute oral presentation. You will then compose a brief (3–4 pages) artist statement that explains and justifies the rhetorical choices you made for each text.

Peer reviewing such a complex project can be daunting, but grounding your comments in rhetoric and focusing on issues of global revision can make the task manageable. Just as every word in a written assignment should be purposeful and focused on the primary argument, all components of a multimodal project should work together to support the rhetor's main claim.

If the rhetor is giving a presentation about the dangers of climate change, for example, but fills their PowerPoint presentation with images of people relaxing on tropical beaches, you could comment on how the images undermine the author's purpose. As another example, maybe the rhetor was a little too enthusiastic about using all of the neat effects included in PowerPoint so that you have a difficult time following the presentation. These problems, while resulting from the visual and aural aspects of the presentation, can be directly related to the issues of organization and clarity we identified earlier in the chapter as key issues to focus on in peer review. A rhetorical approach to peer review makes room for honest reactions, which can be especially helpful when working with a multimodal presentation. Simply telling the rhetor how the presentation made you feel or what it made you think about overall, even if you cannot completely articulate why, can be useful when revising a large project with many parts.

» Using Rhetorical Knowledge to Offer Advice

Now that we have identified some primary areas of concern and explored different types of projects you may encounter in peer review settings, we need to address how to effectively offer feedback. The easiest way to think about offering feedback is to remember the Golden Rule: treat others as you want to be treated. Most of us want to get good grades on our assignments and getting help on a project helps us accomplish this goal.

On the other hand, no one likes to hear that someone does not like their writing or that they have done a bad job responding to a specific assignment. The key to finding a balance between helping your peers and offending them is (surprise!) rhetoric. Remember that your audience for your comments is your classmates, people who, like you, want help improving their papers. This means you should not be afraid to offer feedback, but you should do it in a kind and respectful way. Some guiding concepts for providing helpful feedback are below:

+ **Always be respectful.** In our good-natured desire to be honest and helpful, we can often end up being disrespectful without meaning to. For example, something like "I don't really like your thesis, it sounds too vague," is more constructive than "Your thesis needs some serious work," but still comes off as harsh and judgmental. By focusing your feedback on the rhetorical components and the writing rather on your own personal likes and dislikes, your comments will sound less personal and judgmental: "Your thesis seems a little broad. I think it would really help your paper if you made the thesis more specific by talking about *how* the author is using rhetoric." If you do come across a passage that needs serious reworking, try offering possible solutions rather than just pointing out what is wrong. For example, if the rhetor has a paragraph that lacks focus and contains examples that do not seem to connect with the topic sentence, rather than saying "This paragraph is long and confusing," try something like "I'm getting confused in this paragraph. Is the main point supposed to be Bob Dylan's use of pathos or the importance of rhetorical memory in his songs? Are you trying to say that memory is used to build pathos?" The first response does nothing except embarrass and frustrate your peer, whereas the second example gently points out a place of weakness and asks productive questions that may actually help your classmate during revision.

+ **Always be thorough.** Just as mean and offensive language is disrespectful, one word responses and surface level observations indicate a lack of caring and respect for your classmates. Aside from being disrespectful, one word responses are rarely helpful. If you are not willing to put in the time and effort to help your peers, why should they want to spend time helping you? Even a positive one word comment, such as "good!" is not helpful unless you accompany it with more information that explains what you found useful or well-written. One way to develop more in-depth feedback is to address the "how" and/or "why." This applies to both positive and critical feedback. If you think something really works in the rhetor's paper, point it out and explain *why* and/or *how* it works. For example, rather than just saying your classmate's thesis is "good," explain *why* it is good: "I really like your thesis because it clearly states your position and seems focused without being too narrow."

- **Include positive and constructively critical feedback.** Pointing out where your classmate has done something well can not only serve as an example for future revisions, but also help build confidence. You can even pair constructive criticism with positive feedback: "Your paragraph organization on page two is really great. The topic sentence matches the content well. Maybe try to reproduce this structure in the last paragraph on page three, where your examples don't seem to match up with your topic sentence."

- **Do not be afraid of phrasing your recommendations as comments or suggestions.** After all, the text remains the intellectual property of the rhetor, and they ultimately decide whether or not to use your feedback. Ordering or demanding your peers to fix something will damage your ethos and make your classmates less likely to listen to your advice, no matter how relevant it is. Instead of saying "this example doesn't fit with the paragraph, take it out," try something like "I'm not sure I understand how this example fits in with the rest of the paragraph. Maybe you could add more analysis to clarify the connection, or move the example to the previous paragraph. I think the quote would fit in with that paragraph nicely and support your topic sentence."

> "The great thing about *peer* review is that you are working with people who have a similar knowledge base. You are not expected to know more than they do, so it is fine to not have all the answers."

While these guiding principles seem obvious, they can be difficult to put into practice. Perhaps you think something needs to be changed in an essay, but are not quite sure *how* it should be changed. The great thing about *peer* review is that you are working with people who have a similar knowledge base. You are not expected to know more than they do, so it is fine to not have all the answers. Providing these kinds of specific, probing, and constructive comments not only helps your peers, but also hones your own analytical abilities, which will help improve your own writing in the long run. (For more guidance on how to write helpful peer review comments, see the example critical reflection at Appendix I.)

» Using Rhetorical Knowledge When Receiving Comments

As previously mentioned, peer review can make us feel vulnerable, and this often causes us to act defensively when receiving feedback. Defensiveness, however, can blind us to the usefulness of our peers' comments and inhibits our ability to engage in a productive conversation. Rather than becoming offended and wanting to argue with your peers, ask them to explain in more detail why they responded the way they did. You, as the rhetor, should also feel free to respond and explain what you hoped to achieve with your writing. By having this type of conversation, we can develop a better sense of audience expectations and can recognize where and why our writing is not meeting those expectations. Finally, remember that you are working with your peers, and therefore you should not expect them to find *all* of the strengths and areas that could be improved in your paper. Even if you think you have been paired with someone who is not as strong a writer as you are, they can still offer valuable feedback from the perspective of reader/audience.

Overall, the key to a successful and enjoyable peer review is to ground your review in your rhetorical knowledge. Know your audience (your classmates), know your purpose (to provide and receive helpful feedback), and remember that you are all in this together. Peer review is not a competition to see "who the better writer is"; it is an opportunity for you to critically think about your writing process from all angles, and to help your fellow classmates along the way.

29. Writing about Your Composing Process

Jessica D. Ward

"The first product of self-knowledge is humility."

—*Flannery O'Connor*

Has anyone ever told you they write a perfect essay on their first try? Well, as you probably guessed by reading the epigraph above, they aren't being honest. If you look at some of the greatest English novelists' early manuscripts, you will see from the words added, lines crossed out, and marginal notes that great writing is a process—one that demands constant reflection and revision. Indeed, in his essay, "The Philosophy of Composition," gothic horror writer Edgar Allan Poe explains that it would be fruitful if an author would, or more importantly "could—detail, step by step" their writing process (2746). Poe also mentions in that essay that most writers want their audience to believe that they write masterpieces spontaneously "and would positively shudder at letting the public take a peep behind the scenes" (2746). Although some scholars argue that Poe might be facetious in much of this essay, this sentiment about the necessity of revealing and articulating one's composition process is particularly useful for students of College Writing to think about, especially because students are often asked, and sometimes required, to reflect and articulate in writing about their own composing processes throughout the semester. Of course, the benefits of thinking about one's processes are not limited to the College Writing classroom. Many professions require employees to provide cohesive rationales for the choices they make in their work.

> "Many professions require employees to provide cohesive rationales for the choices they make in their work."

Many students might empathize with the poets Poe speaks about who desire to keep their processes mysterious. They might find themselves cringing when their instructors tell them that they must articulate their rhetorical choices in detail. Instead of wanting to explain all of the choices they made in their works, students might hope their audience will think they produced their brilliant final work (essay, speech, brochure, poster, presentation, etc.) on their first try. Furthermore, students might find it challenging at first to articulate their writing process even if they want to do so.

Although keeping one's process a mystery might seem attractive for a number of different reasons, the work will suffer for it. For one, **College Writing requires that students reflect on their processes throughout the semester, so they must learn how to effectively explain their rhetorical choices,** much like they learn to do in analyzing Sojourner Truth's "Ain't I a Woman?" in Lauren Shook's chapter, "Reading for the Rhetorical Appeals." How might students transfer and apply the skills they learned in that chapter to an argument they make about their own work?

In the essay mentioned earlier, Poe clarifies his particular writing procedure for his infamous poem, "The Raven," which many students probably read in secondary school. He explains that his writing process is more like the steps one takes to solve a math equation than a product of happenstance (2747). Following Poe's example, then, I would like to think with you, in the remainder of this chapter, about how to conceive of your own rhetorical choices as deliberate actions, like the steps you would take in completing a math equation.

How Should I Begin? What Questions Should I Ask?

Students are asked to reflect on their writing at the end of the College Writing course. All semester, they have been furiously drafting pages upon pages or slides upon slides, depending on the genres they are working in, without having much time to consider the cumulative work they have done throughout the semester. Because of this, assignments that ask students to reflect on the choices they make in their works sometimes seem daunting, but they shouldn't be, especially if you generate reflections every time you submit work to your instructor. Some instructors assign a reflection assignment for each essay a student submits, but even if your instructor doesn't do this, you might want to respond to the following questions every time you turn in work.

Reflection Questions

1. What is the greatest strength in this particular assignment?

2. What did not work for you during this assignment?

3. What feedback did you find to be most helpful?

4. What feedback have you given your peers that you should apply to your own drafts?

5. What did you learn about time management in this assignment that you want to continue or do better while working through the next assignments?

If you answer these questions after each project, you should have quite a bit of information to help you reflect on your process throughout the semester. While still expecting well-written prose, instructors often support students in relaxing their tone, style, and formal approach to show their creativity when they write about their process. **If this type of writing makes you nervous, I encourage you to envision it as a letter, blog, e-mail, speech, or some form other than an essay.** This is your chance to make an argument about your creative choices and to practice a more "everyday" style, while still editing for mechanics, redundancy, word choice, intent, meaning, etc. (As with any assignment, always verify your instructor's expectations for the assignment.)

(For more, see Ch. 30, "Reflecting Back.")

What Broader Conversations Should I Engage with When I Write My Reflection?

In addition to your responses for the questions above, consider the following four clusters of questions as you write about your process:

1. **What adjective (or verb) describes you as a writer? What adjective (or verb) describes you as a learner?** For example, as an author, I would choose inviting, and as a learner, I would pick curious.

   As you start to brainstorm about your rhetorical choices, you may find it useful to consider what sort of author you are when you compose and what kind of audience member you are when you learn. Remember that as an author, or rhetor, you may conceive of yourself in an entirely different way than you do as an audience member. On the other hand, the verb you choose that defines you as an author may signal the expectations you have when you are an audience member, like the descriptors I chose as examples above (inviting and curious). As a learner, I define myself as curious; therefore, I want a text to invite me in and pique my curiosity. Of course, your adjectives and verbs may not engage with each other in this way, and that's fine. If it is hard for you to identify one verb for each role, that's okay too. Remember that these words should help you reveal the types of rhetorical choices you are interested in making. For example, someone who defines himself or herself as an inviting author might begin their works with a question or interesting fact or statistic. After you pick your descriptive words, you should provide evidence from your own work to support your choice. These descriptors might also serve as the foundation for your thesis statement for a reflection essay.

2. **What trends do you see in your own work?** Do you find yourself returning to specific techniques? For instance, look at how you start an essay.
Do you tend to start with a narrative or question? Are your introductions
brief? How do you organize your paragraphs? Do you switch from long
paragraphs to short ones or vice versa? Similarly, think about how you
conclude. Do you look forward to another complementary topic that your
audience might want to explore after they encounter your argument?
Finally, consider the ways you engage with secondary sources. For example,
think about how your research alters your overall argument.

After you identify these specific strategies in your own writing, consider
why you make these choices. If you have already chosen verbs that describe
you as an author and learner, consider how these specific examples might
reveal your expectations.

3. **Does your work reflect your comprehension of the rhetorical concepts
(appeals, canons—e.g., arrangement, etc.)? How does your writing or
work in other genres reflect this?**

Now that you have an idea of who you are as an author and learner and
have identified textual evidence to support your verb choice, you may add
even more nuance to your argument about your process when you engage
with the rhetorical concepts you learned this semester. At this stage, you
have the chance to explain in detail the rhetorical strategies you used in
your works. For instance, consider why you arranged your works the way
you did. What appeals did you engage with when you made your argument? Did you favor one appeal over another due to a certain argument's
topic?

4. **How did your arguments become more complex and precise over the
semester?**

What surprised you about your research or the way your project evolved
over the semester? What skills are you still working on? What aspect of
your writing or argument would you like to strengthen in the future? If
you could redo the research for one assignment, which one would it be
and why?

You might look at your thesis statements in particular and see how they
have evolved. Another approach to this question would be to look over
the comments you received on your work from your peers and instructor
and determine if there are any patterns of error that you have addressed
in revisions or subsequent works.

Don't be overwhelmed by the number of questions asked above, and don't feel like you have to answer each one of them in order. Your instructor might also offer you different questions to consider. Therefore, think of the above questions as potential guides. They will help you start to think about specific choices you make when you compose and reveal what is important to you as a writer/speaker/designer. (For more reflection questions and a sample response, turn to Appendix H.)

Consider the Rhetorical Triangle (Rhetor, Audience, Text, and Context)

As I mentioned earlier, **your critical reflection essay should be similar to an analysis essay, or a rhetorical analysis, where you write about others' works.** A few of the main differences between the two essays, though, will be that in a critical reflection essay you will have authorial insight and might have to consider multiple pieces. Despite the differences, however, you should still consider the rhetorical triangle for this reflection. (If you need to brush up on the rhetorical triangle, revisit Ch. 2, "Rhetoric in Academic Settings.")

The most identifiable point of the triangle for this type of writing assignment might be the audience, which you probably assume is your instructor. You might want to think of the audience as your College Writing class, as well. **If you think of your peers and your instructor as your audience members, you can write with the shared rhetorical vocabulary you all learned throughout the semester without worrying about having to define every term or assignment.** Notice how the rhetor has also been identified in the description above. No matter what genre you are working in, for this essay, you will be communicating your ideas to people that, at least superficially, shared a similar experience.

The final aspects of the triangle you should consider are the text and context. The text is the product you are communicating your argument in, be it an essay, speech, poster, etc. The genre you are working in, then, will dictate the possibilities and limitations of your message. It is important that you engage with these aspects, or at least consider them, in your reflection. Finally, the context of this type of assignment will depend on the particular reflection assignment your teacher asks you to complete, as well as the course and the course materials. Be sure to pay attention to specific details on the assignment sheet and to your instructor's rubric for this assignment to ensure that you address all aspects of the assignment.

The Most Important Question—What Is the Purpose of Writing About Composition?

As you have probably discovered by now, College Writing courses require students to interrogate their own composition processes. Much like the purpose of other writing assignments, an assignment that asks you about your own process illustrates your growth throughout the semester and demonstrates your understanding of rhetorical choices. This kind of reflection reveals that you are able to offer an insightful and sustained argument about your own composition and revision process. To return to the epigraph by Flannery O'Connor at the beginning of this chapter, **remember not to be afraid to speak about the hurdles you have had to overcome in your work across the semester.** If you are able to identify these obstacles, you will be able to help yourself transform into an even stronger rhetor. But, perhaps as importantly, remember to take your work seriously and to analyze your own writing as earnestly as you would someone else's.

> "Remember to take your work seriously and to analyze your own writing as earnestly as you would someone else's."

» Works Cited

O'Connor, Flannery. *Mystery and Manners: Occasional Prose*, edited by Sally Fitzgerald and Robert Fitzgerald. Farrar, Straus, and Giroux, 1969.

Poe, Edgar A. "The Philosophy of Composition." *The Heath Anthology of American Literature*, edited by Paul Lauter, 7th ed, Wadsworth, 2014, pp. 2745–754.

30. Reflecting Back:
Compiling the Portfolio and Writing the Critical Reflection Essay

Emily Hall

Immediately after people play a video game or participate in a sport, what do they do? They reflect back on how well they did. Maybe they forgot to go back and collect all the trophies in the level, or perhaps they fumbled the ball at a critical point in their game, which resulted in the team losing a few points. On the other hand, maybe they successfully finished the level or scored lots of points and won the game. Either way, they stopped, reflected, and probably thought about how to improve their actions to do better the next time.

In many ways, revising a project is similar to this moment of reflection after someone has completed a task. After finishing an essay, a student may not feel confident about what he or she has written. There might be a few awkward sentences, some rough transitions, or a too-short conclusion that merely summarizes the essay. At the same time, the essay might have a strong thesis statement, an engaging introduction, and focused organization. By revising the essay, the student can make sure that the entire work is written cohesively and coherently to better match the strong thesis/organization/introduction. The great thing about writing is that everyone can take a step back from their work, think through the ways that the reader might react to it, and revise it, both for larger, higher-order concepts and smaller, lower-order concerns. In order for students to start meaningful revisions, they first have to reflect back on their work, assessing its strengths and weaknesses, before they make changes to the essay.

» The Portfolio: Where Revision and Reflection Meet

A portfolio is a case that holds materials, often paper documents. For artists and architects, this portfolio may be a physical object that collects work samples that demonstrate their capabilities. In other instances, the portfolio may be a metaphorical holding of investments, including stocks and other financial assets. **The College Writing portfolio assignment combines the revision** and reflection process into one unique assignment.[1] Students are given the opportunity to re-write their essays, creating more complex arguments each time they produce a draft. At the beginning of the semester, new terms like "rhetorical triangle" or "context," might seem unfamiliar to most students who have not taken a college-level writing or rhetoric course, and writing about those concepts may be even more daunting. But the benefit of a revision-centered course is that as students learn more and become comfortable with terms, analysis, and rhetorical decisions, they can return to their original essays and add new layers of complexity. At the end of the semester, students can reflect back on their essays and can apply this new understanding to their earlier drafts. **Thus, the portfolio charts the progression of writing skills *and* knowledge of rhetorical concepts and decisions over the course of many drafts.**

"The great thing about writing is that everyone can take a step back from their work, think through the ways that the reader might react to it, and revise it, both for larger, higher-order concepts and smaller, lower-order concerns."

The portfolio also allows students to decide which essays or projects will be revised one more time to better show the students' best understanding of writing and rhetoric. Maybe Devon wants to revise what he considers his strongest and weakest essays, to showcase how he can improve already strong arguments and how he can strengthen weaker arguments into focused works. Conversely, maybe Zoe has a better understanding of organization, so she revises two less focused essays into two strong, coherent drafts. **Students decide which essays should be revised one more time for the portfolio, and this judgment becomes its own rhetorical act,** as students are persuading their audience that they have selected these essays as evidence of their understanding of rhetoric.

» Revising for the Portfolio: Where to Begin?

After collecting and selecting their materials, students next reflect on their work. When students begin reflecting back on their essays and writing process for the portfolio, they may be unsure about where to start. Often, their instructor has encouraged them to think about the revisions they made from draft to draft. Students can think about what changed between drafts of their project: Did the essay have to be re-organized? Why? Did the thesis statement have to be tweaked to better fit the argument? Why? Students are not only thinking about *what* changes were made, but also *why* these revisions were necessary. Maybe the students reflected on a peer's advice, instructor comments, or even

---

1. Nedra Reynolds and Elizabeth Davis define the portfolio in terms of processes: "Without…collection, selection, and some element of reflection, it wouldn't be a portfolio; it would simply be a scrapbook or a storage container" (6).

their own evolving understanding of writing. They thought about why their work would benefit from revision, and then they changed it for the portfolio.

The portfolio thus shows evidence of substantial revision. But what constitutes "substantial" revision versus merely some revision? **Students who substantially revise their projects will look at the work from a myriad of angles and will ask themselves questions** like:

+ Who was my audience?

+ Did I tailor my argument to better persuade this audience?

+ How complex is my argument?

+ Does my essay's organization convey my meaning?

+ Does my thesis statement reflect what I actually write about?

+ How does my tone affect the audience's reception of my work?

+ Do I use evidence successfully?

+ Does my essay have a "so-what" factor?

These kinds of questions lead students to critically reflect on their own work and to make the kinds of revisions that will improve the project's argument.

Writers should be cautious about confusing revision with editing their work. While having a polished essay is important and surface errors should be removed before the portfolio is submitted, these reflect lower-order concerns. Instead of fretting over correct comma placement, students would benefit from putting most of their revision effort into the higher-order concerns, such as arrangement, the strength of the argument, and whether or not they need to use less or more evidence in their essays. The reason why students would want to pay more attention to these facets is that they are the building blocks of a solid argument. If a student's essay lacks a thesis and jumps from one topic to the next, then they probably have a weak argument and thus the essay is not rhetorically persuasive. Although typos and punctuation errors can be distracting and eventually need to be removed from a essay, changing higher-order concerns reflects a deep understanding of rhetorical processes. (For a more detailed discussion, see Ch. 27, "Re-Seeing the Revision Process.")

» Critical Reflection: Where to Begin?

When students turn in their portfolio, they have a chance to explain why they chose to revise particular aspects of their project in a critical reflection essay. **This assignment can also be called a critical rationale, a process essay, or a reflection letter, among other names, but regardless of the term, it prompts the writer to think back on his or her work and to create a convincing argument for the revisions made across the portfolio.** Often an unfamiliar writing assignment, the critical reflection essay may initially seem intimidating. Students may feel anxious about reflecting on their own work and may seem puzzled by their instructor's request to specifically refer to and quote their own essays. But think of the critical reflection this way: By the end of the semester, students have read, rhetorically analyzed, critiqued, and pondered numerous non-fiction works. They have thought about the purpose of a text, considered the context within which it was written/produced, and have perhaps even surmised ways to strengthen the work. These critical thinking skills are extended to the critical reflection as students reflect on their *own* work with this new understanding of what constitutes a stronger text. (For more discussion of reflection, see Ch. 29, "Writing about Your Composing Process.")

In order to better document and explain the changes among drafts, students might want to pause after each draft and make notes about the changes they made to each essay or project and why they changed them. Instructors may have their students practice this kind of meta-reflection throughout the semester by having the student turn in a reflection sheet with each draft where the student notes the changes he/she made and why he/she made them. This is a great opportunity to practice the kind of writing necessary for a critical reflection and to think critically about why the changes were made to each draft. (For an example of reflection, see Appendix H.) Regardless of whether the instructor builds this assignment into the course, students cannot simply turn in a list of observations with their portfolios. Instead, they should produce a thesis-driven essay that uses evidence to back up its claims.

After students take note of the changes made between drafts, where do they go next? By thinking back on "why" they made particular changes to the project, students are already engaging in critical reflection. They have started to think through the rhetorical decisions they made between drafts. The critical reflection, on a prescriptive level, shows the changes that were made to each draft and provides an explanation for these revisions. But the critical reflection also allows the student to make an argument about the portfolio. After all, the portfolio is more than just a collection of drafts; it is a rhetorical act that proves the student's understanding of how his or her writing has improved over time. The reflection essay also enables the student to present claims about how his or her writing can best be understood by the reader. This essay persuades the reader that the rhetorical decisions that went into the portfolio (selecting the essays, focusing on particular revisions, or using particular rhetorical strategies within the included materials) were purposeful and indicative of the writer's improved understanding of rhetoric and growth as a rhetor. Just as they would in a rhetorical analysis, students need to show proof of their claims by using evidence from their own essays. They also need to analyze this proof to persuade the reader that these changes were fundamental to re-shaping their argument. In this way, the student engages with all of the rhetorical appeals, provides evidence, and shows how they can reflect on their own work.

» Writing the Critical Reflection Essay

But how does one go about writing an essay about writing essays? Let's imagine a student, Anna, has to begin writing her critical reflection essay. Where does she begin? After noting the changes that she made between drafts, she might ask herself a few questions: Across all of the projects, what are her strengths? Her weaknesses? How did she improve these weaknesses? How could she still improve upon these revisions? What revisions is she especially proud of? Why? How did she think of herself as a writer at the beginning of the semester? How does she view herself as a writer now?

"The critical reflection provides a justification of the portfolio's organization, and the organization is a rhetorical decision as well."

Addressing these questions is only one way that Anna can begin to reflect on herself as a writer. Maybe after considering these questions, Anna decides that she wants to focus on how her essays' organization exemplifies her new understanding of rhetoric. She then chooses two essays to revise for the portfolio: one of which covered too many topics and had a weak thesis and the other that had a more coherent organization that she further improved. She opts to write about how strengthening her thesis in the first essay made her ideas more cohesive. For the first draft, Anna wrote an essay on cloning that began with a discussion of human cloning, moved towards animal cloning, and ended with a few paragraphs on cloning trees. After receiving feedback from both her instructor and her peers that the essay seemed disorganized and lacked a central idea, Anna edited out one of the sub-topics of the essay, but still could not think of a successful thesis to tie her two ideas together. However, after writing numerous drafts of the next two essays, Anna understood that her thesis should be an argumentative statement that ties together the ideas of her essay and guides her reader through her ideas. When she sat down at the end of the semester and looked back at her first essay, she understood how to easily fix the focus of her essay with a more effective thesis.

But Anna wouldn't simply say in her critical reflection that in her first essay she changed her thesis and then note the changes by quoting the first, second, and third revisions of the thesis. Instead, she would note the changes, quote them, and then explain how these rhetorical decisions shaped her argument. This might seem like a small inclusion in the essay, but it actually impacts the rhetorical message to add more explanation that clarifies for the audience why she made the decisions she did. Consider the following examples:

> **Draft One:** "I realized that the thesis statement in my first essay wasn't very clear. So I added in a new one. The old thesis was 'Cloning can have negative impacts but it can also be beneficial.' The new one is 'Human cloning has moral drawbacks that supersede any positive benefits.' By changing the thesis, I changed the organization, flow, and arrangement of my essay."

> **Draft Two:** "I realized that the thesis in my first draft wasn't very clear, so I adjusted it for the final draft. The first one, 'Cloning can have negative impacts but it can also be beneficial,' did not convey my meaning and made my essay sound general. Since my thesis was vague, my essay turned out to be disorganized, jumping from various topics. My final draft for the portfolio has a revised thesis: 'Human cloning has moral drawbacks that supersede any positive benefits.' This thesis helped me refine my thoughts and produce a stronger essay. By refining my ideas, my organization improved. I didn't jump from topic to topic, which allowed my reader to follow the logical progression of my argument. My reorganization shows how I learned to effectively employ the rhetorical canon of arrangement."

The second draft of this critical reflection section is more rhetorically effective for many reasons. While both drafts successfully *note* that changes were made, the second provides a context for the changes. Anna honed her thesis statement because it not only helped her organization, but it also allowed her readers to clearly follow the argument. The second revision also shows Anna's audience (usually, her instructor and peer reviewers) the rhetorical decisions that she made and how her revisions changed the rhetorical effectiveness of her argument. In other words, Anna did not merely change her thesis because her peer, Writing Center consultant, or instructor advised her to; instead, she changed it to help her convey a different, clearer meaning that meets her intended purpose. (For an example critical reflection essay, see Appendix I.)

» Submitting the Portfolio and the Critical Reflection Essay

After students decide which drafts to improve, make the revisions, and draft the critical reflection essay, they have a few more decisions to make. The critical reflection provides a justification of the portfolio's organization, and the organization is a rhetorical decision as well. Students can arrange all their drafts chronologically, group together all the first, second, and final drafts, or start from weakest to strongest, or conversely, strongest to weakest draft. The organization is purely up to the student, but each organization type conveys a meaning. In many ways, the critical reflection essay is an argument about the portfolio that influences how the reader should think about the project as a whole. It convinces the reader that these essays best reflect improvement and better

> "Writing happens at the crossroads of reflection, revision, conversation, and critical thinking."

understanding of writing, drafting, and rhetorical concepts. The portfolio's arrangement thus influences how the reader interprets the student's progression as a writer. This arrangement will also be affected by how the portfolio will be given to the instructor. If the portfolio is turned in online or includes digital content, students should determine how to best layout their work. Conversely, if the instructor requires a physical copy, students can think about how to order their materials to present a polished document.

» In Reflection

It's worth noting that no one can produce perfect writing that does not need revision. **Every writer, whether they are a novice or a published author, has to go through a series of drafts.** Like anything else, writing can always be improved. No one achieves 100% completion the first time they play a complicated video game, and no one unilaterally wins a game without ever having to improve. **Writing happens at the crossroads of reflection, revision, conversation, and critical thinking.** Instructors, peers, and Writing Center consultants will all provide feedback, but negotiating that feedback and deciding what should be prioritized are the skills that are reinforced in a portfolio-centered class. By the end of the semester, students will better understand how writing works and will be more confident about the revisions they make to their assignments. They will also be able to look back and understand how to improve their work, whatever the task at hand.

» Work Cited

Reynolds, Nedra, and Elizabeth Davis. *Portfolio Teaching: A Guide for Instructors*. Bedford/St. Martin's, 2013.

» Teaching Text

Questions for Discussion

1. For the Portfolio assignment, you will select an essay (or perhaps two) to revise further to demonstrate your writerly growth. How do you decide which essay(s) to revise? What would be the benefit of revising your weakest essays(s)? Your strongest?

2. If you are working with the Curated Portfolio, how do you know what documents to include? What does curation mean? How will you sort among your various in-class writing, free writes, pre-writes, and assignments to create your Portfolio? How will you give it a sense of unity?

3. What does it mean to reflect on your writing? How do you reflect on your writing as you are writing it? How do you reflect on it after you turn it in and receive comments back?

» Class Activities

1. On the first day of class, ask students to write down three characteristics of what they believe constitutes "effective" writing. After a few minutes of brainstorming, the whole class should share the characteristics they came up with on the board, talking through their justifications for each one.

   Two weeks before the semester ends, ask students to take out this list and to re-assess it, adding their more complex understanding of what constitutes "effective" writing underneath their original thoughts in a short paragraph.

2. When students begin the process of selecting their documents to revise, ask them to generate a list of questions to ask themselves as they begin to revise. Try to move beyond obvious questions like "what does my professor mean when they say 'X'?"

   Encourage students to create more reflective and conceptual questions like: "If I make these additions, what will need to change in the rest of the essay?" or "How can I further emphasize what is at stake for my argument now that I have included an opposing side?" As a class, generate a huge list of questions like these so students can begin reflecting on the choices they are making and *why* they make them.

Contributors

Lilly Berberyan
Brenta Blevins
Amanda Bryan
Erik Cofer
Emily Hall
Kristine Lee
Kellyn Poole Luna
Meghan H. McGuire
Lauren Shook
Chelsea Skelley

Appendices

Appendices

Appendix A. An Example of an Annotated Text 219

Appendix B. Sample Prompt for a Rhetorical Analysis Essay.. 221

Appendix C. Sample Outlines... 223

Appendix D. The Annotated Bibliography 227

Appendix E. Sample Pre-Writing Webbing Exercise 229

Appendix F. Transition Words Table..................................... 230

Appendix G. Sample MEAL Plan Paragraph.......................... 231

Appendix H. Sample Self-Reflection Questions
and Answers.. 232

Appendix I. Sample Critical Reflection Essay
with Peer Review... 235

Appendix A. An Example of an Annotated Text

In order to put the close reading and annotating strategies discussed in Chapter 10 into practice, let's look at a brief excerpt from the beginning of Elie Wiesel's famous speech "The Perils of Indifference," delivered to President Clinton, the First Lady, and Congress on April 12, 1999 as part of the Millennium Lecture Series.

> And now, I stand before you, Mr. President—Commander-in-Chief of the army that freed me, and tens of thousands of others—and I am filled with a profound and abiding gratitude to the American people. "Gratitude" is a word that I cherish. Gratitude is what defines the humanity of the human being. And I am grateful to you, Hillary, or Mrs. Clinton, for what you said, and for what you are doing for children in the world, for the homeless, for the victims of injustice, the victims of destiny and society. And I thank all of you for being here.
>
> We are on the threshold of a new century, a new millennium. What will the legacy of this vanishing century be? How will it be remembered in the new millennium? Surely it will be judged, and judged severely, in both moral and metaphysical terms. These failures have cast a dark shadow over humanity: two World Wars, countless civil wars, the senseless chain of assassinations (Gandhi, the Kennedys, Martin Luther King, Sadat, Rabin), bloodbaths in Cambodia and Algeria, India and Pakistan, Ireland and Rwanda, Eritrea and Ethiopia, Sarajevo and Kosovo; the inhumanity in the gulag and the tragedy of Hiroshima. And, on a different level, of course, Auschwitz and Treblinka. So much violence; so much indifference.

Although additional research is often required in order to understand the broader historical or political background of a piece of writing, **a great deal can be revealed by paying attention to basic contextual information like author, title, date, and method of delivery.** This information allows us to determine the intended audience of a piece, and knowing the audience helps us better analyze the effectiveness of the author's rhetorical choices.

For instance, knowing that Wiesel's speech was delivered to an audience of prominent American government officials, including the current President, makes me recognize that the stakes of his argument are high. He is not only speaking to the public; he is directing his argument to specific individuals who are in positions of power. I also recognize Elie Wiesel as the author of the autobiographical novel *Night*, so I know that he is a Holocaust survivor and a credible speaker when it comes to discussions of violence and indifference. The fact that he presented his speech at the very end of the twentieth century also helps explain its nostalgic and hopeful tone. He is reflecting on the past century and imagining what the future one will hold.

Utilizing this basic context information can help me establish a foundation for my reading, and I can approach my annotations with more intention and critical awareness. After closely reading and annotating the text, my copy of the passage might look something like the following:

Audience = President, First Lady, Congress

Interesting | And now, I stand before you, Mr. President—Commander-in-Chief of the army that freed me, and tens of thousands of others—and I am filled with a profound and abiding gratitude to the American people. "Gratitude" is a word that I cherish. Gratitude is what defines the humanity of the human being. And I am grateful to you, Hillary, or Mrs. Clinton, for what you said, and for what you are doing for children in the world, for the homeless, for the victims of injustice, the victims of destiny and society. And I thank all of you for being here.

He's beginning with praise

Repeats gratitude

Important questions | We are on the threshold of a new century, a new millennium. What will the legacy of this vanishing century be? How will it be remembered in the new millennium? Surely it will be judged, and judged severely, in both moral and metaphysical terms. These failures have cast a dark shadow over humanity: two World Wars, countless civil wars, the senseless chain of assassinations (Gandhi, the Kennedys, Martin Luther King, Sadat, Rabin), bloodbaths in Cambodia and Algeria, India and Pakistan, Ireland and Rwanda, Eritrea and Ethiopia, Sarajevo and Kosovo; the inhumanity in the gulag and the tragedy of Hiroshima. And, on a different level, of course, Auschwitz and Treblinka. So much violence; so much indifference.

1999

Global examples

Who are these people? Why are they included?

Powerful example because he's a Holocaust survivor

Notice the different types of annotations present in this passage. I have highlighted important sentences and circled unfamiliar words, and I am making observations as well as asking questions. Most importantly, I am engaging with and talking back to the text.

As you can see, this stage of the writing process is messy, but it is essential! It is the challenging process of thinking through a text, making connections, forming conclusions, and providing interpretations. This skill takes practice, but it will be vital inside and outside the College Writing classroom.

Appendix B. Sample Prompt for a Rhetorical Analysis Essay

Paper 1: Rhetorical Analysis

Due Dates

+ Thursday, Sept. 6—Peer Review

+ Thursday, Sept. 13—Revised Draft for Grade

+ Thursday, Nov. 29—Revised for Portfolio (with both peer-reviewed and graded draft)

Assignment

For this assignment, you can choose to expand on your short rhetorical analysis of Jefferson or Stanton, *or* choose another essay (see below) and write an extensive, 3- to 4-page rhetorical analysis of it. You need to think about the message of the essay and show **how** the author communicates the message to the audience.

Purpose

This assignment specifically corresponds with the following SLOs:

1. Critically evaluate written, oral, and/or visual arguments;

2. Construct cogent, evidence-based arguments;

3. Identify and employ fundamental rhetorical concepts including the rhetorical triangle, the canons, and/or the appeals in both formal and informal discourse;

4. Summarize, quote, paraphrase, and synthesize source material in support of an argument.

Essay Choices
(all found in *50 Essays*)

+ Stanton, "Declaration of Sentiments and Resolutions" (379–382)

+ Jefferson, "The Declaration of Independence" (191–195)

+ Sojourner Truth, "Ain't I a Woman?" (410–411)

+ Audre Lorde, "The Fourth of July" (239–242)

+ Martin Luther King, Jr., "Letter from Birmingham Jail" (203–219)

Writing the Paper

1. Provide a brief context for the essay you are analyzing.

2. What message is the author delivering to the audience and how is this accomplished (Thesis)?

3. Identify and analyze the rhetorical triangle, the appeals, and the canons.

4. For the sake of cohesion, you should consider how you will organize your paper—by the appeals, by rhetorical triangle, etc.

5. Include examples and quotes from your selected essay.

Requirements

+ Title; example: "Ethos in American Spirit Tobacco Ad" not "Paper 1-Ad Analysis"

+ Length: 3–4 pages (this means at least three **full** pages)

+ MLA format

+ Attach grading rubric

+ Staple or paperclip your paper

Student Name

Instructor Name

Course

DD Month YYYY

Outline

Rhetorical Analysis of Sojourner Truth's "Ain't I a Woman?"

I. INTRODUCTION

    A. Establish rhetorical context of Truth's speech

    B. Truth uses rhetorical questions, draws attention to her own body, and employs Christian allusions to persuade her audience to see her as a woman deserving the same rights as white women.

II. BODY PARAGRAPH: Truth's Use of Logos

    A. "Ain't I a woman?" Answer is "yes"

    B. Draws attention to stereotypes, differences in ways women are treated, but argues they're still women

III. BODY PARAGRAPH: Truth's Body as Evidence in Logical Argument, Pathos

    A. Repeats "Ain't I a woman?" (Logos)

    B. Draws attention to physical body: "Look at me! Look at my arm! I have ploughed and planted, and gathered into barns, and no man could head me!" (Logos)

    C. Whipped by a slave-master

        a. Logos: Implicit argument that she's even more deserving of rights because of what her body has endured

        b. Pathos: audience sympathy

    D. Claims motherhood: children sold to slavery (Pathos)

IV. BODY PARAGRAPH: Truth's Use of Pathos

    A. Religious allusions

    B. "these women together"

    C. Uses humor: "out of kilter"

V. CONCLUSION

    A. Persuasiveness of Truth's speech in her context

    B. How Truth's speech is still relevant

Student Name

Instructor Name

Course

DD Month YYYY

MEAL Plan Outline

Rhetorical Analysis of Sojourner Truth's "Ain't I a Woman?"

I. INTRODUCTION

    A. Establish rhetorical context of Truth's speech

    B. Working Thesis: Truth uses rhetorical questions, draws attention to her own body, and employs Christian allusions to persuade her audience to see her as a woman deserving the same rights as white women.

II. BODY PARAGRAPH: Truth's Use of Logos

    Main Point: Truth effectively uses logos as a persuasive tool to argue for African-American women's rights.

    Evidence:

    1) Truth's repetition of the rhetorical question "Ain't I a woman?" as a logical device: Answer is "yes" because she looks like a woman

    2) She points out that man "says that women need to be helped into carriages, and lifted over ditches, and to have the best place everywhere. Nobody ever helps me into carriages, or over mud-puddles, or gives me any best place!" then asks, "Ain't I a woman?"

    Analysis/Linking: Her examples argue that African-American women are women and, like white women, should be treated with proper respect, helped into carriages, and lifted over mud-puddles.

III. BODY PARAGRAPH: Truth's Use of Body for Logos and Pathos

    Main Point: Truth uses her body as part of her argument for African-American women's rights.

Evidence:

1) "Look at me! Look at my arm! I have ploughed and planted, and gathered into barns, and no man could head me!"

2) "and bear the lash as well! And ain't I a woman?"

3) "I have borne thirteen children, and seen them most all sold off to slavery, and when I cried out with my mother's grief, none but Jesus heard me! And ain't I a woman?"

Analysis/Linking: African-American women are emotionally fortified and can endure emotional trauma, making them worthy of the same civil rights as white women.

IV. BODY PARAGRAPH: Truth's Use of Pathos

Main Point: Truth makes effective use of pathos through her religious allusions and humor.

Evidence:

1) Cries out to Jesus with her mother's grief

2) It was Mary that birthed Christ: Christ comes from "God and a woman! Man had nothing to do with Him."

3) If men do not give all women their rights, then women, black and white, will cause more trouble and the state of America will go "out of kilter."

Analysis/Linking: Truth invokes a range of different emotions, effectively using pathos to have her audience relate to her emotionally.

V. CONCLUSION

A. Effectiveness of Truth's persuasion in her time

B. How Truth's speech is still relevant

Appendix D. The Annotated Bibliography

An annotated bibliography can be exceptionally useful for you and your research. It helps you keep track of and manage your sources—not just what they are and where they're from, but also their ideas and uses for your argument. Though creating an annotated bibliography might seem like more work at the beginning of your project, the breakdown and analysis of each of your sources are ultimately incredibly valuable.

» What Is an Annotated Bibliography?

An annotated bibliography is a reference page that is separate from the version used in the final draft of your project. It is a planning document that includes formal citations of your sources (in full, correct format) and a discussion after the citation that summarizes the source and analyzes its usefulness to your project. While there are multiple ways an instructor might ask you to write an annotated bibliography—strictly summary or strictly analysis, among others—for our purposes, we will discuss a style combining those methods.

Once you've included a full citation for the source you're discussing, you should first write an objective, accurate, and thorough summary of its content and argument. In crafting this summary, keep in mind that your readers have not necessarily read the source; therefore, they will need you to provide definitions of key terms and concepts, as well as some specific examples to accompany your generalizations.

Next, you should present your analysis of the source, which should say more than whether or not the source will be useful. It might, for example, indicate *how* or *why* the source will be useful. Or, if the source will not be as useful as you initially thought it would be, you can explain the limitations of the source with respect to your research project.

» How to Write an Annotated Bibliography

Step One: Create the citation for your source in the correct format for your discipline. If you use a citation generator through the library or a database, make sure to double check that the citation is indeed properly formatted. Citation generators are not always up-to-date and often contain mistakes.

Step Two: Next, write a brief statement explaining the main arguments in the article and the importance of these arguments generally for the topic you are writing on.

Step Three: For the second half of your annotation, explain the source's use within your essay. How are you planning to use the article to formulate and support your own arguments? Note that the more clearly you have articulated your argument in your working thesis statement—even if that thesis evolves throughout the process—the easier the analysis step will be.

» Example Entry

Stewart, Susan Louise. "A Return to Normal: Lois Lowry's *The Giver*." *The Lion and the Unicorn*, vol. 31, no. 1, 2007, pp. 21–35. *Project MUSE*, doi:10.1353/uni.2007.0009.

In this article, Stewart describes the *The Giver*'s critical reception, both positive and negative, due to the younger reader audience and topics such as sexual desire and euthanasia. The author includes reviews of the novel that claim young readers who are introduced to utopian and dystopian fictions are better able to comprehend creating a positive influence within their societies, have the opportunity to grasp the enormity of attempting to create a utopian society, and maintain the belief that they can be instrumental in their own societies. However, the author also notes that *The Giver* "reifies several ideological foundations without providing a space to openly interrogate them" and "reinforce[s] our cultural values" (23). Ultimately, Stewart argues that while the text is typically received as a criticism of our society, the novel actually "reinforces culture norms" and "represents a return to normal" as opposed to offering a social critique, thus placing the text outside the norms of dystopian literature (23). Stewart's approach differs from the conversation of breaking out of a totalitarian regime typically found in dystopian literatures.

I will use this article to demonstrate the influence that individual perspective has on lived experience. American culture prizes individuality and the freedom to choose one's lifestyle. If Stewart is correct that *The Giver* represents a return to the norm, how does that change readers' experience of the novel and its dystopian elements?

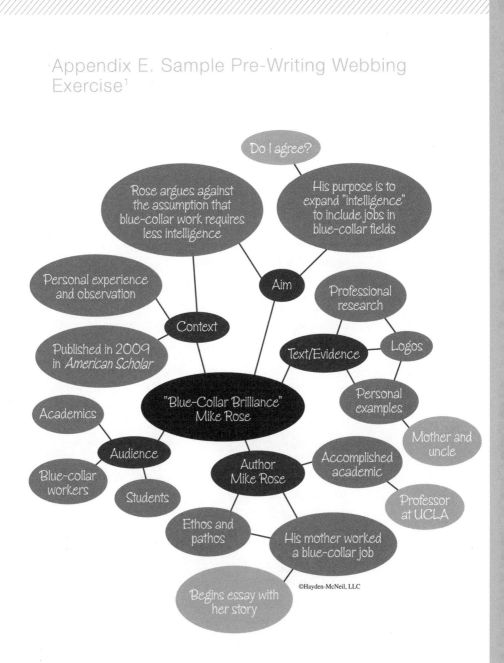

___

1. Based on Mike Rose's "Blue-Collar Brilliance."

Appendix F. Transition Words Table

Logical Relationship	Transition
Additional Support or Evidence	additionally, again, also, and, as well, besides, equally important, indeed, further, furthermore, in addition, moreover, then
Cause and Effect	accordingly, as a result/consequence, because (of), consequently, for this reason, hence, so, therefore, thus
Concession	admittedly, albeit, although, be that as it may, but even so, despite (this), granted, in spite of (this), nevertheless, even though, nonetheless, notwithstanding (this), on the other hand, regardless (of this), though
Conclusion/ Summary	finally, in a word, in brief, in conclusion, in the end, in the final analysis, on the whole, thus, to conclude, to summarize, in sum, in summary, consequently, hence, in short
Digression	by the way, incidentally, to change the topic
Dismissal	all the same, at any rate, either way, in any case/event, whichever/whatever happens
Emphasis	above all, even, even more, indeed, in fact, of course, more importantly, truly
Elaboration	actually, by extension, in short, that is, to put it another way, ultimately
Example	for example, for instance, namely, specifically, to illustrate
Exception/ Contrast	but, however, in spite of, on the one hand...on the other hand, nevertheless, nonetheless, notwithstanding, in contrast, on the contrary, still, whereas, yet
Importance	a more effective..., best of all, even more so, frequently, more importantly, occasionally, still worse
Place/Position	a bit further, above, adjacent, below, beyond, here, in front, in back, nearby, to the right/left, there
Resumption	anyhow, anyway, at any rate, to get back to the point, to resume, to return to the subject
Sequence/Order	first, second, third, next, then, finally, another
Similarity	also, in the same way, just as...so too, likewise, similarly, along the same lines
Time	after, afterward, at last, before, currently, during, earlier, immediately, later, meanwhile, now, recently, simultaneously, subsequently, the following day, then

*Adapted from UNC Chapel Hill, Michigan State, and Southwest Tennessee Community College

[**Main Idea**] America's present failures to adequately care for its veterans should perhaps not be surprising, given the nation's history. [**Evidence**] In his article "The Tragic, Forgotten History of Black Military Veterans," Peter C. Baker chronicles the brutal treatment of black veterans spanning from the Civil War to World War II, highlighting the hostility, racial violence, and inferior government benefits these soldiers faced in this era. Returning home from WWI, black soldiers were met "not with recognition of their civil rights but, instead, with an intense wave of discrimination and hostility" (Baker). [**Analysis**] The experiences of black veterans who fought in these wars signal that they were not suddenly exalted, celebrated figures. Rather, they were still limited by the racial climate of the country. Considering their treatment, why would things be different for other veterans? The reverence we hold for soldiers seems predicated on physical and psychological distance. While they are "away," they attain an almost superhuman quality, but when they return, their value diminishes. [**Linking sentence**] Sadly, the way we care for our veterans today cannot be disentangled from the marginalization of certain groups throughout American history.

In this paragraph, summary, paraphrase, and quotation are used to communicate evidence in support of a main idea. Furthermore, this evidence is analyzed in a way that illustrates the connection to the broader topic of the paper. The last sentence then links this analysis back to the topic sentence. While not all paragraphs have to match this formula exactly, the MEAL Plan is a useful guide for working evidence into your paper and enhancing your rhetorical position.

In this sample reflection, the student has created reflection questions based on feedback received or the student's own observations. Although instructors may assign their own reflections, students should engage in this sort of reflection throughout the course to consider their own learning progress and how to apply their learning to future occasions.

Q. **My peer said that my essay lacked "flow." What does that mean and how can I improve it?**

A. When my peer said the essay could "flow" better, she probably meant that I could work on two areas: transitions and arrangement. When I looked over the paper, I realized that I jump from topic to topic. In my mind, each idea was connected, but when I thought about how a reader would understand my argument, I understood how this could be better organized. I went in and made sure that I did not start or end paragraphs with quotes from other sources. Instead, I added strong topic sentences to the beginning that outlined what I would argue in the paragraph and at the end I transitioned to the next topic. I made sure to make connections for the reader that made it clear how each idea was connected. I re-arranged my paper so that I was building towards an argument rather than making points that were loosely connected. I think my paper now is more organized and easier to read.

Q. **When I read my essay out loud, I realized that my thesis was too vague. How do I make a more focused thesis?**

A. Initially, I thought I had to write the most perfect thesis before I started my essay. I realize now that I needed to go back after the essay was written and double-check my thesis to make sure it still connected the ideas in my essay. My first thesis "The author uses all three appeals to make an effective essay" was broad, vague, and lacked specificity. When I looked at my essay, I realized that most of it talked about how Michelle Obama referred to herself as a mother and how she did this to shape her ethos and to have the audience better consider her argument about childhood obesity. I changed my thesis to: "Michelle Obama emphasizes her role as a mother to appeal to her audience's ethos, helping her more effectively establish herself as a credible and relatable speaker." The essay covered the many instances where she uses her role as a mother to gain the audience's sympathy, to show that her problems are relatable, and to minimize any intimidation her audience might feel. This new thesis is general enough to cover these topics but specific enough to signal to the reader what I will discuss. In the future, I'll think about waiting to write the thesis until after I've finished the essay or I'll go back to the thesis and re-assess whether it fits my finished essay.

Q. **My instructor said that I needed "more evidence" in my essay. What does that mean? How do I analyze without just summarizing the material?**

A. Looking back over the paper, I realize that most of what I argued lacked context. I wrote about what the author stated but never showed proof. Also, even though I noted that the author appealed to pathos, logos, and/ or ethos, I forgot to explain why. In turn, the paper was vague and acontextual. I made sure that when I critiqued an author's language, I used a direct quote and then explained how her tone and diction appealed to ethos or pathos. From there, I made sure to identify which emotion she wanted us to feel and why she would want to evoke that emotion. For less specific material, like discussing the author's use of evidence, I paraphrased, but made sure to cite the material and to still refer to specifics from the text. Again, I explained what appeals were used, how they were used, and why they were used. Now, the reader of my paper can understand which aspects I was referring to and can follow my argument.

Q. **I'm worried my essay summarizes rather than analyzes. How can I make sure I'm following my assignment?**

A. I know that I'm not supposed to summarize heavily in an analysis. But how can I tell when I'm analyzing and when I'm summarizing? Looking back over my essay, I noticed that in some paragraphs, I only re-worded what the author said, so I summarized. While I need to use evidence to support claims, analysis happens when I push myself past observations in the text (like: the author appeals to pathos when he encourages us to feel inspired about the American Dream) towards thinking about why the author would want readers to feel a particular way (like: the author wants to inspire us because he believes we have already given up on the dream. Being inspired helps us re-consider the possibility of making our dreams happen). When I analyze, I'm thinking about *how* an author creates an argument, *why* the author crafts the argument a particular way and *what* larger comment, theme, idea, or message the author wants us to take away from the piece. By contrast, a summary just tells us *what* an article says. Once I understood this, I went back in and removed the excess summary and expanded my analysis.

Q. **My reflection assignment asks me to think about how I used the appeals: how can I assess my own writing? Can I quote myself as proof? What does that even mean?**

A. Throughout the semester, I thought about how authors of texts (essays, speeches, commercials, even blogs) constructed arguments. While I used similar techniques—making my paper more interesting, more focused, and better researched—I've never had to think about *how* I use rhetoric. I took a step back from my paper, examined it through a critical lens, like another reader would, and realized that, like other authors, I also constructed my ethos, appealed to logos, and wanted to inspire emotion. As I took note of how and why I did this, I looked at specific examples. For instance, in a research paper I wrote, I began the paper with an anecdote about how I personally connected with the issue. This not only showed my reader I had credibility to talk about this issue, it also made them feel sympathetic towards me. In this way, I appealed to both ethos and pathos. When I sat down to write my reflection, I used the example of the anecdote and quoted myself. At first, quoting myself seemed strange, but I realized it was the best way to show the reader the exact location in the essay where I was appealing to my reader. By meta-reflecting, I had a better sense of how readers would react to my argument and this gave me even better ideas about how to improve the paper for future drafts.

Appendix I. Sample Critical Reflection Essay with Peer Review

S.B.

Professor Berberyan

English 101

8 November 2016

Peer Review Draft: Critical Reflection Essay

When I came into this class, I didn't know what rhetoric

was. I'm not even sure I could have spelled rhetoric, but

if I thought anything about it, I probably thought rhetoric

was negative. I associated it with politicians who lied or car

salespeople who told you whatever, whether or not it was

true, as long as it would sell you a car. Fortunately, Professor

Berberyan is great and I learned a lot! Since then I've decided

that rhetoric is still some of those things, and I'd define it as

More formal tone

persuasion, <u>sure</u>, but I'd also define it as coming up with ways

to be persuasive, ways to be effective in persuasion, and ways

replace with comma?

to analyze my own work—whether in writing or speaking.

But the most important thing I've learned about rhetoric is that

we use rhetoric all the time. We even use rhetoric for school.

My portfolio will show that I've learned to use rhetoric to

make my writing more effective, all of which I used to fulfill

English 101's six different learning outcomes, even as I realize

that writing and speaking are lifelong processes—but at least I

know what areas I'm still working on.

One of the first ways I started developing as a rhetor in

this class was in our first assignment which had me analyze

a TED talk. This essay required me to fulfill English 101

Student Learning Outcome 1, which is that students will

"Analyze the content and structure of complex texts (written,

oral, and/or visual in nature)." For this essay, I learned that

---

Margin notes:

I like that you start with your own understandings of rhetoric at the beginning of the semester, but I don't think you should say that you didn't know what it was at all or that you didn't know how to spell it. I think you should take out that information and keep the politicians/car sales people.

I really like this definition.

You should be more specific about what these areas are. That way your argument would be even stronger!

I agree! Professor Berberyan is great! But I think this sentence should be removed for your final draft because the assignment says the critical reflection should NOT "assess the capabilities of the instructor of the course."

I really like the previous statement but this sentence weakens the overall statement you're making.

235

analysis means to break down. In other words, I broke down

a TED talk by Sherry Turkle. The talk was "Connected, but

alone?" and she gave it in February 2012. This talk was a

combination of oral, visual, and written. Turkle delivered her

talk orally, showed pictures to support her argument, and the

TED talk also had some words displayed on screen. I analyzed

the essay using rhetoric. To do this, I fulfilled student learning

outcome 3 "Identify and employ the rhetorical triangle,

the canons, and the appeals in both formal and informal

discourse." For example, in my analysis essay, I wrote in my

final draft,

> Turkle's audience is multiple. She addresses both the
> people in the TED audience, but she also addresses I
> think her message is targeted toward a variety of age
> ranges. For example, she shows a picture of a couple,
> parents, I guess, who are part of her audience. She also
> shows a picture of her daughter and friends who are not
> talking, but staring at her phones. These images and
> comments point out how Turkle is addressing a range of
> people in her comments that we are connected, but more
> alone. ("Final Draft, Analyzing TED," 2)

I analyzed who Turkle was as the rhetor and how she

established ethos: "Turkle is a professor at Massachusetts

Institute of Technology and even Director of MIT Initiative

on Technology and Self Program in Science, Technology, and

Society ("Sherry Turkle"). Because of this, she has credibility

to present. She delivered more evidence than other TED

speakers we watched" ("Final Draft, Analyzing TED," 1). My

favorite point from my rhetorical analysis was one about the

appeals: "Overall, I think Turkle presented a logical argument

with good evidence. In fact, Turkle included so much evidence

from her own research that the E in TED stood in Turkle's

presentation for Evidence, not Entertainment, which is what

Citation?

the E in most TED talks stands for." I think that I used good style, which is one of the rhetorical canons. In that essay, I both analyzed and used rhetoric.

I've learned a lot about the rhetorical appeals. In my first draft of the Turkle analysis essay, I really didn't understand how ethos, pathos, and logos worked. I didn't understand how they could work together. I thought they were separate. For example, I wrote, "Turkle used logos to argue that because if parents didn't put down their phones, they were setting a bad model for their children. Turkle used pathos when she pointed out that children felt bad because their parents were texting and emailing instead of paying attention to them." But now I

Citation?

see that they work together, as I show in my final draft of the analysis essay:

> When Turkle says, 'Parents text and do email at breakfast and at dinner while their children complain about not having their parents' full attention,' she's making a logical argument that parents should put the technology down and make eye contact with their children. Then she says, 'But then these same children deny each other their full attention.' That's when the viewer might have an emotional response, especially if they're a young person, and might think they should change their use of technology. Turkle's next line really tries to logically persuade us to take action by causing an emotional reaction; she says, 'And we even text at funerals.' I don't think there's anyone who doesn't understand that we should put our phones down . (Blevins, "Final Draft, Analyzing TED," 4)

I really like this example. It's so much better than the previous ones. I think you should use this to show that you have mastered the appeals.

This seems too short—you need to add more information here explaining why you used such a long quote.

By the end of the semester, I have a much better understanding of how the appeals work together.

I've used more drafting than ever have before. This whole portfolio shows how I have met Student Learning Outcome 5, "Employ drafting, peer review, and revision techniques in order to improve content, style, and structure of their own writing." The 70 pages of drafting, peer review, and all the different drafts, including writing center drafts, my invention exercises. But as the example I just referred to from my Turkle essay shows, revision really helps. I revised based on a comment on that paragraph from my instructor, who said, "Consider how the appeals never exist in isolation." Because I had to revise from the graded draft, I had an opportunity to learn more about rhetoric and to think through the comments and what I'd written before. The extra time it took to revise also gave me a chance to get new perspective on what I thought and to show how much more I knew about rhetoric.

Every essay I turned in in this class helped me fulfill the second English 101 Student Learning Outcome: "Composed cogent, evidence-based, argumentative texts." I learned how to write essays far better than I ever did before. The longest essay I wrote in high school was 3 pages. When I saw that I had to write four essays in this class, I didn't know how I would write that many pages over the semester. But I've learned about rhetoric and invention and now I use those to write my essays.

After each essay, we engaged in critical reflection, which is just like the term suggests, an opportunity to look book analytically. This helped me in two ways: it helped me think about the revisions I could do for the final portfolio and it also helped me get some perspective on my writing that I'd never had before. For example, after my first essay, I decided that I needed to procrastinate less. It was a real struggle for me to get to the page limit. Part of the reason for

Margin comments:

You should add drafting to one of the skills that you have developed in your argument.

I think this is a fragment.

Writing Center

In this paragraph you talk about drafting AND revision. I think they should each be a separate paragraph.

Do you mean "back"?

Do you want to tie this to SLO 6 like you mentioned SLO 5 in the previous paragraph?

that was that I didn't give myself enough time before I had the peer review draft. For future essays in the class, I engaged in the brainstorming described in Kristine Lee's chapter in "Rhetorical Approaches to College Writing." Freewriting worked best for me. I set my timer for five minutes, put a piece of paper over my monitor, the assignment sheet on my desk, and then I wrote whatever came into my head that might fit the assignment until the timer went off. That worked well—sometimes I wrote 300 words in that time—which is a FULL page. I did that several times in a row, then I used the reverse outline. The reverse outline helped me to arrange my ideas into a draft. Once I realized this technique worked well for me, I began using this technique every time I had to turn in an essay. You can look at scanned copies of my freewriting with reverse outline notes in this portfolio; I even included a copy of the freewriting and outline I put together for this critical reflection essay in the portfolio. Reflecting is nothing I've done for writing before, but I did learn from it.

> I think book titles should be in italics without quotation marks.

> This paragraph begins with reflection and analysis but most of the examples you use are about drafting. I think you should move those to the drafting paragraph.

The most important thing I learned in this class is that I'll be using rhetoric the rest of my life. In fact, I'd always used it before, but, now, because I've studied rhetoric, I'll be able to use it more effectively. I don't think as long as you're writing and speaking and communicating, you ever stop using rhetoric. I think I need to work on my revision more. Revision is hard. In future classes I'll have to make sure I leave myself more time for revision even for classes that don't have revision as a student learning outcome. I will continue to get peer review by going to the Writing Center and talking to the consultants there. I even took this critical reflection essay to the Writing Center.

> I think you could rewrite this sentence to take out the "don't think" part because it gets a bit confusing. Like, "I think as long as you're writing and communicating, you always use rhetoric."

> I think this conclusion could be stronger—you end up reflecting about your struggles with revision, but your conclusion should be wrapping up your reflection as a whole.

> Where's your Works Cited?

239

Index

Academic Integrity 43
    Citations 46, 99
    Ethos 45
Annotated Bibliography 227
Annotation 96
Argument 122
    Claims 83, 122
    Counter-Argument 123
    Rogerian. 8, 120
    Strategies 126, 177
Assignment Sheets 26, 82, 221
Audience 17, 20, 125
Brainstorming 109
Citations 99
Collaboration 48
Conclusions 123, 143
Conferencing 37
    Ethos 40
Context 14
Critical Reflection 205, 212
    Sample 235
Editing 188, 211
Feedback
    Peers 202
Freewriting 95, 111, 124
Genre 176
Introduction 138
Logical Fallacies 132
MEAL Plan 140, 225
    Sample Paragraph 231
MLA 99
Multiliteracy Centers 109
Multimodal 49, 171
Narrative 127, 177
Organization 138, 192

Outline 112, 223, 225
Peer Review 189, 195
    Example 235
    Reflection 232
    Visual and Multimodal Texts . . 199
Plagiarism 43
Portfolio 209
Presentation 169
Reading
    Active 95
Reflection 203, 212
    Questions 204
    Rhetorical Appeals 132, 134, 136
    Sample 232
Research 95, 128
    Research Question 84, 122
Reverse Outline 113, 142, 192
Revision 23, 187, 209
    Portfolio 210
    Strategies 190
    Thesis 120
Rhetoric
    Defined 3, 6
    Persuasion 5
Rhetorical Analysis
    Appeals 132
    Audience 13
    Context 15
    Rhetor 11
    Text 14
Rhetorical Appeals 16, 129
    Ethos 130
    In Speech 136, 169
    In Visual Design 136, 170

Logos 129
Pathos. 130
Rhetorical Triangle. 130
Rhetorical Canons 16, 19
   Arrangement 21, 192
   Delivery 21, 169
   Invention 5, 20, 109
   Memory 20, 21
   Style 21
Rhetorical Situation. 17
Rhetorical Triangle. 10
   Audience 12, 195
   Context 14
   Rhetor 10
   Rhetorical Appeals 130
   Text. 13
Sources. 94, 99
Spoken Rhetoric. 119, 169
Syllabus 24
Synthesis 128
Thesis. 115, 122, 225
   In Conclusion 143
   Revising 191
   Spoken 119
   Visual 118
Title 120
Tone 163
Topic Selection 82
Transitions 142, 230
Visual Rhetoric. 118, 170
Voice. 163
Writing Center . . 47, 106, 175, 181
Written Communication. 38
   Emails. 38